Writing Under the Influence

ALSO BY AUBREY MALONE
AND FROM MCFARLAND

*Hollywood's Second Sex: The Treatment
of Women in the Film Industry, 1900–1999* (2015)

The Defiant One: A Biography of Tony Curtis (2013)

*Censoring Hollywood: Sex and Violence in
Film and on the Cutting Room Floor* (2011)

Writing Under the Influence

Alcohol and the Works of 13 American Authors

Aubrey Malone

McFarland & Company, Inc., Publishers
Jefferson, North Carolina

LIBRARY OF CONGRESS CATALOGUING-IN-PUBLICATION DATA

Names: Malone, Aubrey author.
Title: Writing under the influence : alcohol and the works of 13 American authors / Aubrey Malone.
Description: Jefferson, North Carolina : McFarland & Company, Inc., Publishers, 2018. | Includes bibliographical references and index.
Identifiers: LCCN 2017044126 | ISBN 9781476667409 (softcover : acid free paper) ∞
Subjects: LCSH: Authors, American—20th century—Alcohol use. | Authors, American—20th century—Biography.
Classification: LCC PS129 .D53 2018 | DDC 810.9—dc23
LC record available at https://lccn.loc.gov/2017044126

BRITISH LIBRARY CATALOGUING DATA ARE AVAILABLE

ISBN (print) 978-1-4766-6740-9
ISBN (ebook) 978-1-4766-2787-8

© 2018 Aubrey Malone. All rights reserved

No part of this book may be reproduced or transmitted in any form or by any means, electronic or mechanical, including photocopying or recording, or by any information storage and retrieval system, without permission in writing from the publisher.

Front cover: Mickey Rourke as Henry Chinaski, the role based on poet and author Charles Bukowski, in the 1987 film *Barfly*

Printed in the United States of America

McFarland & Company, Inc., Publishers
   Box 611, Jefferson, North Carolina 28640
     www.mcfarlandpub.com

Table of Contents

ACKNOWLEDGMENTS 6

INTRODUCTION 1

1. Eugene O'Neill 5
2. Raymond Chandler 21
3. Edna St. Vincent Millay 35
4. Dorothy Parker 45
5. F. Scott Fitzgerald 58
6. William Faulkner 81
7. Ernest Hemingway 90
8. John Cheever 107
9. John Berryman 126
10. Carson McCullers 139
11. Charles Bukowski 155
12. Anne Sexton 176
13. Raymond Carver 193

CHAPTER NOTES 205

BIBLIOGRAPHY 217

INDEX 223

Acknowledgments

Special thanks to Derek and Debbie Savage
for their great help in preparing this book,
and to Al Berlinski of Sun Dog Press.
Thanks also to Mary Hunt, to the librarians from
Pearse Street and also to those from the ILAC Center.

Introduction

In the following pages I investigate the connection between drinking and writing as applied to thirteen American authors. Though the chapters are separate from one another, the themes embedded in them overlap—as do the people.

Most of the thirteen experienced mood changes with drink. Many of them underwent personality changes. A number of them attempted suicide, and three succeeded—if that's the appropriate word. With a number of them one can see the positive and negative effects of drink on the page. Some of them wrote before drinking, some after it, some during. Some used drink to inspire them, some to increase that inspiration, some to change their perspective of the world or their attitude toward it. In every case we can witness the impact of alcohol to some extent in what they wrote, even if only between the lines.

Faulkner's stream-of-consciousness style seemed made for a man who liked to drink. Writers like Hemingway and Raymond Carver, who held more store by formal discipline, did not. F. Scott Fitzgerald's florid writing flourished briefly under the influence but he usually conked out after a glass or two, thereby knocking on the head whatever heightened sensations might have been created by the gin he so loved.

There are stories of cure as well. A handful of the writers attended Alcoholics Anonymous meetings on a regular basis. A few became sober after a lifetime of excess. More common, though, were the half-hearted attempts to go cold turkey and then fall off the wagon.

Shakespeare once ruminated on the connection between drinking and sex, concluding that alcohol increased the desire but diminished the performance. Perhaps the same is true of drinking and writing, though writers possess the ability to edit the following day—failed lovers don't have the same facility.

Four high-profile Americans to win the Nobel Prize for literature were alcoholics: Sinclair Lewis, Eugene O'Neill, William Faulkner, and Ernest Hemingway. An argument could be made for the fact that a fifth, John Steinbeck, was one, too. "Some American writers," said James Thurber—himself no stranger to the bottle—"who have known each other for years have never met when both were sober." Sinclair Lewis once asked: "Can you name five American writers since Poe who *didn't* die of alcoholism?"[1]

The Irish writer and filmmaker Neil Jordan once posited the notion that the reason so many writers were alcoholics was because one could write with a hangover. Such a convenience perhaps makes a better case for why so many alcoholics were writers rather than vice versa. This book is replete with writers who wrote drunk (usually badly) and with hangovers (not quite as badly). It also, needless to say, features many of them writing sober. For some, sobriety seemed to take the spark away, Charles Bukowski being the most notable example.

I've structured most of the profiles in a cradle-to-grave manner, focusing primarily, though not exclusively, on the drinking escapades that punctuated the lives in question. In some cases, I've suggested the trigger for the alcoholism was a dysfunctional childhood. Elsewhere, it came from a self-destructive personality. Many of the people featured experienced both, either as cause and effect, or incidentally. Many of them also suffered from depression. Was depression behind the alcoholism, or did the alcohol lead to depression? We might as well ask how long is a piece of string. It was usually both, in varying doses.

James Dickey said that the two things that go along with poetry are alcoholism and suicide. Bukowski adapted that statement:

> Drinking joggles you out of the standardism of everyday life. It yanks you out of your body and mind and throws you against the wall. I have the feeling that drinking is a form of suicide where you're allowed to return to life and begin all over the next day. It's like killing yourself and then you're reborn. I guess I've lived about ten or fifteen thousand lives.[2]

Alcoholism is sometimes referred to as slow suicide, but many writers died young and quickly. As Donald Newlove elucidated:

> Jack London did it on a morphine overdose. Malcolm Lowry got his Golden Eternity Mask on fifty sodium amytals after his wife smashed his gin bottle. Hart Crane jumped unknowingly into a shark's mouth in the Caribbean. Lucky James Agee felt his heart go, and F. Scott Fitzgerald keeled over, knocking his head on a mantle.[3]

Most of the writers mentioned above are not included in this book. There were many others I could have chosen as well—Hunter S. Thompson, O. Henry, Edgar Allan Poe, Sherwood Anderson, Theodore Dreiser, Ambrose Bierce, Frederick Exley, Stephen King, Ring Lardner, Theodore Roetke, Tennessee Williams, Truman Capote. But the line had to be drawn somewhere.

One of the reasons I didn't include Williams or Capote is because their drinking was tied up with the ingesting of other substances. This clouded the issue somewhat. The same applied to Jack Kerouac. That isn't to say all three weren't rabid alcoholics or that drink didn't have a huge effect on them. The first time Kerouac became intoxicated he thought he saw God. He went on to breakfast on bourbon. He drank a quart of Cognac brandy a day, followed by beer chasers.[4] Similar stories could likely be told about Williams and Capote.

Writing Under the Influence is replete with tales of the duplicitous stratagems heavy drinkers employed to camouflage their condition from their loved ones—or even their hated ones. No conclusions have been drawn from such behavior. Neither has any attempt been made to engage in any facile character assassination. Alcoholism is a disease rather than a flaw. It has no cure but it can be managed. Some of these thirteen people chose to manage it; others, to curl up under it. Each followed his or her own path to recovery or decline. The advice they received from the medical establishment and those in their immediate circles was usually ignored.

Drinkers, like writers, tend to be a very stubborn breed.

Eugene O'Neill
(1888–1953)

Addiction was in O'Neill's blood. His father, James, was a heavy drinker; his mother, a morphine addict. She developed the addiction after giving birth to him.

He was born in a hotel. It was a hard birth. His mother asked for morphine for the pain, and it was given to her. O'Neill always blamed himself for this. He wrote about it in *Long Day's Journey into Night*, though that play wasn't totally autobiographical. In real life, contrary to what happened in it, Ella O'Neill conquered her addiction.

It's not known if morphine passes into a nursing woman's milk. O'Neill would have been exposed to it when his mother was breastfeeding him. Could this have been the beginning of his own addictive personality? It's possible.

His father helped, too. As a baby, whenever he had a nightmare or a stomachache, James gave him a few drops of whiskey in water to soothe him. O'Neill's mother believed alcohol to be "a healthy stimulant."[1]

Thus were the habits of a lifetime laid down. If his mother's problems with addiction began when she was pregnant with him, his own started in early adulthood. O'Neill was withdrawn as a child, like many writers—and many drinkers. His mother protected him excessively on this account. The more he evinced signs of weakness in childhood, the closer she held him. This trait continued when he developed a drinking problem. It was shared by his elder brother Jamie.

O'Neill's drinking got so bad at times in his youth, his friends had to lock him in bedrooms and basements to keep him away from alcohol. This was occasionally done at his behest.

He started drinking at the age of fifteen. That was when he was a student at Princeton. One night he lit some incense in his room. He then covered a light bulb with red paper and started drinking absinthe. It drove him half crazy with "absinthmania." He emptied out the drawers of his bureau and scattered the contents all around the room. He then tried to throw a chair out the window. He even put a gun to his head and pulled the trigger (luckily, it wasn't loaded at the time). He was eventually thrown out of Princeton. The reason, the rumor goes, is that he threw a beer bottle at the window of one of the professors, Woodrow Wilson, the future president of the U.S. O'Neill denied this. His biographer Stephen Black claimed the reason was simply his poor scholastic record.[2]

His father was an actor. His most famous role was in *The Count of Monte Cristo*. This became almost like a pension to him over the years. Now and again he tried to break away from it, but he always went back. It made him a fortune but destroyed whatever versatility he might have once possessed. In time, the typecasting became a burden to him.

Although James drank heavily, he never missed a performance. Eugene was different: drinking all but took over his life. He goes into this in some detail in *Long Day's Journey into Night*. His mother says to his father about him in that play, "You brought him up to be a boozer." The same applied to Jamie, who, unlike his brother, frequented high-class bars. Eugene, in the words of one biographer, found "his niche in the lower depths of society, on Buenos Aires' waterfront and New York's Lower East Side. He lived with bums, drank with bums and ultimately wrote about bums."[3]

Sometimes he did meaningless things when drunk. One day he punched a bartender for no apparent reason, after which he was descended upon by bouncers and beaten up. On other occasions he was even more outrageous. When asked to explain his behavior, words failed him. He didn't deny his actions, nor could he throw light on his motives, if there were any.[4]

He did most of his youthful drinking at a bar called Jimmy's Hotel, in Fulton Street, New York. It was nicknamed Jimmy the Priest's. O'Neill attempted suicide there in 1911. He described it as "a saloon of the lowest kind of grog shop."[5] There were beds upstairs which one could rent for as little as $3 a month. A shot of whiskey cost a nickel. Violence erupted frequently. When it did, the perpetrators were simply thrown out by the proprietor, James Condon. O'Neill described the clientele as just his kind of people. He saw decency in them, a consistency: "They were sincere, loyal and generous. I learned at Jimmy the Priest's not to sit in judgment on people."[6] He also learned to drink without stopping.

Condon was forced to shut the bar in future years after four people died while drinking on the premises. One of them was found in a back room, another upstairs in bed, and two more in a comatose state outside the building. They were all taken to Bellevue Hospital, but none survived.

Condon was arrested for homicide and charged with serving what was termed "coroner's cocktails," a type of wood-alcohol moonshine. He escaped jail, but his bar never opened again. (In 1966, it became part of the grounds of the World Trade Center).

O'Neill continued to drink absinthe after the Princeton experience. At times it seemed to have an almost hallucinogenic effect on him. This was how he described it:

> The earth is a sun-struck bee, its wings sodden with golden pollen.... Green parrots in the green of the orange trees gossip like deaf people; a discord rasps sawteeth in the keen blue blade of silence.[7]

He was also fond of a brew vulgarly termed Tiger Piss, a Cape Cod cocktail that tasted so vile it had to be consumed in one gulp. O'Neill once urinated in a half-empty bottle of it and then slugged it back.

He became a sailor for a time. He mined for gold. He lived in derelict buildings and outhouses, soaking up experiences from the seamy side of life—his basic raw material. He wanted to write for a living, but didn't know how. While he was waiting to find out, absinthe (or Tiger Piss) filled in the blanks.

He married Katherine Jenkins in 1910. The reason, he said, was simply that she was pregnant with his child. They never lived together. The baby was called Eugene Junior. He didn't see him until the boy was twelve. Eugene Junior would grow up to be an alcoholic like his father.

By his early twenties, O'Neill was drinking from dawn to dusk in various New York hellholes. He suffered from blackouts, memory loss, and the dreaded DTs. In 1912, he took an accidental overdose of an opiate called Veronal, which he was using to combat hangovers. If a friend hadn't woken him up, he might well have died. He might also have died from tuberculosis that year, but he was treated successfully in a sanatorium. When he came out he decided to become a full-time playwright.

In the fall of 1914 he studied dramatic technique at Harvard but didn't complete the course, leaving after a year. He wrote prolifically at this time (mainly poetry), but had little success finding a publisher.

Drinking seemed to affect his mind more than his body. As he admitted years later:

> After I'd had a quart and a half of bourbon, I could walk straight and talk rationally, but my brain was nuts. If anybody suggested that I climb up the Woolworth Building, I'd be tickled to death to do it.[8]

One night he said to a bartender, "I want something to knock the top of my head off."[9]

He contemplated suicide often; he even attempted it a few times. He toyed with the idea of swimming to his death in the ocean. This was ruled out due to his prowess as a swimmer. (He thought his instinct of self-preservation would probably have kicked in).[10]

Eugene and Jamie sometimes appeared onstage in minor roles in support of their father. There were nights when the young men were too drunk to deliver their lines or even to stand upright. To teach them the benefits of moderate drinking, James took them to bars after the performances, offering them one drink each before departing. This was somewhat aspirational on his part as they used the openers as mere preludes to another night of drunken debauchery—often involving ladies of the night. Their frustrated father would groan, "God deliver me from my children."[11]

Jamie appeared in many productions but Eugene in only a few. Sometimes Jamie went on the road with a touring company, always packing a few bottles of whiskey to help him on his way. One time when he was traveling from Denver to Salt Lake City his suitcase opened and two bottles fell out, smashing on the ground. He was inconsolable for the remainder of the tour.[12]

Under Jamie's streetwise tutelage, O'Neill blended into New York's seedy underbelly. He took him into showgirls' dressing rooms and brothels to "wise up his kid brother to the ways of the world."[13]

His friend Art McGinley bragged, "Gene and I wanted to drink America dry. When we read somewhere that there were two thousand distilleries and four thousand breweries in the country, we realized we'd never make it."[14]

McGinley was even fonder of drink than O'Neill, if that's possible. O'Neill liked to tell a story about his friend climbing the stairs of an apartment once with a quart of whiskey under each arm. He fell from the top step and crashed through a window, eventually landing on the roof of a store outside. Undaunted, he got to his feet. He then went back in through the broken window and climbed the stairs again, entering the apartment with the words, "Well thank Christ the whiskey didn't break its neck!"[15]

O'Neill's friend Mary Vorse described how he looked after a night on the town: "There was no such darkness as Gene's darkness. You could have taken the air he breathed and carved a statue of despair of it."[16] Gastritis and excruciating abdominal pains were the only things that seemed to keep him away from the bottle.[17]

He often woke in rooms—and indeed on trains—without remembering how he had gotten there. There were times when he woke with bruises from fights only dimly remembered, what small amount of money there might have been in his pockets pilfered.

Sometimes he squatted in empty houses. A favorite ruse employed by his friend Terry Carlin was to send one of his respectable friends to a real estate agent in Greenwich Village and ask to view a flat. As soon as he was leaving, he'd press a lump of clay against the door latch which prevented it from locking. He would then tell Carlin and O'Neill the address and they'd make their way there, armed with mattresses and whiskey. If they couldn't find mattresses they slept on piles of sacking. They used newspapers for bed linen and drank the night away. The next morning they'd buy more whiskey. The first drink of the day, the hair of the dog that bit them, was the hardest to get down. O'Neill was often so weak from the previous night's exertions he had to have Carlin help him lift the glass—or bottle—to his lips. It was like medicine to set him up for the next day's insanity.[18]

By 1916, O'Neill was in an advanced state of suicidal melancholia. "I wandered in that grey country of alcohol," he said, "in which all worldly hopes are as naught and the great longing one for annihilation. Ah, to fall asleep and never wake again to cower before the fetish of life."[19]

Aware that he was in danger of dying, he told Carlin he was thinking of going on the wagon. Carlin waned him against going cold turkey, fearing the devastating effects of the DTs, but O' Neill wouldn't listen. To persuade him to quit gradually, Carlin went out on the streets and brought home an array of the most unsavory characters he could find—a number of thugs, a trembling drug addict, an aging prostitute—to give O'Neill an inkling of the kinds of visions he might have with sudden withdrawal. By now the situation had become almost comic. O'Neill gazed at this colorful entourage through bleary eyes and saw Carlin's point. Result? He asked him for a whiskey. Carlin was only too willing to oblige.[20]

Another problem of sobriety was the resulting convulsions. They were cured only by more alcohol. He often shook so much that barmen gave him towels to put around the glasses he drank from to prevent unwanted spills. He drank anything he could find, the stronger the better. He even sampled the camphor-flavored wood alcohol, a drink taken—often fatally—by waterfront outcasts at the end of their tether. O'Neill lived with such outcasts off and on for many years. He slept in their shacks with them and shared their park benches, cadging food off sailors on leave on the odd occasion that he decided to replace liquids with solids.[21]

One of the reasons he drank so much, he said in later years, was from the frustration of not being able to establish himself as a writer. O'Neill was now twenty-eight. Many of the writers in this book found success early in their careers, even with drink, but it hampered O'Neill. He was thirty before he started to produce his best work.

In 1918 he married Agnes Boulton, a writer of commercial fiction. They had two children, Shane and Oona. Boulton once claimed she married him not despite his drinking problem, but because of it. He was weak, she said, and needed somebody to take care of him.[22]

She knew she was going to have her work cut out for her keeping him sober. Shortly after she married him she tried to get him on a train from New York to Provincetown. He was drinking with Jamie at the time. Both of them were sharing a bottle of whiskey in a hotel. They didn't want to leave, so she had to cancel the tickets. The next morning O'Neill was hungover. He asked her to go down to the bar and get him a milk shake with a shot of brandy in it. When she came back with it he drank it in one gulp. He then asked her to go down to the bar again, this time for eggnog with two eggs in it and two shots of brandy. After he finished these, Jamie came into the room with a fifth of Old Taylor. They spent the rest of the day trying to polish that off. And so on. Each day's hangover "cure" began a new binge. It was a week before they finally boarded the train. Said Boulton, "What I didn't know then was that after one drink, the cycle had to be fulfilled."[23]

He used to say to his wife, "One drink and I'm off."[24] In time she became more of a nurse than a wife to him, soothing him through his blackout periods, smoothing out the effects of his hangovers, tolerating his tantrums when the morning after brought out his latent anger about big things and small. Sometimes he hit her when she tried to prevent him from drinking. If he was drunk enough, he would accuse her of having affairs behind his back.

He often escaped from Agnes to frequent yet another dingy bar. One was called, appropriately, The Hell Hole. He usually became ossified there and then retired upstairs to a room to sleep it off. If Agnes came looking for him, barmen covered for him. It always helped to have friends like that.

The arrival of Prohibition in 1919 might have been expected to get him to draw in his horns but it didn't. His years fraternizing with those on the fringes of society helped him build a coterie of people who supplied him with bootleg liquor. Sometimes he got doctors to write prescriptions for whiskey. It helped if they were Irish, like his father, and regarded the substance as a palliative. One night he had a party that went on for two days. At the end of it he hurled the empty bottles into the fireplace, enjoying the crashing sound they made. Then he threw the household china in, plate-by-plate and cup-by-cup. Not satisfied with that, he began throwing in the lamps that were in the room and any other furniture not nailed to the floor. By his standards it was a good party. His friend Frank Shay—another Irish-American—was with him. They understood the importance of such behavioral patterns. It meant nobody had to wash the dishes after dinner.

Eugene O'Neill's writing talent flowered as the new decade was ushered in. His first full-length play, *Beyond the Horizon*, opened on Broadway in February 1920. But tragedy was to follow. A week later his father suffered a stroke and died soon afterward. He lived just long enough to see Eugene make a success of his writing. He felt a certain amount of guilt over the fact that he'd given more attention to Jamie over his more gifted son. Eugene had just won the Pulitzer Prize. He said, "I can die happy because I think Gene is going to be all right."[25]

He got drunk with Jamie at the funeral. Afterward, they were joined by Art McGinley. Over a drink, O'Neill showed him a royalty check he had for $1,700. McGinley was suitably impressed. The three of them got blotto on the strength of it. McGinley couldn't understand how O'Neill managed to drink so much and still produce literature. O'Neill wasn't able to explain it either. After his father died he seemed to write even more feverishly than before.

His writing was infused with raw passion. This intensity bled into the plays. He felt the old man had sold out his integrity for the treasure of Monte Cristo, i.e., his paycheck. He was determined the same thing wouldn't happen to him.

But such conviction came with a price. He may have avoided the snare of artistic compromise, but the temptation of the bottle continued to be an issue. One night he grimaced when he was polishing off a glass of whiskey. Boulton was surprised that he didn't seem to be enjoying it.

Like many writers, he drank to gain confidence. Whiskey was a prop to meet a situation. It enabled him to do what he wanted to do rather than what was expected of him. His friend Harry Kemp said he kept to himself at parties if he wasn't drinking: "When he spoke it was hesitantly and haltingly. It was only when he drank that he expressed himself fluently."[26] Another person took over, a superman that hid all his insecurities.

He put his alcoholism down to various root causes—his highly strung personality, his parents' addictions to drink and drugs, even the fact of having been thrust into a boarding school before his seventh birthday. His friend Clayton Hamilton, a theatre critic, thought he had an Oedipus complex, a view with which O'Neill himself agreed. "All he had to do was read my plays," he remarked.[27] The psychiatrist Louis Bisch believed he had a homosexual attraction towards his father and that he carried this into some of his friendships with other men. Bisch believed he had revulsion towards his mother and, by a similar process of osmosis, other women as well.[28]

His Irish heritage was cited as another factor. By the middle of the 20th century, the Irish in America were statistically proven to be twenty-five times more likely to succumb to alcoholism than any other group.[29] A love for alcohol, indeed, seems to be hardwired into the Irish DNA, as well as a pronounced tolerance for its excesses. Gross indecencies and crimes are often excused for being only a drink. In *Long Day's Journey*, James Tyrone dubs it "the good man's failing." In this sense, he was doubly damned; drink being the writer's curse as well.

Art McGinley said O'Neill was a "periodic" drinker, a man who couldn't stop once he started, at least until he got sick. On the morning after a binge he would be disconsolate: "He would gloom up and not say a word or else talk of suicide." At times like this his writing was virtually non-existent. But when he stopped drinking he had immense discipline and would work around the clock.[30]

Donald Newlove thought one could smell alcohol from him as soon as he put pen to paper: "You can't watch a play from his greatest period without knowing exactly where the bottle is. It's the silver pivot of the action and makes everything high-flown, fantastic and grim."[31]

As well as this affliction, O'Neill suffered from a tremor in his hands. Many people took this to be the early onset of Parkinson's Disease. (It wasn't). It was intensified when he was drinking, causing his hands to shake violently as he drank. This often resulted in his spilling drinks all over himself. (If he was drunk enough he did that even *without* the tremor).

The tremor also affected his writing. Perhaps his penmanship even contributed to it. It was so intricate, he was once reputed to have composed an entire three-act play within two and a half pages.

The plays came fast and furious. In the 1920s alone he wrote over fifteen that were produced—and God knows how many more that never were. His mind was on fire. His masterpiece was *Long Day's Journey into Night*. He believed this to be too personal a work to be staged in his lifetime. In his will he stipulated that the book of the play wasn't to be published on any account until twenty-five years after his death. One of the main reasons for this was a fear of upsetting Eugene junior. As mentioned, he became an alcoholic like his father. In his case, the disease had even more traumatic repercussions: he committed suicide in 1950 at the age of forty, drinking a full bottle of whiskey before cutting his wrists in a bath. His suicide note read: "Never let it be said of an O'Neill that he failed to empty a bottle."[32]

Long Day's Journey is a play about a family, the members of which are in denial about their addictions. The irony is that it's also the play where O'Neill confronted such denial, thereby negating it. In his other plays he used alcohol as a crutch if not a theme. Here it's both.

There's ambivalence about alcohol that runs through *Long Day's Journey*. The characters insult one another for their drinking but still egg one another on. At one point James and Jamie Tyrone try to prevent the tubercular Edmund, another brother, from drinking. But a few moments later they change their minds and *encourage* him to drink. Such inconsistent behavior informs the play in general. This combination of guilt and need create the heightened drama.

Life was to mirror art in terms of its tragic elements. O'Neill's mother died in 1922, an event that traumatized him. To Jamie was entrusted the task of bringing her coffin from California to New York for burial. The train journey took five days. He brought ten bottles of whiskey with him, a diet of two per day, and polished them all off in record time. When he reached New York, where the body was to be interred, he was too drunk to attend her funeral. Many of her possessions were stolen en route, Jamie diverting his attention from her to a prostitute who was also on the train. Jamie was always falling in love with prostitutes. He had to be pried away from her.

Before his mother died, Jamie tried to persuade her to bequeath all of her property to him, leaving Eugene out of the equation. When Eugene heard about this he exploded. He could never feel the same way about Jamie afterward. The man who was once his role model now became a base individual. He told him he wanted nothing more to do with him. He went on a massive bender, feeling a double legitimacy to do so.

He disgraced himself even by his own standards in the summer of 1922. One night he appeared at a costume party in Provincetown wearing nothing but a leopard skin loincloth and an orange wig. His body was deeply tanned. A woman standing beside him at the party thought this was makeup. She wiped a piece of paper against his arm to satisfy her curiosity. O'Neill reacted by hitting her so hard he sent her flying across the room.

Jamie died the following year, his body and mind destroyed by drink. Only 45 years old, he looked 60. There was even a suggestion that he committed suicide. Eugene didn't go to the funeral, but he was still grief-stricken. "After my mother's death," he said, "Jamie gave up all hold on life."[33]

Things looked grim for the embattled playwright. "I've lost my father,

Sophia Loren and Anthony Perkins in *Desire Under the Elms* (1958), one of O'Neill's most highly regarded plays.

mother and only brother within the last four years," he said, adding, "Now I'm the only O'Neill of our branch left."[34] In a strange way this gave him the will to carry on—for his children as much as himself. His writing continued with *Desire Under the Elms*, one of his most highly regarded plays. It would be made into a 1958 film with Anthony Perkins and Sophia Loren.

At the end of 1924 he made a gallant effort to stay dry. After knocking back a bottle of whiskey one night he became disgusted with himself. He resolved to reduce his drinking on a systematic basis: five drinks one day, three the next, and one the next. On New Year's Eve, he wrote in his diary, "On wagon." The following day he wrote: "Welcome in a new dawn and pray."[35]

On New Year's Day 1925, he cut his drinking down to a glass of ale with his dinner. This, he said, didn't create "the slightest yen for more." He told a friend his mother's conquest of her morphine addiction had been the catalyst. He said his main temptation to drink always came when he finished his plays because they never turned out the way he wanted.[36]

After he became sober he forbade any liquor in the house. That included any Agnes might drink. Her function as his nurse and caregiver now became defunct, and with it much of her relevance to him.

When their relationship deteriorated beyond repair, O'Neill asked her for a divorce. Boulton was slow to consent, which angered him. She then grudgingly acquiesced, but wanted more alimony from him than he felt was fair. This angered him even more. He threatened to stop writing so he would have no income. Lawyers became involved. The situation rumbled on, tempers frayed. By now he had fallen in love with another woman, Carlotta Monterey. Monterey was a minor actress. She'd appeared in his play *The Hairy Ape* in 1922. They had a tempestuous relationship, much of it conducted on the move as they journeyed from country to country. He told her she was his substitute for drink: "You are my passion and my life-drunkenness and my ecstasy and the wine of joy to me."[37]

O'Neill developed an addiction to alcohol almost from birth. He was one of the few writers in this book to kick the habit but never quite lost the longing for it (*Writer Pictures*).

He knew he was an extremist by nature. He once said to Monterey:

> I have always been hilariously shooting in on the crest of a wave or else bogged down to my neck in a swamp. The dry, warm, sure-footed middle ground was the one place I was never taught to walk. I finally escaped onto the plane of my work where I can always dance and drown and be re-born to dance and drown again. When work wouldn't come I had to escape via masks of solitude, alcoholic and otherwise.[38]

He admitted alcohol had prevented him from producing better work. "I've never written anything good when I'm drinking," he said, "or even when the miasma of drink is left."[39] He was also aware of the terrible effects it had on his health. A doctor told him the brain had the texture of "raw egg white." If it was exposed to enough alcohol and the tissue tightened, it more closely resembled a cooked one.[40]

He only fell off the wagon on a few occasions. After he moved to France with Monterey, he had a visit from an old friend, Louis Kalonyme.

They got drunk together one night as they recalled the good old days—or, rather, the bad old days. Monterey saw the danger signs. She tried to frighten him by telling him she was leaving him. She even went so far as to pack her bags and leave the house for a night. But O'Neill hardly noticed: he was too busy nursing a hangover. She returned the following morning.[41]

Afterward, they went to the Far East. There he tried to keep his mind off booze by gambling in Saigon. Monterey castigated him when she saw all the money he was losing; he refused to listen to her. Things got worse on a trip to Shanghai. After one row, he hit her. She thought she might have to go to the hospital, but it was he who ended up there, attempting to dry out. After being released, he continued drinking. Monterey had had enough by this stage and went home alone. This time O'Neill was shocked enough by her departure to sober up. He sent her a series of radiograms, begging her to forgive him. When she did, they were reunited in Port Said. He now told her he was going to give up drinking for good, speaking with such conviction that she believed him. Her leaving him was the spur, he said. They then sailed to France together. They got married there in September 1929. The following year, they moved back to the U.S.

After O'Neill embraced sobriety, he blamed the woman he drank with for his drinking. (F. Scott Fitzgerald also did this, as did Raymond Carver.) Boulton, he said, "urged" him to drink, "because when I drank she could feel a bit superior, a martyr." Further, "She liked to get drunk herself." And then came the final blow: she "stuck" with him because he represented "bread and butter and luxuries."[42]

As O'Neill aged, he became a total recluse. This suited Monterey. Now she had him to herself, away from all the acquaintances of his past. If they appeared at his door she became like a sentry, fending them off. People thought she exerted too much influence over him. If so, he was a party to it.

Being on the wagon after so many years of constant drinking felt alien to him: "One feels so normal with so little to be normal about. One misses playing solitaire with one's scales."[43]

He wrote to his friend Frank Shay in 1930: "I haven't had a drink in nearly five years, so help me. Booze was getting sick of me. After a long huddle with my liver I decided to throw in the sponge—and mean it. Life since then has lacked the uproarious but I must admit I feel better."[44]

When George Bernard Shaw heard that O'Neill had forsaken the booze, he said he would probably never write a good play again. How wrong he was. On the dry, his writing prospered. In 1931, he wrote *Mourning Becomes Electra*, a mammoth work. There were others as well but his hand tremor continued to slow him down. He won the Nobel Prize in 1936, a long-overdue honor.

He wrote one of his last major plays, *The Iceman Cometh*, in 1939. It was first staged in 1940 but didn't attract much attention. A later production, in 1946, however, drew rave reviews. These meant a lot to him as he hadn't had much theatrical success in the previous decade. This was largely because his plays were too long-winded. Such a charge could also have been leveled at *Iceman*, but it had an intensity that grabbed the public's attention, an intensity borne of his pain.

O'Neill drew on many of the experiences he'd had in Jimmy the Priest's for the play. At one point a character drunkenly remarks, "Don't you notice the beautiful calm in the atmosphere? That's because it's the last harbor. No one here has to worry where they're going next because there's no farther they *can* go."[45] That was exactly how O'Neill felt during his drinking days. Bars were Last Chance Saloons for him. They were havens, mother's wombs, ultimate escapes.

Though he remained sober, his writing continued to be suffused with the subject of alcohol. As one critic remarked, his last two full-length plays (*A Touch of the Poet* and *A Moon for the Misbegotten*) are as saturated with alcoholic guilt as *Long Day's Journey* and *The Iceman Cometh*.[46]

Despite managing his problem and having an artistic Indian summer, his last years were anything but happy. In 1943, he disowned his daughter Oona for marrying Charlie Chaplin, a man thirty-six years older than she. He never saw her again. As was the case with his other children, he felt used by her. They all leaned on him for money and, to his way of thinking, sought the easy life.[47] So had Agnes Boulton, fleecing him for alimony payments and then refusing to work. He was disgusted with the lot of them.

A Moon for the Misbegotten was his final play. It dealt with the last drunken days of Jamie. Putting these memories down on paper brought them all back to him—the craziness, the never-thinking-about-tomorrow, the irresponsible highs and lows. The play wasn't staged for many years after its completion. When it was, the production was poor and it flopped. O'Neill became disconsolate. He felt he was finished with the theatre—or, rather, the theatre was finished with him. He panicked. How was he going to spend the rest of his life if he couldn't write?

His moods darkened. He saw no one. At times he seemed to be waiting to die. He even composed the words he wanted on his tombstone: "Eugene O'Neill: There Is Something to be Said for Being Dead."[48] Doctors prescribed sedatives and sleeping pills to try and anaesthetize his overwrought mind. They did to an extent, but the effect soon wore off.

Jason Robards, Katharine Hepburn and Frederic March in *Long Day's Journey into Night* (1962), a film based on the play in which O'Neill laid bare all the alcoholic demons of his family.

Life held few pleasures for him now. The world around him seemed bland. He feared dementia. The suicidal impulses that had dogged him in his youth returned. Would he have been better off to go out on a bender with his faculties intact?

Reminiscing on his past one day, he wrote bemusedly to a friend:

> Men were men in those days. When they decided it was fitting to go on a drunk, they went on a drunk. Not like the weaklings of today who after ten days of mixed drinks have to have an animal trainer bed them down in Bellevue and gently subdue their menagerie visions. In the old days a man went on a five-year drunk and finished by licking four cops. Then he went home to raise hell because dinner was late.[49]

His last years with Monterey were painful. They argued more than ever and many times seemed on the point of divorcing. But somehow they stuck together. As they got older, health worries became added irritants. Monterey suffered badly with arthritis, and O'Neill had a host of problems, many of them souvenirs of his wild past. There were days when he was totally incapacitated, when he could only hobble about with a cane. Monterey had to lift him, which caused her great pain.

She took sedative bromides, developing paranoid symptoms as a result. They caused her to become unpredictable in her behavior. At one stage, believing O'Neill to be unfaithful to her, she went so far as to hire private detectives to follow him. In 1948, she left him for a time. In her absence, he fell and broke his shoulder. He wrote to her from his hospital bed, begging her to come back. She did, but their relationship continued to be tempestuous.[50]

When Eugene junior killed himself in 1950 it was the last straw for O'Neill. He had always had a special affection for him. He was the only one of his children, he thought, who never exploited him for money. The tragedy of losing him was one from which he would not recover. The man who loved words couldn't even talk about it. His collected letters—which are as fascinating as any play he ever wrote—capturing almost every mood he had since the day he was born, but when something affected him too much—like the estrangement from Oona—he drew a line under it. So it was with Eugene junior.[51]

His despondency spilled over into his relationship with Monterey. He had a fierce quarrel with her the following year which resulted in his falling and breaking his leg. He looked to her to help him, but she refused. Her paranoia was worse now. She was even placed in a mental hospital for a time. O'Neill's friends urged him to leave her. He told them he was considering it but that he couldn't take this final step.[52]

When she came home, they fell into each other's arms. They didn't seem to be able to live with or without one another. They were like mutual bad habits, the blind leading the blind into an uncertain old age.

The more infirm he became, the tenderer he seemed towards her. In 1951, he drew up a will that made her his sole heir and executrix. He cut Shane and Oona out altogether and also "their issue now or hereafter born."[53] (Shane committed suicide in 1977. Oona stayed married to Chaplin until his death, on Christmas Day of the same year. They had eight children together. Oona, who reportedly lapsed into alcoholism after her husband's passing, died of pancreatic cancer in 1991; she was sixty-six.)

O'Neill had become almost a total recluse now, seeing nobody but his doctors and lawyer. He spent a lot of his time sitting by the window, watching the sailboats on the river and recalling the halcyon days when he sat aboard such vessels. Life was like a banquet then, which he was about to sample in all its riches. As for now, all he could think of was "The Reaper."[54]

Monterey found it difficult to deal with his gloomy moods. His health deteriorated further, making him reluctant even to eat. She thought if she got him to read something his spirits would improve. She was a fan of detective novels and showed him some. O'Neill read them and decided they were poor, that he could do better himself. He told her he was going to write one, but nothing came of it.

As he became weaker, he knew the end was near. His thoughts turned to his uncompleted plays, of which there were many. "Nobody must be allowed to finish them," he said. He believed that after he was dead someone would try to, so he decided to burn them. Monterey told him she wouldn't allow this to happen, but he didn't listen. "It isn't that I don't trust you," he said to her on a dark winter afternoon in early 1953, as she brought him the plays he wanted burned, "but you might drop dead or get run over and I don't want anybody else working on [them]." Said Monterey, "He could only tear a few pages at a time because of his tremor so I helped him. We tore up all the manuscripts together, bit by bit. It took hours. After a pile of torn pages had [been] collected, I'd set a match to them. It was awful. It was like tearing up children."[55]

Toward the end of that year he developed pneumonia. He had shortness of breath and a cough and his temperature reached 104 degrees. He knew he was slipping away. "I want a simple burial," he told Monterey, "with no priest present." He wasn't sure how he felt about the hereafter. He's always described himself as a bad Catholic. As Brendan Behan said, it was the religion of all great writers. If he had the courage in the past, he claimed, he would have killed himself. For Catholics this was a mortal sin, so they preferred to drink themselves to death instead. When asked about a divinity, he quipped, "If there is a God and I meet Him, we'll talk over things man to man."[56]

He died at the age of sixty-five in the Shelton Hotel in Boston. His last words were said to be, "I knew it. Born in a goddamn hotel room and died in a hotel room."[57]

Raymond Chandler

(1888–1959)

Chandler was born in Chicago but spent his early years in Nebraska. His father abandoned the family in 1900. His mother then moved to London, feeling her son would receive a better education there. He returned to the U.S in 1912. When World War I broke out in 1914, he joined the armed forces.

Chandler's fondness for drink started early. "When I was a young man in the RAF," he said, "I would get so plastered I had to crawl to bed on my hands and knees." But his recuperative powers were strong: "At 7.30 the next morning I would be as blithe as a sparrow, and howling for my breakfast."[1] As the years went on the binges became greater and the breakfasts (and blitheness) diminished.

After the war ended in 1918 he began a love affair with Cissy Pascal, a married woman eighteen years his senior (although she only admitted to seven of these on their wedding day). She divorced her husband in 1920, and she and Chandler married four years later. By now he was working as an auditor and bookkeeper with the Dabney oil syndicate.

In the 1920s he began to drink more consistently. There were many reasons. It was partly due to the trauma of the war and partly childhood memories of his father, an alcoholic who physically abused Raymond's mother.[2]

Much of young Chandler's social life revolved around alcohol. He drank at football games and tennis events, often behaving in bizarre manner as a result. He got drunk at the home of a tennis friend once and tried to drag his wife out of bed to join him on the court. When she refused, he took a gun from the living room and threatened to shoot himself.[3]

Some of his drinking was done out of frustration over Cissy's age. At times she seemed more like a mother to him than a wife. He had affairs with some of his secretaries at his workplace, going away with one of them on a long weekend once and getting into trouble upon his return. Incidents like this fueled his writing. He wrote in *The Lady in the Lake*:

> You know how it is with marriage—any marriage. After a while a guy like me, a common no-good guy like me, wants to feel a leg. Maybe it's lousy but that's the way it is.[4]

In 1930, Cissy walked out on him, unable to deal with his drinking and infidelities. She came back to him when he threatened suicide—a familiar ploy he used to get his way—but the tensions remained. The fact that Cissy was so much older caused her to live her life at a slower pace than he was accustomed to. It also meant she was prone to more health problems. This depressed him and made him moody. When her health began to decline it seemed to give him yet another reason to drink, yet another reason to be unfaithful. His drinking contributed to an unhappy home life, and his unhappy home life contributed to his drinking.[5]

He described his drunken behavior graphically in a letter he wrote to a friend:

> I can remember sitting around with two or three congenial chumps and getting plastered to the hairline in a most agreeable manner. We ended up doing acrobatics on the furniture and driving home in the moonlight filled with music and song, missing pedestrians by a thin millimeter and laughing heartily at the idea of a man trying to walk on two legs.[6]

He made weekend trips to football games that involved lots of drinking—and often no football. With a colleague from Dabney's he sometimes chartered a small airplane. They used to fly down the coast towards Mexico. On one occasion he got so drunk he undid his seatbelt and tried to stand upright in the open cockpit. In hotel rooms he made more suicide threats, varying from moments of high elation to dark despair. His booze-soaked frenzies found their way into his fiction, as in this passage from *The Lady in the Lake*:

> I smelled of gin. Not just casually, as if I had taken four or five drinks of a winter morning to get out of bed on, but as if the Pacific Ocean was pure gin and I had head-nosed off the boat deck. The gin was in my hair and eyebrows, on my chin and under my chin. I smelled like dead toads.[7]

He drank through Prohibition, as had Eugene O'Neill. If possible, he drank even more during this time. Speakeasies seemed to be everywhere. They were America's open secret. It was much more fun going in the back door of an establishment than the front. There was the thrill of possibly getting caught.

He continued to top up his glasses at home. If visitors called, he let

Robert Montgomery and Audrey Totter in *Lady in the Lake* (1946).

them know in no uncertain terms that they weren't welcome. One unwanted caller was given a none-too-subtle hint to leave by Chandler donning his pajamas in mid-visit.[8]

He was promoted to vice president of Dabney's in 1931 but lost that title the following year. He could hardly complain: he'd been making a nuisance of himself for some time there. This wasn't only because of his drinking; it was his absenteeism as well. He was also predatory with his female employees, not all of who responded favorably to his advances. To save face, he told people the reason he was being let go was because of the Depression. (It wasn't, unless we spell that word with a lower-case "d.") His gruff manner with certain staff members had been another bone of contention.[9]

Life outside Dabney's was difficult. He'd been earning almost $3,000 a month before he left. That was all gone now. He looked to his friends for a helping hand, but few were forthcoming with loans. Perhaps this was the beginning of his cynicism concerning his fellow man. He was reminded of Orson Welles's remark, "When troubles come, something always turns up, and it's usually the noses of your friends."[10] Having no children eased the burden but it was difficult to meet daily expenses on the lean pickings from the literary table. It was tough on Cissy, too. He knew that the reduction in their quality of living was his doing. She had pneumonia at the time he was fired. They moved in with her sister Lavinia until she recovered. "Raymio," as she called him, promised her he'd go on the wagon and stay away from other women.[11]

They moved into a cheap apartment in Santa Monica. He started submitting stories to crime magazines. Some writers believed inspiration came from poverty; Chandler thought that idea was rubbish. Not having the comforts of yore was just an inconvenience. The lack of money was a distraction to inspiration, a lack of an incentive to sit at his desk.

He did his best to resist the temptation to drink. Sometimes he made his characters big drinkers instead, as if to live vicariously through them. This was especially apparent in his most famous character, Phillip Marlowe. Marlowe personified many of Chandler's qualities, with his sense of isolation, idealism, and his penchant for sarcastic putdowns.

"The toughest thing about trying to cure an alcoholic," a doctor once said to him, "is that you have absolutely nothing to offer him in the long run. He would like to be cured of it if it is not too painful and sometimes even if it is. And it always is. But we forget pain. The alcoholic then looks around him and what does he see? A flat landscape through which there is no road more interesting than another. His reward is negative."[12] This wasn't always the case but it explains why many alcoholics—including Chandler—slip after appearing to be cured. They may have temporarily escaped alcohol hell, but they replace it with something nearly as bad: a limbo of dryness.

He compared drinking to sex: "The first drink is magic," he said, "the second intimate, the third routine. After that you just take the girl's clothes off."[13] The less Chandler drank, the more Marlowe did. It was a form of sublimation for him. Blackouts occur in all of the Marlowe novels. They were telegraphed as early as 1938 in one of his pulp magazine stories. A detective says, "I'm an occasional drinker, the kind of guy who goes out for a beer and wakes up in Singapore with a full beard."[14]

He was once asked how close he was in personality to Marlowe. The way he answered the question showed a humor we don't usually associate with him:

> I am very tough and have been known to break a Vienna roll with my bare hands. I live in a French provincial chateau on Mulholland Drive. It is a fairly small place of 48 rooms and 59 baths. I dine off gold plates and prefer to be waited on by naked dancing girls. There are times when I am entertained in the drunk tank of the city jail. My filing cabinet opens out into a very convenient portable bar, and the bartender, who lives in the bottom drawer, is a midget named Harry Cohn. I am 38 years old and have been for the last twenty years. My favorite weapon is a $20 bill.[15]

Freudians may tell us he wanted to *be* Philip Marlowe. He discovered he could—with a pen in one hand and a bottle in the other. The former accountant morphed into a rumpled anti-hero with a bruised dignity and weary hope. The main thing they had in common was the belief that life was a bad joke. You were best off to go along with it, the hand-me-down existentialism went, if you wanted to beat the rap. All other roads led to destruction.

Cissy tried to persuade him to make his writing more upbeat. She didn't say much but, when she did, he listened. Wives, he felt, made much better literary critics than literary critics.

The 1930s were his happiest years with her. Her health was good then, which helped his demeanor. The fact that he had cut back on his drinking made him more relatable, easier to be around. They lived a quiet life but a romantic one. He tried to compensate for the drinking and womanizing of the Dabney days. Each year on their wedding anniversary he filled a room of their home with red roses. He bought her perfume and jewelry. He wrote love poems to her.[16]

His writing went on without the catalyst of drink. He published many stories in a magazine called *Black Mask*, some in the tradition of Dashiell Hammett, a writer he much admired.[17] There was also a magazine called *The Dime*, to which he contributed various pieces. His writing was disciplined, pared-down. It was also very stylized. One imagined him filing his nails as he documented gruesome murders. He seemed removed from the experiences he wrote about, formalizing the horror into noir vignettes. His mode of narration confused readers who hadn't expected their nickel-and-dime magazines to be this abstruse. His writing had class.

It was difficult to pigeonhole Chandler. The layman felt he was a smart aleck, whereas the snobs saw him as lowbrow. Fellow writers thought he was too good to be writing mysteries; they thought he should try "straight writing." Chandler wasn't sure what that meant, except that it was an insult to mystery writers. Why shouldn't his genre be allowed to embrace life as richly as any other?

By the early 1940s he had attained a modicum of respectability. Intellectuals—"the people who wore soup on their vests"[18]—started to write about him in the Sunday supplements. He had outgrown the pulp tag, at least to an extent. He became best known for his vivid depictions of Los Angeles, a city he once defined as having "no more personality than a paper cup."[19]

He was now invited to Hollywood to work on the 1944 Billy Wilder film adaptation of his novel *Double Indemnity*. He had mixed feelings about the idea. As he put it: "If my books had been any worse I should not have been invited to Hollywood and if they had been any better I should not have come."[20] Between that Scylla and Charybdis he sculpted his syllables for the delectation of those filmgoers who probably didn't read books, who tolerated speeches in films only if they didn't go on too long or sound too literary.

He hadn't been drinking much since he left Dabney's, but he began again on the set of *Double Indemnity*. He was insecure with Wilder, a much younger and brasher man than he. And of course he was also worried about whether he could be a good screenwriter. It was a different situation to being at home with Cissy. That had been the case with all his writing up to this time.

Sometimes, Cissy joined him in his drinking now. Maybe she felt it would keep him closer to her. She knew she couldn't stop him anyway so she adopted an "If you can't beat 'em, join 'em" approach.

Alcohol helped to relax him on the set of *Double Indemnity*. He wrote excellent dialogue for the film's two main stars, Barbara Stanwyck and Fred MacMurray, who were cast as his characters Phyllis Dietrichson and Walter Neff. He was less comfortable with the storyline. There's a funny story told about Howard Hawks cabling him once and asking him who pushed one of his characters off a pier in *The Big Sleep*. Chandler is alleged to have wired back, "No idea."[21] The things that mattered to him were mood, imagery, and the rhythm of speech. He liked the fact that when he was writing, he didn't know how his books would end. That stopped readers guessing "whodunit"—because he didn't know himself until he came to the page in question.

He had a strained relationship with Wilder on the set of the film. Wilder thought his dialogue was too long-winded. Chandler, for his part, felt Wilder cut too many corners and lost character consistency. Whenever they argued, Wilder left the room—ostensibly to go to the men's room but really to have a cigarette. When he was gone, Chandler turned to a pint of bourbon he kept in his briefcase. "It gave him the strength to bear Billy's abuse."[22]

Some commentators on Chandler's life have drawn a parallel between his relationship to Wilder offscreen and the onscreen relationship between insurance agent Neff and his boss, Barton Keyes (Edward G. Robinson). The two characters had an uneasy friendship. Neff hid a deep secret from Keyes: he was a murderer. Chandler's relationship with Wilder was also affected by a secret—his drinking.[23]

As was the case with his time in Dabney's, heavy drinking led to lust. Chandler started looking at other women again now. There were pretty

Fred MacMurray and Edward G. Robinson in *Double Indemnity* (1944). Their relationship paralleled that between Chandler and Billy Wilder.

secretaries walking up and down outside his office every day. He propositioned one of them and she accepted, leading to a brief affair. Cissy found out about it and raised hell. She was now seventy-three; he, only fifty-five. He could deal better with the age gap when he was working in seclusion than he could when in the full glare of the public. It didn't look good, his having an elderly wife in trendy Hollywood. When he escorted her to the premiere of *Double Indemnity*, he left before the lights came on, so ashamed was he of her age and appearance.[24]

Double Indemnity made him rich and famous. He would never reach these heights again. The film also changed the careers of MacMurray and Stanwyk. Suddenly it was cool to be evil. But the film was too hot for the Hollywood Academy to honor. Instead, the more insipid *Going My Way* took the major Oscars that year—seven of them, in fact, including Best Picture, Best Director (Leo McCarey) Best Actor (Bing Crosby), and Best Supporting Actor (Barry Fitzgerald). Chandler and Wilder were shocked at being overlooked, but they still drew some positives from the experience. A seismic shift had taken place in what could be done on screen. MacMurray and Stanwyck had lit the film up with sex and murder, without really showing either. Noir would never be this blistering again. (The acid test is that over seventy years on, nobody has ever dared to remake the movie, at least on the big screen.) It's interesting that the project Wilder took on after *Double Indemnity* was *The Lost Weekend*—the study of an alcoholic played by Ray Milland (who won Best Actor honors for his performance). Was he thinking of Chandler when he made it?

The following years were stop and go for the writer. He liked movie money but did not respect it. He couldn't help seeing screenwriting as a lower art form than the composition of novels. Writers were also the Cinderellas of the movie world. They were expected to do their job quietly and then get out. Stars *made* movies; writers only wrote them. Producers, he remarked, were "low-grade individuals with the morals of a goat and the integrity of a slot machine."[25] But he continued to work in the field. He wrote the original screenplay for *The Blue Dahlia*, which he sold to Paramount in 1946.

His drinking made it difficult for him to function on the Paramount lot or even get to it. Things got so bad at one point that he asked John Houseman, the film's producer, if he could work from home. Houseman said yes. Emboldened by this, he then told Houseman he wanted six secretaries, a cab driver to take he and Cissy to the doctor when necessary and someone to drive his maid to and from the market. Again, Houseman concurred. Chandler added one last request: He was suffering from writer's block and needed to be drunk to get out of it. Again Houseman agreed.[26] So that was the way he finished the script. He always claimed it worked for that reason. The only problem he had with the film was its female lead, Veronica Lake, whom he referred to as "Moronica" Lake.

The Blue Dahlia contained over thirteen references to drinking, an indication of where Chandler's head was when he wrote it. The Production Code Administration (then known as the Breen Office) clamped down, demanding revisions and/or retractions. Chandler grudgingly agreed, though he insisted on keeping the film's last line: "Did somebody say something about a drink of bourbon?"

He worked on *The Big Sleep* that year as well, earning many plaudits for it, but after his contract was completed, he announced his intention of leaving Hollywood for keeps. How would he survive without its money? More importantly, would he be able to become sober again?

Later that year the couple moved to La Jolla, a coastal district 100 miles south of Los Angeles. He described it as "nothing but a climate and meaningless chi-chi."[27] The mean streets of Los Angeles weren't here, just "old people and their parents."[28] But Cissy liked it as somewhere she could put down roots and call home. That was more important to her than to him. He enjoyed the nomadic lifestyle. It fed his imagination.

Cissy's age was working against her more and more now. In her seventies, she developed fibrosis of the lungs. She had to take sedatives to kill the pain. As a result, she was groggy much of the time. The pair of them grew more distant from one another. She started dressing younger in an attempt to look better, but this tended to have the opposite effect. She looked pitiful in her suggestive chiffon, although Chandler appreciated her motive for wearing it.

He returned to Hollywood briefly in 1950, working with Alfred Hitchcock on the script for *Strangers on a Train*. This wasn't a happy experience for him. He wouldn't have been the first (nor last) writer to find Hitch too mechanical. Neither was the director satisfied with Chandler. In the end, Hitchcock actually fired him. But he was well paid for the indignity—$40,000 for just eight weeks' work.

He started to tire easily now, to become jaded. He dramatized himself like a character from one of his novels. "I have lived my life on the edge of nothing," he pronounced, with mock-solemnity.[29] He wasn't sure if he could produce good work anymore. He was ready to throw in the towel and many people felt he would indeed do so. But Chandler rarely did what people expected of him. Instead, he embarked on his last Marlowe novel. It was appropriately titled *The Long Goodbye*.

As the novel germinated in his mind he sailed for London with Cissy in 1952. It was a trip they had been planning for years. She was now eighty-two, but Chandler was unaware of her actual age; he still believed she was at least seven years younger. She became sick on the boat, and sicker still in London. Chandler became frustrated by this and did what he always did when he was under pressure—drink. A trip that was meant to add luster to their marriage instead brought tension to it. They still loved each other dearly, but not even love could fight the infirmities of age. The vacation ended as a non-event, a dress rehearsal for the bad times ahead.

Cissy's health worsened back in the U.S. As Chandler struggled with the final pages of *The Long Goodbye*, he took to sleeping on a couch outside her room so he could be ready to tend her at a moment's notice. He wasn't drinking now, nor was he eating. His weight dropped so much that he was reduced to punching two holes in his belt to tighten it.[30]

Everything seemed to be leaving him: his wife, his protagonist, his will to live. Cissy worried about how he might be if anything happened to her. She knew how dependent he was. She died at the end of 1954 and Chandler went to pieces. He arrived drunk at the funeral. Maybe that was the only way he could have gone at all.[31] Afterward, he continued to drink. Going into her room, picking through her clothes—everything brought her back in a way that was unbearable for him. He sat among her effects trying to remember the good times, but he felt only pain.

He had spent his life writing about tough guys. Now he was called upon to show the greatest strength of all: that of the mind. He once said that Humphrey Bogart was his favorite movie hero because he was "tough without a gun."[32] Could Chandler be tough without a wife? To the outside world he'd always seemed to be the dominant member of that relationship. Few visitors even got to see Cissy; fewer still ever actually heard her talk. But Chandler knew who the *real* boss was. The silence of her death was deafening.

Chandler was never able to handle his drink. When he got older it took over his life completely.

On February 22, 1955, just ten weeks after Cissy died, he rang the police station in La Jolla to say he was about to shoot himself. He was drunk when he made the call. Neither was it the first of its kind that he made. When the police arrived at the house they heard two shots coming from the shower area. They followed the sound and found Chandler slumped on the floor with a .38 caliber revolver in his mouth. They told him to surrender the weapon; he did so peacefully.

The first shot, it turned out, had been fired by accident when he fell getting into the shower. The second misfired, ricocheting off the walls. It was an old revolver and the cartridges were weak. Had it been a genuine attempt to kill himself? He didn't even know himself. He was too drunk to remember. He was placed in a psychiatric ward of the San Diego County Hospital for the night.[33] The attention he received from the nurses during his hospital stay after this farcical episode persuaded him that it might be better hanging around a while longer.

The character of Roger Wade made a half-hearted suicide attempt in *The Long Goodbye* by trying to shoot himself. It was "just a wild shot at the ceiling," he tells Marlowe, who replies, "You were just swimming in a sea of self-pity."[34]

Back home, though, his gloom returned with a vengeance. In a drunken stupor, he called people in the middle of the night, often staying on the line for ages without speaking. If he did speak it was usually in morose tones about death. Or suicide. Or Cissy. All three topics were really the same conversation.

He knew he had to leave La Jolla. Every room in the house screamed at him with her memory. As he wrote in one novel: "Whenever I went, whatever I did, this was what I would come back to: A blank wall in a meaningless room in a meaningless house."[35] He sprang from it "like an animal released from a trap."[36]

Where would he go? He decided on London, where he had been with Cissy just a few years earlier. He was, of course, half-British himself and had a fondness for Britain in general. "In England I am an author," he once remarked, "in the U.S.A. just a mystery writer."[37]

He stayed at the Connaught Hotel, spending money like it was going out of style. Maybe he suspected time was running out for him and he wanted to be rid of it. After a month he was asked to leave because of his drunken behavior. He moved to the Ritz but drank even more there. Again, he was asked to leave. His agent, Helga Greene, helped him find a flat. There, amazingly, he stopped drinking. His friend Natasha Spender brought him to Italy on a trip. He stayed sober on it even though he was bored to tears.[38]

His visa ran out in October 1955. He returned to the U.S., but two months later he was back in London again. He said he had come over to see Spender, who was about to have surgery. As she waited for her operation, he took her to Tunisia to repay her for the Italian trip. There he became morose and philosophical, spending most of his time in a whiskey-soaked funk.[39]

Spender, Green and others formed what they called a "shuttle" service, geared toward his emotional regeneration. He assigned them all special roles in this. "In his mind," Spender remarked, "we all became characters in a Raymond Chandler novel."[40] Part of their function was to monitor his drinking, but this ambition was doomed to disaster. Alcohol helped him make sense of the world. A swig of a martini made him feel he could roll back the years, take on a new guise, blot out the feeling that he was half in love with death. Or that he wanted to join Cissy on the "other side."

He kept up a pose of debonair charm in London, but sometimes the mask slipped, as when he broke down crying one day when speaking about his late wife to a *Daily Express* reporter.[41] He couldn't get over her. "She was the beat of my heart for thirty years," he said.[42]

Wherever he went he praised her grace and dignity, usually doubling the blow of her demise by focusing so much on it. The people he met were kind but, if they were female and pretty, he sometimes mistook this for interest. He made a fool of himself with many women in this way. If drink was involved, which it usually was, the situation became even messier. He tried to talk his way into their beds but cut a sorry figure as he did so. He tried to be gallant with them, as he had once been with Cissy, but he was really just going through the motions. He once saw it as "treason" to look at another woman, but after the slow torture of Cissy's death—"I watched my wife die by half-inches," he sobbed—suddenly he seemed to be in love with all of them.[43]

On went the drinking. There were accidents and some hospital stays courtesy of these. When doctors suggested he cut down he ignored them. Eventually he found one who thought sobriety made him melancholic. He liked the diagnosis and continued to visit this doctor, who effectively gave him a license to imbibe. Maybe he felt he was going to drink anyway, so he might as well make it pleasurable for him.

He documented his average day to Jessica Tyndale in a 1955 letter:

> I start off with a drink of white wine and end up drinking two bottles of Scotch. Then I stop eating. I have to quit and the withdrawal symptoms are simply awful. I shake so that I can't hold a glass of water. One day I vomited eighteen times. My father was an alcoholic and I have lived my whole life in fear of becoming one but until my wife died I always quit drinking on my own power when I felt there was a real need for it. For three years before she died I was as dry as a bone.[44]

Taking care of her had given him a role, but now that role was gone. And with it the motivation to stay sober.

He returned to the U.S. in May 1956. Shortly after getting there he fell downstairs in New York and had to be taken to a hospital. His spirits now revived. He always enjoyed the attention of medical staff, particularly female medical staff.

His doctor told him it was bad for him to live alone. He agreed he needed female company. He didn't care if it was "one woman or twenty." If he was on his own, he thought, he would drink and then get sick. The problem was, Chandler drank *anyway*—maybe even more so with company. When people told him he was on the verge of alcoholism, he replied, à la Marlowe, "That's a nice little verge."[45] Curiously, he didn't see himself as an alcoholic.

Natasha Spender visited him at the end of 1956. He drove to meet her at Phoenix airport—a bad idea. He was drunk behind the wheel, so drunk that as he drove her from the airport she seriously considered throwing herself from the car to save her life. After they got to the house— miraculously—she told him he needed to dry out. Chandler wasn't interested in this kind of talk. She was ready to scream, but liked him too much to do that.

When he found himself able to write again he resurrected an abandoned screenplay from 1947 called *Playback*. This was the only one of his books (as opposed to screenplays) that he finished drunk. He had a throat infection at the time. He mixed alcohol with penicillin, giving himself a double high. Maybe this explains the amount of comedy in the book.

He now placed an advertisement for a secretary in the *San Diego Tribune*. Jean Fracasse, an Australian woman, answered it. Chandler proceeded to fall in love with her and proposed marriage, as well as announcing plans to set up a trust for two children she'd had from a previous marriage. He also fell in love with Helga Greene at this time, and even with Green's colleague Kay West, proposing marriage to her as well. Raymio was making so many betrothals of undying troth it was difficult to keep up with them.[46]

Greene asked West to stay with him for a while to look after him, worried as she was about his erratic behavior. One night she woke up in the middle of the night to find him on the landing of the stairs, crawling on all fours towards the liquor cabinet. The next morning, he had no recollection of the incident.[47]

Ian Fleming interviewed him on BBC Radio in 1958. He was drunk during the interview and appeared uninterested in Fleming's questions. The liquor, as ever, took over.

Towards the end of the year he switched from Scotch to champagne at the suggestion of a doctor, a decision that made about as much sense as it sounded. The "cure" was worse than the disease.

The more he drank, the less he ate. Malnourished and morose, he wandered around the house, searching for the magic of his past and finding only dried relics. On the rare occasions he saw people he tried to affect the craggy dignity of a Marlowe, but those who knew him realized what a poor actor he was.

His last—unfinished—novel had Marlowe getting married. He called it *Poodle Springs*—a play on Palm Springs. Maybe it was better that he didn't finish it. A married Marlowe was like a widowed Chandler: a fish out of water. He intended to have Marlowe drink himself to death in it, which might have been slightly more likely.[48]

The creator of the iconic private eye died in 1959. It wasn't a dramatic death, just an inevitable one. The death certificate gave a medical explanation for his demise, but most people knew what the real killer was—drink.

But what did it matter how he died, Marlowe would have said, whether it was from drink or a gunshot wound or heartbreak or any of the other natural shocks that flesh is heir to. It didn't matter whether he died on a dirty dump or a marble tower at the top of a high hill.

He was dead and he was sleeping the big sleep.

Edna St. Vincent Millay

(1892–1950)

Serenity shot out of Edna St. Vincent Millay's eyes, but behind them lay passionate intensity. A free spirit before that term was coined, she strode like a Colossus through the early years of the last century, burning the candle at both ends with her intoxicating personality.

From a young age she uttered a great "Yea" to life in all of its vicissitudes. Daniel Mark Epstein outlined this in no uncertain terms:

> If beauty is dangerous, if it is a poison, then she will sip at it drop by drop until she can enjoy more of beauty than any man alive. If sex is dangerous, she will study and practice it until she has mastered all of its holds, feints and attacks, and until she has learned to escape from sex without injury. If men say alcohol is deleterious she will drink with such gusto and diligence, her tolerance for beer, wine and gin will render her free from every effect but the liquor's pleasure. And when alcohol has been tamed, there will always be hashish and morphine.[1]

Many people regarded her as the most seductive woman of her era. More pretty than beautiful, she exerted an almost hypnotic influence on men—and on women, too. Nothing seemed to be beyond her ambit. She became enraptured by desire and pushed it to its limits, often to her detriment. An electrifying personality, she lived life from the ground up.

She was born in Rockland, Maine, on February 22, 1892, the daughter of a schoolteacher, Henry, and a nurse, Cora. Her middle name derived from St. Vincent's Hospital in New York. It was there that her uncle's life had been saved just before her birth.

Her father was a spendthrift. When Edna was four, Cora told him to leave the house. To the surprise of all, he acceded to her demand. Cora loved literature and transmitted such a love to Edna and her two younger sisters, Norma and Kathleen. They grew up with strong wills and minds, especially Edna. They were as unified as the three sisters of Anton Chekhov's most famous play.

Cora had once dreamed of being a writer herself, but it didn't happen.

To make up, she was determined to give her daughters all the artistic opportunities she missed.[2] She taught Edna to write verse at four. At seven she was playing the piano. She was only fourteen when she won her first prize for poetry. A year later she was being published in various magazines. She often sent her poems out using the initial "E" instead of Edna, to suggest that she might have been a man. She felt this would increase her chances of publication.[3] Cora, in fact, brought her up like a man. This was because she'd been expecting a boy when she had her.[4]

She entered a national poetry competition in 1912 with a contribution entitled "Renascence." It only came in fourth, but most people—including the three poets who placed ahead of her—agreed that her work was infinitely superior to theirs. Congratulatory letters poured in from around the country, making her into a celebrity of sorts. Nobody could believe that a nineteen-year-old girl could have written such an "astonishing" poem.[5]

Millay combined her love of drink with a simultaneous addiction to morphine, which she used to combat the pain that dogged her for most of her life, being intensified by a horrific car accident. The combination of the two fed into her writing with sometimes brilliant and sometimes disastrous results (*Writer Pictures*).

She entered Vassar College in 1913 and shook it to its foundations. She was a maverick, a radical whose intellectual brilliance threw the authorities. She smoked and drank when she felt like it, cut classes, played hooky from compulsory chapel, spearheaded classroom insurrections and went AWOL with frequency. She broke every rule in the manual and then turned in papers that were so brilliant her teachers had no choice but to give her top grades.[6] Some of them were tempted to threaten her with expulsion, but the college's president, Henry MacCracken, thought differently. "I know all about poets at college," he said. "I don't want a banished Shelley on my doorstep."[7]

She didn't like Vassar,

complaining that it was run like an orphan asylum, with "its inmates pacified by ice cream and candy."[8] But she managed to do her own thing there, including having some lesbian romances and campaigning on social issues. When World War 1 broke out in Europe, she marched against it.

She moved to Greenwich Village in 1917, managing the transition from bluestocking to *gamine* with some relish. Norma stayed with her in a cramped apartment. She was happy there even though money was scarce. A new world was dawning and she wanted to be part of it. Young women were bobbing their hair and giving up corsets. They were also taking lovers and speaking their mind. Her mother had prepared her for such a life. Now she was living it.

Prohibition had come in but there was always bootleg gin to be found in the speakeasies that proliferated around the Village. Swilling it was one way to overcome the wartime blues.

In the winter of that year she joined a drama group, the Provincetown Players. They would soon stage the works of none other than Eugene O'Neill. She auditioned for a role in a play called *The Angel Intrudes*. Floyd Dell was the director. She was attracted to him; he soon became her lover.[9] Afterward, she had many others as she boldly proclaimed the right of a woman to love "as willfully and capriciously as a man."[10] She always made mistakes with men, she said, but never the same mistake twice.[11]

Dell tried to get her to go to a psychoanalyst to "cure" her of her "Sapphic tendencies."[12] She didn't want to do this, for two reasons. First, she didn't think there was anything wrong with them; second, they inspired her poetry.

She next became infatuated with the poet Arthur Ficke. He proved to be the one that got away, which made her desire him even more. The pain of the loss is evident in many of the sonnets she wrote at this time.[13] She wrote by day and acted by night. When she wasn't acting she cruised the local bars in search of another kind of stimulation. If she was having her period she sipped some "anti-cure gin."[14]

After she received news of the armistice in the fall of 1918, she cavorted with friends until dawn, riding back and forth on the Staten Island ferry and drinking from a jug of wine. Afterward they clambered up and down the shoreline of the island, dancing on the beach and chasing one another through the dunes. She stumbled home to her cold-water flat the next morning to compose more poetry, keeping herself warm by chain-smoking cigarettes and drinking endless cups of tea.

Her first poetry collection, *A Few Figs from Thistles*, was published in 1920. It created much controversy, largely because of its sexual undertones—and overtones.

Fortunately for her, A *Few Figs from Thistles* was indeed a good book. This wasn't Wordsworth's emotion recollected in tranquility but rather the emotion itself, raw and unvarnished. The words leapt off the page in all their melodious grandeur. Her next book, *The Ballad of the Harp Weaver*, was equally passionate and was awarded the Pulitzer Prize. She was only the third woman to be so honored, following Sara Teasdale in 1918 and Margaret Widdemer the year after that.

Drinking had not become a problem as yet, despite her near-constant imbibing. Alcohol helped her fly on wings of poesy to her preferred land of the imagination. This she captured in the sonnets that became the treasured love fugues of a generation. Such fugues were generally inspired by the romances she was having in her life.

In one of her most famous poems she wrote,

> My candle burns at both ends
> It will not last the night
> But ah, my foes, and oh, my friends
> It gives a lovely light.

Such lines became anthemic to budding writers. With them, Millay turned into the "It Girl" of the hour, the "Miss America of 1920," as far as writing was concerned.[15] Dorothy Parker remarked, "She did a great deal of harm with her double-burning candles. She made poetry seem so easy that we thought we could all do it. But of course we couldn't."[16]

She received marriage proposals from Floyd Dell and also from the writer Edmund Wilson, but she turned both of them down for Eugene Boizzevain, the man she married in 1923. He had formerly been married to the labor lawyer Inez Mulholland, who died in 1916.

Boizzevain was a prosperous Dutch businessman who made his money importing coffee and other products. A bombastic character, he had a great curiosity about life. Unlike Millay's other lovers, he was no fan of poetry, but he enjoyed hearing her talk about it—and indeed about everything else. Mulholland had been rather dour, having little time to enjoy life between her various crusades—the repeal of capital punishment, securing the vote for women, etc.—but Millay was different. She was both a feminist *and* fun to be with.

They bought a 600-acre farm in Austerlitz, New York, calling it Steepletops. Millay grew her own vegetables there. She wrote in a cabin on the grounds. It also had a tennis court. In the summers, the newlyweds repaired to Ragged Island, their summer retreat at Casco Bay, Maine.

Her life was a round of tennis matches, parlor games, nude swimming parties. Domesticity bored her, which meant Boissevain took on the role of househusband. "If I let her struggle with the problems of order," he said, "she doesn't write, so I solve it quite simply. I look after everything."[17] Millay appreciated this. She liked order, but "if I had to live in a mess or live in a neat room and give up my writing, I prefer the mess."[18]

Boissevain had had an open relationship with Mulholland. A marriage that didn't allow both parties the freedom to cavort with other lovers was, he believed, "like an ice box with always the same cold chicken in it."[19] Such a practice continued with Millay. If she wanted to be with another man he got out of the way. Her sexual appetite was so large she could have been classified as a nymphomaniac.[20] She plotted "with the precision of a French *farceur*" the entrances and exits of her lovers so they wouldn't collide.[21] A lot of the time it was mixed in with emotional need. Maybe she never quite learned to separate the two.

Her poetry trailed off a little after she got married, the tension of her life up to now being more conducive to inspiration than domestic stability.[22] Boissevain wasn't to blame for this. He accepted the fact that she was more important than him. "Anybody can buy and sell coffee," he remarked, "but not anybody can write poetry."[23] He was blithely lacking in ego and slapped his thigh in delight anytime he was referred to as "Mr. Edna St. Vincent Millay."[24]

This was magnanimous of him, but it took an edge of excitement away from the marriage, and Millay needed excitement. In the words of one writer, love was her religion. Such a compulsion was combined with the knowledge that most love affairs ended badly. In modern parlance, love was a dangerous game for her, but one she continued to play both on and off the page, whatever the consequences.

She met the poet George Dillon at a reading at the University of Chicago in 1930 and fell headlong for him. He was fourteen years her junior, a fact she tried her best to ignore. Despite her devotion to him she continued to have other lovers. In May of that year she went to the apartment of a man called John Bishop and slept with him. Before doing so, she informed him that he was just one of three men she planned to bed that day.[25] But Dillon meant more than sex to her. He became an obsession.

He meant more to her than any man she'd met up to now, including Boissevain. Her love for Boissevain was too bourgeois for her. That, for Dillon, was more like an "enchanted sickness" which came over her, "as if I had drunk a witch's philter."[26]

She said she loved Boissevain but that she was *in* love with Dillon. This could be construed as wanting to have things both ways. Boissevain fed into such duplicity, if such it was. Her affair with Dillon progressed with his blessing. He conducted himself almost like a gooseberry with the couple rather than a chaperone or cuckold. This freed him up for dalliances of his own, which Millay accepted with equal grace. "Eugene and I live like two bachelors," she boasted.[27]

Her mother died in 1931. She blamed herself for having neglected her in recent times, obsessed as she was with her affair with Dillon. She never really recovered from this death, and neither did her sister Kathleen, whose marriage broke up afterward. Kathleen then descended into clinical paranoia, eventually drinking herself to death. Millay outlived her sister but, for the next twenty years, she sought to block out the tragedy in drink, drugs, and "playing Russian roulette with death."[28]

Part of the reason she drank was because she was plagued with headaches, a condition she eased with alcohol. It also relieved the pain induced by accidents, like the time she scratched her cornea. But there was a price to be paid: "The pain made her irritable; alcohol relieved her for the evening and a hangover made her short-tempered again."[29]

By the early 1930s she was sorely in the grip of alcoholism, suffering blackouts that took her "right out of the picture" as she frequented one speakeasy after another, hardly knowing who was accompanying her to them. One night she got so drunk she boarded a train and then fell face down on her berth. When the conductor asked her for her ticket she passed out. She woke up a few hours later in her night attire. She couldn't remember undressing, so she assumed the conductor did the honors.[30]

Her love for Dillon inspired the sonnets in her 1931 collection, *Fatal Interview*, but he distanced himself from her as time went on. Her grief fed into the work and caused her to drink more. She may have been the most adored poet of her time but inside she felt like a broken woman. She pined for him and also for her mother. Alcohol seemed the only poultice she could put over these emotional scars to soothe them. She had champagne for breakfast, gin fizzes for lunch, martinis in the afternoon, wine with dinner, and brandy nightcaps. Her doctor told her she'd have to change her lifestyle or die.[31]

Her failure to hold on to Dillon was a watershed for her, a signal that she was losing her "animal" appeal. Age had entered the equation. No longer could she assume her personality alone could captivate and hypnotize.[32]

She knew she was too old for him but, still, couldn't let go of him.

She tried to write her way out of her pain, but couldn't. Drinking her way out of it proved easier. By 1935 she was hooked on Fleischmann's gin. She wrote to her friend Witter Bynner in May of that year, "I am at present under the influence of hashish, gin, bad poetry, love, morphine and hunger."[33] It was quite a cocktail. Even though morphine was a controlled substance, Boissevain was able to procure it from a pharmacy in the nearby town of Great Barrington.

She traveled to France with him at the beginning of 1934. After they docked at Marseille she wrote in her diary that she sat at the bar all afternoon getting "tighter and tighter."[34] She didn't remember leaving the bar or going to her cabin. "Got to cut it out," she finished, "Not only that the doctor says so but I'm getting a tummy."[35] The following morning, however, she forgot her promise to herself and had "seven gin-rickeys" for her sojourn there.[36]

At Cap d'Antibes she started living a healthy life. She rose at sunrise each day to play badminton and take long walks by the sea. But then the violent winds of the mistral began to blow and she couldn't go outdoors anymore. She also had "the curse"—another excuse to imbibe. "You have to do something to fight off the mistral," she wrote in her diary. "I have a headache and feel nervous and irritable. Think I'll get drunk."[37] Later on in the trip she said she drank "buckets" of champagne cocktails. On a trip to Paris by train the mistral continued to blow and she was also unhappy with the bed in her compartment. "The sheets are of cotton and I hate cotton sheets," she wrote, "Thank heaven I have a flask of gin along."[38]

Her problems were increased a hundredfold in 1936 when she was in the car with Boissevain and the door swung open. She was leaning against it, not realizing it wasn't properly closed. She was thrown down a rocky embankment, rolling over several times before she was able to catch hold of a tree and stop.[39] Her injuries would have long-lasting consequences. "We are not pleased with God," said Boissevain.[40]

The main problems she sustained were to her back and shoulder. The pain was so bad, her doctor prescribed Dilaudid and morphine. Boissevain injected the morphine into her. All forms of treatment were used to try and alleviate the pain: X-rays, surgery, massage, infrared rays and so on, but none of them really worked. She slept on a plank for five months. She found it difficult to use a typewriter or even a knife and fork to eat.[41]

She changed doctors. A year after the accident, her new doctor increased her dosage. He also augmented it with a cocktail of other drugs, including barbiturates, to help her sleep. She topped these up with alcohol. For the next four years she was in and out of the hospital, ostensibly suffering from "recurrent depression."[42] Her real problem, however, was drug addiction.[43]

She cut a sorry figure at the inception of World War II. "Her body sagged, her lips shriveled, her teeth were discolored and pain had engraved her face.... Then there was a steady stream of alcohol."[44] Despite all this, her enormous resilience caused her to forget her problems enough to become a war activist. She joined the Writers' War Board, the Red Cross, and the wartime *New York Times* Conference of Women.

By 1941, she was addicted to morphine, which she took in conjunction with codeine and Nembutal. She was in denial about her addiction, claiming she took these substances to combat the pain she was getting from headaches, backaches, shoulder aches, and menstrual cramps. She was more honest about her addiction to alcohol, which was on its way to destroying her liver.[45]

As would be the case with Anne Sexton some years down the road, she found it difficult to do a reading without some liquid stimulation. Boissevain was usually on hand with the trusty hip flask before she went on. She'd knock back a swig of it as a matter of routine and have some more afterward as the applause rang in her ears.[46]

Afterward came the hangovers and low moods. Her depression was mistaken by some for aesthetic haughtiness. She received an anonymous letter that stung her deeply:

> You and Mahatma Gandhi would make a first-class team. You could give him some of your hair and some of your rags. Come down to earth. Be yourself. After all, you are not a Second Messiah. The Lord have mercy on your husband.[47]

Her intake of morphine rose to three grains a day. Her friends tried to persuade her to put herself under the care of a more stringent doctor but she resisted this, fearful that any diminution would take away her intensity of spirit. She was also injecting herself with insulin now.[48]

She stopped writing poetry, spending most of her time lounging around the house in a daze. On St. Patrick's Day in 1944 she swallowed a cocktail of Nembutal, codeine, and Dilaudid, as well as consuming five grains of morphine.[49] She was lucky to survive this overdose.

Boissevain lost most of his wealth in the war and their massive medical bills drained his resources even further. Steepletops had to be remortgaged. To swell their coffers, she prevailed upon her publishers to give her advances upfront. Eugene had funded her generously in the past. Now she felt it was her turn to pony up on their living expenses.[50]

Her work was suffering at this time, being criticized for its war-fueled propagandist import. As Paul Engle wrote, it was doubtful that a bad poem could help a good war.[51] She was aware of this and suffered a breakdown as a result of it. "There is nothing on this earth," she said, "which can get on the nerves of a good poet as the writing of bad poetry."[52]

These years posed a bigger challenge to her psychological stability than anything she had experienced so far. How could she have gone from the vivacious Vassar graduate to a reclusive agoraphobe who rarely dressed? Life became dull, repetitive. "It's not true that life is one damn thing after another," she reflected wryly. "It's one damn thing over and over."[53]

She went to the hospital in 1944 in an attempt to deal with her various addictions. The doctors managed to wean her off morphine, but held less hope for curing her drinking problem. Her report upon leaving read, "Patient discharged. Still an alcoholic—initial condition unimproved."[54]

It would have been easy to go under but, once again, her fighting spirit came to her rescue. She tackled her problems by going cold turkey in the following years. After coming home from a summer in Ragged Island in 1947 she said, "I am strong and brown from months of swimming in the sea and working in the hot sun.... I am clean of drugs now and clean of alcohol. Eight months without a drink, six months without even a drop of wine."[55]

She had two years of relative happiness with Boissevain in her reformed condition, but he contracted lung cancer in 1949 and died from it in the same year. Millay had another nervous breakdown as a result and went back on the bottle.

Her doctor permitted her a liter and a half of wine per day when she was admitted into a hospital that year suffering from depression. It was unlikely she'd keep to that limit, especially when visitors started sneaking in bottles. These she dispatched to the top shelf of her closet and soon had quite a stash. When news of it reached her doctor he signaled his disapproval. She replied defensively that wine wasn't injurious to her. Rather, it was "a beautiful amber and rosy liquid that inspired the literary imagination." When he said she needed to practice moderation, she told him he was being "too medical" and treating "this beautiful liquid of the Gods like a common medicine."[56]

Drinking moderated her grief, but it wasn't able to take it away. She couldn't stop thinking of Boissevain. What an irony that the woman who talked so much about the necessity to have other men outside marriage should feel her life was over now that her husband was gone. He had, of course, overprotected her. She compared the anxiety she felt without him to a child's fear of going to the dentist.[57]

By 1950 she was beginning to deal with her loss, and even get back to writing, but on October 18 of that year, after staying up all night reading the proofs of a translation of *The Aeneid*, she felt ill while going up the stairs. After sitting down to rest she suffered a heart attack and died. She had a glass of wine in her hand when she got her attack. It was perhaps the only time in her life she ever left a drink unfinished.

Dorothy Parker

(1893–1967)

Parker was born Dorothy Rothschild in New Jersey in 1893 to a Jewish father and a Scottish-American mother. She was two months premature. "It was the last time I was early for anything," she joked.[1] Her mother died in Dorothy's infancy, and her father remarried. She was raised by her stepmother, whom she referred to as "the maid." Dorothy was enrolled in a Catholic school, where, she claimed, the only thing of note she learned was that if you spat on a pencil eraser it erased ink as well. She was eventually expelled for suggesting that the Immaculate Conception was nothing more than "spontaneous combustion."[2]

In the summer of 1916 she fell in love with Edwin "Eddie" Pond Parker II, a stockbroker. When the U.S entered the war the following year, Parker enlisted as an ambulance driver. Before he went away they decided to marry. "We were married for about five minutes," she sighed, "then he went off to war."[3]

Her first literary post was as a caption writer for *Vogue*. She then became a reviewer for *Vanity Fair*. Robert Benchley was her editor. The two became friends and, for a time, shared an undersized office off Times Square. "One cubic foot less of space," Benchley quipped, "and it would have constituted adultery."[4]

Both of them soon became members of the famed Round Table set at the Algonquin Hotel. Charter members of the Round Table included: Franklin Pierce Adams, columnist; Heywood Broun, columnist and sportswriter (married to Ruth Hale); Marc Connelly, playwright; Ruth Hale, freelance writer who worked for women's rights; George S. Kaufman, playwright and director; Brock Pemberton, Broadway producer; Harold Ross, The *New Yorker* editor; Robert E. Sherwood, author and playwright; John Peter Toohey, Broadway publicist; Alexander Woollcott, critic and journalist; Membership was not official or fixed for so many others who moved in and out of the Circle. Some of these included: Tallulah Bankhead, actress; Noël Coward, playwright; Blyth Daly, actress; Edna Ferber, author and playwright; Eva Le Gallienne, actress; Margalo Gillmore, actress; Jane Grant, journalist and feminist (married to Ross); Beatrice Kaufman, editor and playwright (married to George S. Kaufman); Margaret Leech, writer and historian; Neysa McMein, magazine illustrator; Harpo Marx, comedian and film star; Alice Duer Miller, writer; Donald Ogden Stewart, playwright and screenwriter; Frank Sullivan, journalist and humorist; Deems Taylor, composer; Estelle Winwood, actress; and Peggy Wood, actress.[5]

His marriage to Eddie was marred by his drinking. In the army he was called "Spook," a reference to his ghostlike appearance when hungover. This was a frequent condition of his. (He drank a pint of whiskey once on a furlough, passed out, and then drank another one after he woke up). His friends felt sorry for Dorothy, unaware of the fact that she would develop habits even worse than these in the years to come.[6]

When Eddie came back from the war he was out of his depth with his wife and her sophisticated Round Tablers. By now she'd developed the caustic style of writing—and speaking—that would become her trademark. Nuggets of wit emanated from her almost without her being aware of them.

The first thing she did when she got up in the morning, she said, was brush her teeth and sharpen her tongue.[7] She described Channing Pollock's *House Beautiful* as "Play lousy."[8] A novel she reviewed wasn't to be tossed aside lightly but rather "thrown with great force."[9] The actress Marion Davies, she said, had just two expressions: "Joy and indigestion."[10]

Like Parker, the Algonquin members were all big drinkers. Heywood Broun carried a hip flask around with him out of which he poured generous amounts of alcohol at regular intervals. Edmund Wilson stumbled away from the hotel most nights in a decrepit state. One of Robert Benchley's most famous quips was uttered after being caught in the rain: "Let's get out of these clothes and into a dry martini." Scott Fitzgerald once said to Benchley, "Bob, don't you know that drinking is slow death?" Benchley replied, "So who's in a hurry?"[11]

Parker enjoyed bantering with this set but she was also aware such banter was often a substitute for work. The Round Tablers, she said, were "famous for being famous."[12] She debunked them for being self-serving: "Think of who was writing in those days—Lardner, Fitzgerald, Faulkner and Hemingway. Those were the real giants. The Round Table was just a lot of people telling jokes and telling each other how good they were. Just a bunch of loudmouths showing off, saving their gags for days, waiting for a chance to spring them." She described the women of the Round Table as "little black ewes that had gone astray," a sort of "ladies' auxiliary of the legion of the damned."[13]

But she enjoyed their cordiality. Most people who drop acid with the facility she did feed off the oxygen of laughter. Not Dorothy Parker, however: she felt her one-liners obscured her more serious work. It would have been a terrible thing, she averred, to be remembered for her repartee rather than her verse.[14] Sadly, that's what happened. When she said something like, "Men rarely make passes at girls who wear glasses," it became more quoted than any of her poems or stories.[15]

People also grew fearful of her venomous wit. They knew vitriol lay behind her surface charm; there was an iron fist in that velvet glove. Ernest Hemingway noted: "She had a soft side, like blackberry pie. But the bitch was always there, ready to rise with the heat."[16] George S. Kaufman underlined that estimation: "If she didn't take to you, she bit you, digested you and spat you out.... You looked at her and you knew she was sizing you up for a straight left at the appropriate time."[17] Dashiell Hammett said she carried "brass knuckles" on her tongue.[18]

It was even worse when she was drinking—which was most of the time. Part of the appeal of alcohol for Parker was the fact that when she started drinking seriously it was illegal. "Bootleg hooch" became her poison of choice, the forbidden fruit displayed so prominently in speakeasies for liberal souls like hers. She wrote of a character in one of her early stories:

> She commenced drinking alone, little short drinks all through the day. Alone, it blurred sharp things for her. She lived in a haze of it. Her life took on a dream-like quality. She was never noticeable drunk and seldom nearly sober. It required a large daily allowance to keep her misty-minded. Too little and she was achingly melancholy.[19]

One imagines her own experience to have been similar to this.

She first became aware she was taking too much in the early twenties. This was when she started using a substance called tuberose to mask its smell. Tuberose was so strong undertakers used it for embalming purposes.

As was the case with most of her problems in life, she tried to hide this one under a carapace of humor. She told her friends her hangovers were so bad they should be preserved in the Smithsonian Institution under glass. The best way to avoid hangovers, she added, was to stay drunk.[20]

Her friend Vincent Sheen thought she drank to dull her perception of life. It was more likely she did so to enhance it. "Three highballs and I think I'm Francis of Assisi," she crowed.[21]

Sometimes she drank to absorb the pressure that came from being "the wittiest person in New York"—if not America. Such a tag carried responsibilities. Even actors rested when they came offstage, but being a wit was a twenty-four-hour-a-day job. What if she couldn't think of a sharp *rejoinder*? Would she be seen as "past it"? She was "on" all the time and drink fed into that intensity, giving her the adrenaline she needed to keep her mind on red alert. People at parties would say things to her like, "So you're Dorothy Parker. I dare you to say something nasty."[22] And she would.

Hers was a restless spirit. Like many drinkers she was searching for something that always eluded her in life. One night in an especially inebriated condition she kissed a cab horse on Sixth Avenue. She said she'd kiss him again if he asked her, and even go to Atlantic City with him. All the same, she refused to put the horse under pressure. She didn't want to have him going around the place feeling he had to marry her.[23]

Her favorite drink was Haig & Haig. She was also partial to a rotgut Scotch whiskey she called White Hearse. If whiskey wasn't available on a given night she'd take anything else that was on the menu except gin, which always made her ill. "I'd rather have a bottle in front of me," she declaimed à la Groucho Marx, "than a frontal lobotomy."[24] Drinking caused an increase in her sexual activity, as was transmitted by one of her most famous quatrains:

> I like to have a martini,
> Two at the very most.
> At three I'm under the table,
> At four I'm under the host.[25]

She fell head over heels for the playwright Charles MacArthur in 1922. Unfortunately, her devotion wasn't reciprocated. After she became pregnant by him he ran for the hills. "It serves me right," she sighed, "for putting all my eggs in one bastard."[26] An abortion followed.

She attempted suicide afterward by slashing her wrists in a hotel room with one of Eddie's old razors, but she wasn't really serious about the attempt. Before cutting herself, she phoned a local restaurant and asked them to deliver dinner to her room. The deliveryman found her and got her to the hospital before any serious damage was done. "The trouble with Eddie," she reflected afterward, "was that he hadn't even been able to sharpen his own razors."[27]

Later attempts to do herself in seemed similarly halfhearted. She once diluted large doses of a sedative in a glass of water, but then threw it out the window. She also swallowed a bottle of shoe polish and a glass full of sleeping powders one night but neither of these proved lethal. By now her attempts to kill herself seemed as much the stuff of humor as tragedy. "Dottie," said Benchley when he visited her once after yet another aborted effort, "If you don't stop this sort of thing you'll make yourself sick."[28]

She published her first book of poetry, *Enough Rope*, in 1926. She wasn't totally happy with it, thinking it derivative. "I'm always chasing Rimbauds," she droned.[29] The drinking was getting a bigger grip on her by now, but she refused to do anything about it.

At a party one night in 1926 she met Alvan Barach, a psychotherapist. The following morning she saw him for a consultation. He immediately diagnosed a serious drinking problem. She was hardly surprised. She wasn't even enjoying alcohol at this point, just drinking for the sake of it. Neither did it produce an automatic high. She

Dorothy Parker, a woman who was corrosive without drink and even more corrosive with it.

had to work at it, increasing her dosage to get the same sensation: "What frightened her most," one of her biographers wrote, "were those times when the effects of the whiskey suddenly deserted her without warning and she would be swamped by anxiety so powerful she seemed to be sinking in her tracks, literally unable to move backward or forward."[30] At times like this she felt misery crushing her "between great smooth stones."[31] Because the whiskey wasn't giving her the sensations it used to she started to see it as an old friend who'd betrayed her.[32]

But a night out was still inconceivable without it. Having fun meant getting drunk. Having a lot of fun meant getting *very* drunk. Life was like one continuous, never-ending party. She cavorted with her literary friends by day and at night rang room service to have whiskey and ice set up to her room. There, the banter continued with the likes of Irving Berlin, Harpo Marx and Tallulah Bankhead—a woman, arguably, even more daring than she.

By now she'd become fascinated by the work of Ernest Hemingway. His collection of short stories, *In Our Time*, had become a *cause célèbre* among writers.[33] She admired his minimalism, his talent for describing without describing, his ability to throw so much material out and still leaves the essentials. Hemingway liked her but he made fun of her in a poem he wrote. It contained the following lines:

> Little drops of alcohol
> Little slugs of gin
> Make the mighty notions
> Make the double chin.[34]

Parker was shocked that he had turned on her like this. It was similar to the way he turned on another former friend, F. Scott Fitzgerald.

Parker actually had a fling with Fitzgerald, each seeing in the other one a mirror-image of an alcoholic. Like many of the subjects of this study, they enjoyed drinking with people who had the same problem as themselves. It legitimized it: one was never going to be judged by a fellow lush for over-imbibing. But Parker was uncomfortable with Fitzgerald: "She despised in him the very qualities she hated in herself—sniveling self-pity, the way they both wasted their talent, their lack of self-discipline. And, like herself, Scott could be tiresome when he was drinking."[35]

After Parker became famous she began to be invited to more functions. Unfortunately, most of these filled her with disdain. She attended literary gatherings "filled with people who looked as if they had been scraped out of drains."[36] Most such soirées she avoided like the plague. You lost your soul if you became too much of a public figure; it ate into your writing time. Or worse, it took away the will to write. The media also sucked this will out of her. Reporters asked her stupid questions, like what she thought of the New York skyline. She fended them off by saying things like, "Put a little more gin in mine."[37]

In 1930, she made the statement that she hated writing more than anything in the world.[38] She wrote a collection of short stories called *Laments for the Living* that year but when it came time to proofread it she shied away from the task. Her editor, George Oppenheimer, recalled that the only way he could persuade her to correct the proofs was to lock her in a room with a bottle of whiskey. "The more she drank," he said, "the less she liked what she'd written, "but a few drinks more and she mellowed."[39]

In 1931, she published a collection of poems, *Death and Taxes*. Two years later saw *After Such Pleasures*, another collection of stories. The reviews were respectable if not exuberant. Many people regarded her more as an epigrammatist than a "pure" writer. For this she had only herself to blame: her one-liners were absolutely irresistible. When, in 1933, it was reported that the moribund Calvin Coolidge had died, her response was, "How can they tell?"[40]

She met the writer Joseph Bryan at a dance one night and they discussed collaborating on a play together. Bryan was excited by the idea and wanted to know when they might start. When Parker said "Tomorrow" he was elated, leaving the dance "floating on a pink cloud." But when he called her hotel the following morning and asked the doorman to ring her room, spelling out the letters of his name slowly, they meant nothing to her. Bryan was distraught. Not only had she forgotten their plans to work together, she'd been so drunk she couldn't even remember meeting him.[41]

Benchley asked her whether she was interested in joining Alcoholics Anonymous. She told him she regarded it as an "admirable outfit" but there was a problem with the people running it. "What's that?" he asked her. "They want me to stop drinking," she replied.[42]

It was around this time that she met the writer-cum-actor Alan Campbell, a man eleven years her junior. They were attracted to one another immediately and began a relationship. Part of the attraction was the fact that he liked drinking just as much as she did. He had ambitions to make it in Hollywood. She agreed to accompany him out there and do some screenwriting with him. This, despite the fact that she'd never had any love for the place. She described it as a "cultural boneyard"—an expression that would be taken up by no less than Marlon Brando two decades later. "The only 'ism' Hollywood believes in is plagiarism," she rasped.[43]

When they arrived, an MGM representative asked her what kind of office she wanted. Her reply: "All I need is a room to lay my hat and a few friends."[44] Life in the movie capital became just as riotous as it had been in New York. There was a rumor Campbell was gay, but she didn't let that bother her. They lived for the moment, going to bed at all hours and sleeping through much of the day.[45]

Their parties were boisterous. Parker drank Manhattans; Campbell, Scotch on the rocks. A friend recalled: "They'd bring it in by the case. Both of them used to run around with drinks in their hands even when there was no company there."[46] Guests drank whether they felt like it or not, because they knew it was expected of them. The food at such soirées was like an optional extra. Those who wanted some had to wait a long time for it to be served—or not served. A casserole was sometimes stuffed into the oven as a token gesture. It often resembled a "congealed morass" due to the oven being turned off too soon. As the hungry wondered if they would risk eating it, Campbell would say to Parker, "Dottie, don't you think we could have one more pitcher of martinis?"[47]

Despite all the carousing, some writing did get done. Both of them were paid handsomely for it as well. Parker was on $1,000-a-week salary, and Campbell on $250, though he was expected to act as well as write.[48]

Because of their lifestyle, such salaries didn't go very far. "Hollywood money is like congealed snow," Parker declared, "It goes so fast it melts in your hands."[49] She once expressed the view that the two most beautiful words in the English language were "Check enclosed,"[50] but now she was more dispassionate about the subject: "If you want to know what God thinks of money," she remarked, "just look at the people he gave it to."[51]

Though she spent a lot of money on herself, she spent a lot on others as well. She was very generous to her friends and a sucker for hard-luck cases. Her heart and soul were always with the cause of socialism.[52]

In this she resembled Hemingway more than Fitzgerald. All three of them spent much of their time in the company of the affluent, but only Fitzgerald was dazzled by this ambience. A famous exchange between Fitzgerald and Hemingway had Fitzgerald saying, "Let me tell you about the very rich. They are different from you and me." Hemingway replied, "Yes, they have more money."[53]

She became close to him during the Spanish Civil War. She went to Spain when he was there and was shocked by the horrors she saw, joining him in his support for those opposing Franco. Harold Ross, her editor at the *New Yorker*, was unimpressed by her political diatribes. When she wrote about the war, he chastised, "Goddamnit, why can't you be funny again?"[54] But that Dorothy was a thing of the past now. The war scarred her and dragged her down. A reporter visited her at her home in early 1939 and asked her to say a few words about her life. "It was terrible," she snapped back. Was there anything she enjoyed? Yes. "Flowers, French fried potatoes, and a good cry."[55]

She found it difficult to put her socialist sympathies in abeyance when she returned to Hollywood's cotton candy world. There was also the danger of being called out as a "pinko" by Joseph McCarthy's "red-baiting" army at the House Un-American Activities Committee (HUAC). (That would eventually transpire). But she was never militant. "Do I look like someone who would overthrow the government?" she asked. "I can't even get my dog to stay down."[56]

The Parker that returned from Spain was more reclusive. She was a socialist, not sociable. As one writer put it, "The champagne of the twenties had gone flat for her."[57] Like Scott and Zelda Fitzgerald, what she was experiencing was the hangover from a two-decade party. She still drank a lot, but more often alone.

By the early 1940s she was, to use her own expression, "waking at the crack of ice." She usually began the day with what she called "an eye-opener."[58] She would then drink steadily until bedtime or a blackout, whichever happened first. Campbell was a partner-in-crime in this respect. He was as much in denial about her alcoholism—and his own—as she was. In today's parlance he would be called an enabler. He brought home recipes for cocktails as well as expensive ice crushers and bar paraphernalia. When she came to the end of a drink, all she had to do was hold it out and he'd refill it. The more they drank, the more they argued. They sparked off each other like the couple in Edward Albee's *Who's Afraid of Virginia Woolf?*, at times appearing to take pleasure in their spats.

She had a miscarriage in 1939, followed by a hysterectomy. She no longer felt like a sexual being, and turned her frustration on Campbell. After the invasion of Pearl Harbor, she encouraged him to enlist in the army. He did this, serving with Army Air Force intelligence, both in London and Paris.[59]

She turned fifty in 1943. She was starting to put on weight now, which made her less attractive to him. Towards the end of World War II he told her he'd fallen in love with another woman. The affair didn't last long but when the war ended he came home to a dead marriage. They divorced shortly afterward.[60]

In 1947, Susan Hayward won an Oscar nomination for *Smash-Up*, a film based on a story Parker wrote. Its theme of a woman with a drinking problem trying to haul herself back from the brink was one which struck a chord with her. John Howard Lawson adapted her words in a rare example of Hollywood fidelity to a text. Both he and Parker were nominated for Oscars that year but didn't win. Neither did Hayward: Loretta Young won instead for *The Farmer's Daughter*.

Parker remarried Alan Campbell in 1950. The idea seemed to be a triumph of optimism over experience. Since it hadn't worked the first time, why should it now? A slew of famous people attended the wedding—Humphrey Bogart, James Agee, Howard Dietz included. When a guest remarked that many of those in attendance hadn't spoken to one another for years, Parker shot back, "Including the bride and groom!"[61]

The problems that dogged them the first time around re-surfaced. An added irritant to the relationship was the fact that Campbell now felt himself in danger of being blacklisted by the HUAC. He blamed this on Parker. He'd developed his left-wing conscience, he grumbled, to please

Susan Hayward played an alcoholic in *Smash-Up* (1947). Parker's screenplay for the movie was said to have been based largely on her own life.

her. HUAC cited her for being a communist the following year, and Campbell felt the heat of this. Within a year they were separated again.[62]

She wrote *Ladies of the Corridor*, her final play, in 1951. It dealt with a group of women whose husbands died young, which plummeted them into loneliness, depression and desperate actions. One of them took a young lover. Another developed a drinking problem and committed suicide. It was an unusual theme, an interesting porthole into a neglected area of life, but it flopped when it was staged. Parker took this badly. She felt herself finished as a serious writer. The following outpouring from one of the characters might make one believe the play was semi-autobiographical. Alcohol, she says, "makes you a different person. You're not yourself for a little while and that's velvet…. A couple of drinks and I've got some nerve. Otherwise I'm frightened all the time."[63]

She became a recluse in the 1950s. Friends called occasionally, but she was rarely glad to see them. If she was sober, she was easily bored. If drunk, she repeated the same stories over and over. After a time, fewer and fewer old friends dropped by. That was the way she preferred it.

The writing continued, albeit in truncated form. She wrote some pieces of short fiction for the *New Yorker*, but they lacked her old fizz. In 1956, she wrote a song lyric for the Leonard Bernstein musical *Caddie*, but this flopped too. The following year she was contracted to do some book reviews for *Esquire*. In 1961, she reconciled with Campbell and moved from New York to Los Angeles.

She drank so much in the early '60s that it completely destroyed her talent. *Esquire* still sent her monthly check in the hope that she'd sober herself up enough to write for them again. She rarely did: indeed, she missed five deadlines in 1962 alone. The interest in blackening pages—or wowing readers with her nuggets of wit—had disappeared. Asked by a reporter what she did for fun, she replied, "Everything that isn't writing."[64]

Campbell tried to revive her interest but failed. Annoyed by his interference, she lied about her output. One day when he was going out he placed a hair on her typewriter keyboard when she was due to write a piece for *Esquire*. When he came back he asked her if she'd done it. "Yes," she replied. But the hair was still there.[65]

Her moods continued to darken and her drinking increased. Part of her depression was due to the fact that so many of her friends had passed away: Heywood Broun, Dashiell Hammett, and Robert Benchley. "If I had any decency," she said, "I should be dead. Everyone I ever cared about is."[66]

Campbell died in the summer of 1963 of an overdose of Seconal. Parker found his body. He'd been drinking heavily in the leadup to his death. If she had any doubts that it was an accident, these were dispelled when she saw a dry cleaning bag around his head.

She refused to grieve in the conventional way. When a friend asked if there was anything he could do for her she said, "Get me a new husband." He was shocked by her reaction. "That's the most callous remark I ever heard in my life," he said. "Okay," Parker snapped back, "Then run down to the corner and get me some ham and cheese on rye and tell them to hold the mayo."[67]

If she'd failed to take care of herself while Campbell was alive she let herself go even more now. Sally Foster, a friend of hers, came to the rescue. She stopped by every other day to cook and clean and to feed Parker's dogs. She had less luck feeding Parker. She begged her to cut down on her drinking. To facilitate this, she hid booze on high shelves that were out of Parker's reach. Parker wasn't impressed. What good was it up there?[68]

Campbell's death affected her more than she admitted. She couldn't stay in Los Angeles, so she moved back to New York after his affairs were settled. It was a time of confusion and dismay. As her biographer John Keats wrote,

> She sat at home with two black French poodles who ate more than she did. She chain-smoked cigarettes which blunted the edge of hunger, and drank neat whiskey which blunted the edges of many things.[69]

Shortly afterward she turned seventy. She didn't feel seventy, she said, she felt more like ninety.[70] A reporter from the Associated Press was sent to interview her. She drank Scotch, neat, throughout the interview.

For the next few years she saw herself as an anachronism. Most young readers didn't know who she was, or, if they did, whether she was alive or dead. She promised her doctor she wouldn't drink at her seventy-second birthday party in 1965. She kept the promise but was miserable as a result. Sipping a consolatory glass of ginger ale spoiled the day for her, but she accepted it. Apart from the obvious risk to her health she also feared drinking-related accidents.

Her birthday resolve was short-lived. In the following months she went into bars for the proverbial one drink but couldn't stop there. Many times she was hospitalized as a result.

One night, towards the end of 1965, her friend Parker Ladd tried to curtail her drinking by sharing a bottle of whiskey with her. He thought she would stop when the bottle was empty, but she had other ideas. She jumped to her feet and started rummaging around her closet. On the floor she found another bottle of Scotch, lodged between some pairs of shoes. She held it up triumphantly to a dejected Ladd. That Christmas she spent in the hospital, drying out.[71]

She knew she was nearing the end of the road but didn't seem to care. When a doctor told her she could die within months if she didn't go on the dry she looked at him and said, "Promises, promises."[72]

Lillian Hellman visited her after she went to the hospital. They'd always been close, though Hellman's husband, Dashiell Hammett, didn't like her. Shortly before, Hellman had sent her a check for $10,000 having been aware (like most people) that she was short of cash now. In the course of the visit, Parker told Hellman she was broke. Hellman said she couldn't be, not with the $10,000 she'd sent her. Parker didn't seem to be aware of this. When Hellman said, "Where is it?" Parker replied, "I don't know." She'd put it in a bureau drawer and forgotten about it.[73]

She pined for the past. When she was living it she was critical of it but now that it was gone she realized how much richer it was than the present. The Algonquin Circle may have had their faults, but its members were alive, original, daring. Contemporary writers, on the contrary, were staid and bland. "I don't read the *New Yorker* much these days," she said, "It always seems to be the same old story about somebody's childhood in Pakistan."[74]

Feeling intimations of mortality, she wrote her will. She bequeathed her estate to the Reverend Martin Luther King, Jr., and, upon his death, to the National Association for the Advancement of Colored People (NAACP). After she'd made it she said, "The least I can do now is die." Money had never been important to her, and it was even less so now. What could she use it for at her age, she asked, except to buy a diamond-studded wheelchair?[75]

Her manner became remarkably gruffer in her last years. Some friends who visited her towards the end of her life found her sitting on the floor, surrounded by empty bottles. When they walked in she looked up at them from a rug strewn with dog feces and rasped, "You're Jew Fascists, get out of here."[76]

On the afternoon of June 7, 1967, Parker suffered a massive heart attack and died. She had said to her friend Fred Shroyer, in the mid-'60s, "Don't feel badly when I die because I've been dead for a long time."[77]

The media were generous in their eulogies. This was surprising as she'd been quiet in recent years. It was gratifying to see that people remembered back to the time before "the champagne went flat." A reporter for *Vanity Fair* wrote, "Her acidic *bons mots* were the olives of the martini age."[78] The *New York Times* gave her a full-page tribute.

There were various suggestions she had made regarding her epitaph. One was: "If you can read this, you've come too close."[79] Another was, "Wherever she went, it was against her better judgment."[80] Most people think her chosen wording was "Excuse my dust," but a more favored—and appropriate—epitaph was, "This one is on me."[81]

Because, all too often, it was.

F. Scott Fitzgerald

(1896–1940)

Fitzgerald wasn't popular as a child. He threw a party for a number of chums when he was six, but nobody showed up. In a temper, he ate the birthday cake himself, and even the candles.[1] He was already etching in the kind of behavior that would characterize his future.

He grew up in St. Paul. He was writing stories for the school magazine there from a young age. He even wrote a play in 1911. He was sampling sherry by that time, too, and getting merry enough to earn the reputation of "a man who drank."[2]

When he entered Princeton in 1913 he developed a taste for champagne, but it wasn't until the 1920s that he started to drink in earnest. After a while the beverage in question didn't matter: he enjoyed everything from home brew to bathtub gin to absinthe.

At the beginning, drinking was fun. It had no repercussions. "Pardon me if my hand is shaky," he wrote to a girl from Princeton, "but I just had a quart of sauterne and three Bronxes."[3]

He fell in love with society belle Ginevra King at Princeton, but she may have been out of his league. Fitzgerald wasn't quite poor but, compared to her, he was. He never got over her and used her as the template for many of the characters in his stories and novels—including the Daisy Buchanan of *The Great Gatsby*.[4]

After leaving Princeton he joined the army as second lieutenant. While stationed at Camp Sheridan in Alabama he fell in love with Zelda Sayre. Their pairing seemed ideal. They were like something from a comic book, a real-life symbol of dashing '20s optimism. They had a swish and dare that acted like a clarion call to youth to slough off the shackles of the past, sobriety being one of those shackles.

The new decade was ushered in with the publication of *This Side of Paradise*, his first novel, in 1920. A month later he married Zelda. They soon became famous figures in New York, an iconic party couple. When their daughter, Scottie, was born the following year, it hardly put a dent in their high-flying lifestyle.

Fitzgerald was still drinking heavily, but it hadn't impacted on his writing as yet. When a reporter suggested to him that *This Side of Paradise* didn't read as if it was written on coffee, he replied, "It wasn't. It was written on Coca-Cola."[5]

Such flip comments concealed an already growing disenchantment with life. Bizarrely, he wrote to his Scribner's editor Maxwell Perkins in 1921, "I should like to sit down with a half-dozen chosen companions and drink myself to death. I am sick of life, liquor and literature."[6] This, it should be remembered, was long before his well-documented crack-up, and equally long before his famous statement: "In a real dark night of the soul it is always three o'clock in the morning day after day."[7]

Scott and Zelda pose with Scottie, their beloved daughter. The family unit was strong then but it would soon be riven by their demonic indulgences.

His second novel, *The Beautiful and the Damned*, was published in 1922. He followed it with *Tales of the Jazz Age*. Things seemed to be booming for him. The words flowed out and the drink flowed in—though not necessarily in that order.

Gin was his favorite tipple. He liked it because it didn't smell. This seemed to suggest he knew he was developing a problem, one that he needed to conceal from others. He told people it inspired his muse but more often it became an end in itself. If he had enough of it, the writing soon became forgotten. "First you take a drink," he announced, "then the drink takes a drink. Then the drink takes you."[8]

An alcoholic can feel more comfortable about his drinking if his wife shares such a habit, and Zelda certainly shared her husband's during the Jazz Age. Their life together was a continuous round of parties. Often the couple ended their evenings by falling out of taxicabs after they were driven home. Or falling asleep on the deck of a yacht. Or on the floor of a casino.

Zelda's capacity was only slightly better than Fitzgerald's. They often passed out together at parties, being put to bed by their hosts. They became very good at apologizing to such hosts on the mornings after parties—probably because they had so much practice.

Donald Goodwin posited the theory that Fitzgerald had a greater capacity for drink than most of his biographers assume. He was a performer, he alleged, and liked to pretend he was drunker than he was. Like most alcoholics, Goodwin contended, he also hid his drinking, so had consumed more on a given night than the people in his company suspected. The latter part of this argument seems to hold water. Either way, his tolerance increased in the thirties. During this decade he was capable of downing thirty bottles of beer a day, and/or a quart of gin, and still write.

Sometimes he introduced himself at parties as, "F. Scott Fitzgerald, the well-known alcoholic."[9] This was a jab at the manner in which attendees introduce themselves at AA meetings. It was an amusing ploy and also perhaps a Freudian one: when someone called themselves an alcoholic it prevented other people from doing so. It also gave him a license to misbehave. When a party was going well he did things like pour soup down the hostess's back, kiss the serving maid, or pass out in the dog kennel.[10] His friend Elizabeth Lemmon thought his histrionics resulted from insecurity: "Scott's inferiority complex made him always the show-off."[11]

Outrageous stories circulated about him. John Dos Passos was once alleged to have seen him staggering out of a bar in broad daylight and kicking a tray of cigarettes from the hands of an old woman selling tobacco on a street corner. While vacationing in Cannes, he was reported to have stepped into a resort café one day and roughed up a group of waiters, dragging one of them to the foot of a cliff and threatening to drop him down into the cold waters of the Mediterranean.

Another time he was rumored to have overpowered the bartender of a restaurant, spread him across two chairs and threatened to saw him open to see what his insides were made of. At this point Zelda intervened, cheerily assuring her husband he would find nothing inside the man except broken porcelain, cardboard menu scraps, and pencil stubs.

It's most likely these stories are apocryphal. What's more probable is the fact that Zelda confided to a friend that two drinks were enough to put her husband into a manic state, making him want to fight everyone in sight, including her.[12]

Drink seemed to turn him into a totally different person. Sober, he balked when he heard somebody say, "Damn it." Drunk, he swore like a stevedore. Sober, he dressed like a clotheshorse. Drunk, he put on any old rags that were ready to hand.

As he got older he found it more difficult to deal with the effects of liquor. With the DTs he saw beetles and pink mice crawling all over him. Hangovers were equally horrendous, as was the embarrassment engendered by his antics. One night he dove into a swimming pool, fully clothed. Another time he urinated in front of horrified guests at a party, leaving Zelda to deal with the fallout.[13]

Like many heavy drinkers, Fitzgerald often forgot what he had done when he was in the grip of a binge, waking up the following morning to hear news of it from Zelda, who may well have been a part of it. People eventually ran scared of them, leading to the familiar groan, "Here come the Fitzgeralds."[14] The couple, according to Ernest Hemingway, "fed off the festival conception of life."[15] He thought they were both wired to the moon in their respective fashions. Not for them the dull discipline of rising at dawn to get a paragraph right. They were too busy sleeping off the previous night's entertainment.

Fitzgerald said to a friend once, "I couldn't get sober long enough to be able to tolerate being sober."[16] He left Zelda at the dead of night on many occasions to go on benders. Sometimes when she woke up she'd find him asleep on the front lawn. When they entertained, he did things like cut off his tie with a kitchen knife for a jape, or else he might crawl around on all fours under the table tickling people. Occasionally, he tried to eat his soup with a fork.

When he partied with Zelda in the early years he drank not so much because he craved it but because he felt it was expected of him. It was part of his image. People laughed along with him, even if they had to pick up the pieces afterward.

Later on, the repercussions became more palpable. "If you want to get your furniture antiqued up," a friend remarked, "get the Fitzgeralds in—they'll antique it in a single night."[17] Zelda, too, was prone to outrageous pranks, like parking her car on railroad tracks or threatening to drive it off a cliff. One night he drove his car into a lake after a party.[18]

He also liked to throw things at people when under the influence. Anita Loos remembered a night when he bombarded herself and Zelda with "two enormous candelabra with lighted candles, a water carafe, a metal wine cooler and a silver platter." The two of them hid under an oak table until the deluge stopped.[19]

There were many reasons why he drank: a wish to be more confident,

Scott and Zelda, party animals extraordinaire. In time people would groan, "Oh no, here come the Fitzgeralds."

manlier, more outgoing. Alcohol also made him more relaxed with women. When problems occurred in later years, like his waning talent or the hospitalization of Zelda, it comforted him, telling him he wasn't responsible. A psychiatrist he saw in the 1930s thought his need might have been the result of the fact that his body produced excessive amounts of insulin, thereby causing a craving for sugar. Subsequent pathologists discounted this theory. It would, in any case, have been a purely physical phenomenon. Alcoholism generally runs much deeper than this. It's even arguable that he drank to make the world commensurate with his romantic expectations of it. Sadly, it had the opposite effect.

He also believed drinking helped his writing, at least if it occurred before he sat down at his typewriter rather than during the actual writing itself. When he started writing he disputed the notion that alcohol could summon the muse; coffee, perhaps, but not whiskey. Later on he changed his mind about this. "Can you name a single American artist except James & Whistler," he asked an acquaintance, "who didn't die of drink?" He told his friend Laura Guthrie: "When I drink it heightens my emotions ... my stories written when sober are stupid—all reasoned out, not felt."[20]

Fitzgerald and Zelda moved to France in 1924, imagining they could live more cheaply there. The following year he published *The Great Gatsby*, his most acclaimed book. Shortly afterward he met Ernest Hemingway, a writer he admired hugely.

He was so excited the day he first met Hemingway—then regarded as one of the most exciting young writers around—that he drank too fast and it went to his head. He embarrassed Hemingway by over-praising him and asking him questions like "Did you sleep with your wife before you were married?"[21] Their meeting was a precursor to many they would have in the succeeding years, where the older man behaved like a younger one, and vice versa.

Fitzgerald had a much higher place on the literary ladder at this point but didn't act like it. He was awed by Hemingway and showed this too obviously. Hemingway lost respect for him as a result. He always had an aversion to people who couldn't hold their liquor. In later meetings, Fitzgerald gave Hemingway some good advice about his work, but Hemingway, already cocky, usually ignored it. He felt Fitzgerald was too "soft" a writer to be important, even debunking *Gatsby* to him.[22]

Hemingway described Fitzgerald's reaction to the champagne he drank at their first meeting like this: "The skin seemed to tighten over his face until all the puffiness was gone, and then it drew tighter until the face was like a death's head. The eyes sank and began to look dead. The lips were drawn tight and the color left the face so that it was the color of used candle wax."[23]

He didn't regard Fitzgerald as a drunkard since he was affected by such small quantities of alcohol. As he got to know him better, though, and saw him passing out at dinner tables, he began to revise his opinion. Sometimes he had to undress him and put him to bed. Anything he drank, he concluded, "seemed to stimulate him too much and then to poison him."[24]

Hemingway visited Scott and Zelda once at their flat on Rue de Tilsitt. Zelda had a hangover. She was needling Scott about not drinking enough the night before on Montmartre. She called him a killjoy, a spoilsport. At this time Scott was making an effort to cut down on his drinking so his writing would improve. Hemingway thought Zelda was jealous of this. Scott wrote in his memoir of that time, "Zelda would begin complaining about how bored she was."[25] She would then persuade him to go to another party, where each of them would misbehave. They would quarrel and then make up. Afterward, Scott would sweat out the alcohol on long walks with Hemingway ... until the next drunken party.[26]

Scott and Zelda excused their misbehavior, according to Hemingway, by passing out: "Becoming unconscious when they drank had always been their great defense." They went to sleep like children, he claimed, or like two people who were anesthetized. When they woke up the next morning they would be "fresh and happy, not having taken enough alcohol to damage their bodies before it made them unconscious."[27]

Zelda's capacity was greater than Scott's. Scott drank more than he wanted to because he was bored. He needed to escape the rut he was in, to escape Zelda, to escape his demons. He tried to work, but he could only write in snatches. This made him get drunk again. If he was drunk enough, he sought out Hemingway. He took "almost as much pleasure interfering with my work as Zelda did interfering with his," Hemingway declared.[28]

Hemingway believed Fitzgerald rarely drew a sober breath in the twenties. Fitzgerald disagreed, despite his previous "boast" that he was an alcoholic. The reason Hemingway saw him tipsy so often, he pointed out, was because they mostly met at parties.[29] He took to describing this time of his life as "1,000 parties and no work."[30] A night without a party wasn't a proper night in his view. (But a day without a drink wasn't a proper day either.)

He went on vacation to the Pyrenees with Zelda in the winter of 1926 to get away from the party scene and its attendant excesses, but the plan didn't work: "Wherever you go, you take yourselves and your faults with you. In the mountains or the city, you make the same things happen."[31]

As time went on, his behavior became unacceptable even to his rich society friends Gerald and Sara Murphy. When they gave a party for Hemingway and his then-wife Hadley at Juan-les-Pins that year, Fitzgerald spent most of the evening throwing ashtrays at people. In the end, Murphy left his own party. At a later one, Fitzgerald threw Sara's favorite Venetian glasses over a wall. This got him banished from their villa for three weeks.[32]

Drinking had transformed Fitzgerald into a fool, Hemingway believed. It was poison to him, but he was addicted to it.

When Fitzgerald went out socializing with Hemingway, more often than not he disgraced himself, often getting into scrapes from which Hemingway had to extricate him. Fortified with drink, he tried to become Hemingway at such times, aping his macho demeanor. But he was no match for anyone he might challenge to a fight. They'd have decked him if Papa had not intervened.

On other occasions, Fitzgerald called to the Hemingways in the middle of the night to chat about something. Hadley had a baby now, Bumby. As ever, he would be abject in his apologies the following day.

"I was quite ashamed of the other morning," he wrote to Hemingway after one unexpected visit in the small hours. "However, it is only fair to say that the deplorable man who entered your apartment Saturday morning was not me but a man named Johnston who has often been mistaken for me."[33] The Hemingways weren't amused by his attempt at wit.

Hemingway grew more and more impatient as he

Fitzgerald looked angelic without drink. With it, his personality completely transformed itself.

watched Fitzgerald do things like stand on the top of his staircase and throw a toilet roll down, enjoying watching it unravel. "Scott would take one drink," said an equally impatient Hadley, "and pretty soon he'd turn pale green and pass out. His system just couldn't stand it."[34]

One day Fitzgerald told Hemingway his latest tendency was to "collapse about eleven o'clock with tears flowing from my eyes, with the gin rising to their level and leaking over." The morose tone continued: "I haven't a friend in the world and likewise care for nobody, generally including Zelda and often implying current company, after which current company tend to become less current and I wake up in strange rooms in strange places."[35]

Hemingway felt Fitzgerald took pride in his problems. He thought of him as a defeatist. "He would quit at the drop of a hat," he said, "and even borrow someone else's hat to drop." He thought he had a "cheap Irish love of defeat."[36] He accused him of writing glorified pulp fiction for the easy money and running away from the talent that made him famous.

Drunkenness was an easy alibi for him, he believed. It stopped him having to go to the well again, stopped him having to challenge himself. It was all part of the boozer's need for a hard luck story to excuse laziness. He told Fitzgerald his idea of heaven was probably "a beautiful vacuum filled with wealthy monogamists, all drinking themselves to death."[37]

Hemingway maligned Fitzgerald in his 1926 story "The Snows of Kilimanjaro." He wrote about "poor" Scott Fitzgerald (mentioning him by name) and his foolish adoration of the rich. "He thought they were a special glamorous race," he wrote, "and when he found they weren't it wrecked him just as much as any other thing that wrecked him."[38] Fitzgerald was shocked by the reference to him, especially as the story was published in *Esquire*, the magazine in which his talent had shone so brightly in years gone by. He wrote a harsh letter to Hemingway, but Hemingway never really apologized. He told Maxwell Perkins, their mutual editor, that he had done it to shake Fitzgerald up, to shock him out of his tendency towards self-pity. Fitzgerald's name was changed to Julian in subsequent publications of the story, but the damage had been done.[39]

Shortly afterward Fitzgerald was interviewed by a journalist by the name of Michael Mok—a 'c' could perhaps have been added to his surname—for the *New York Post* on the occasion of his fortieth birthday. Mok went for the jugular, depicting Fitzgerald as a broken-down man. When he saw the article he was so devastated he swallowed an overdose of morphine. He might well have died had he not vomited. The article was reproduced in *Time* magazine. Shortly afterward, he fired a revolver in a hotel

F. Scott Fitzgerald (1896–1940)

after a suicide threat. The manager threatened to have him thrown out unless a nurse was brought in to take care of him. This was duly arranged. A lady named Dorothy Richardson filled the post. Her main function was to keep Fitzgerald's drinking to a minimum rather than anything more medical. In time, they became friends.

Towards the end of that year he organized a tea dance for his daughter, Scottie. He got tipsy at this, perhaps inevitably. When he danced he started weaving around the floor with some of Scottie's friends in a manner that embarrassed her. It wasn't the first time she saw him drunk but this was different: he was infiltrating her circle.[40]

In the end he told all the guests to leave. He had employed a band to play music. After everyone was gone he sat listening to them, paying them extra money to keep playing as he stayed alone in the middle of the room, a bottle of gin in his hand. He spent that Christmas in St. John Hopkins Hospital drying out.[41]

"My life has a cycle," he said. "Work, drink, love." If he had enough money, Scott Donaldson claimed, it would have been just drink and love.[42]

Fitzgerald went to Hollywood in 1927, believing that writing screenplays would be easier than novels. While he was there he became infatuated with the teenage actress Lois Moran. Zelda was so enraged at this she burned her clothes in a bathtub. He then took a screen test with Moran in the hope that they might make a film together. Moran was more amused by this than anything else. She didn't reciprocate his feelings for her but liked him nonetheless. One evening she invited him to tea at her parents' house. Fitzgerald drank too much. After the guests finished eating he asked them all to give him their watches and wallets. Then he proceeded to try and make soup from them.

Fitzgerald met James Joyce in 1928. He was greatly impressed by his work and told him so. In fact, he offered to jump out a window to manifest his adulation of him. Joyce was flattered, if rather nonplussed, by the offer. Around the same time his friend Sylvia Beach (one of Joyce's many subsidizers) introduced Fitzgerald to the French novelist Andre Chamson. Fitzgerald gave Chamson the jitters while standing on a window ledge. It happened at his apartment one day when he stood on the balcony after one too many glasses of gin. He shouted down to passersby on the street below, "I *am* Voltaire! I *am* Rousseau!" He subsequently tried to wrest two bicycles from a pair of gendarmes. Chamson had a tough time trying to prevent him from being arrested.[43]

By the late 1920s, Zelda stopped drinking with Fitzgerald. She wrote the following to him about his behavior in 1928: "You didn't work and were dragged home at night by taxi-drivers when you came home at all.... You were literally eternally drunk the whole summer."[44] Things didn't improve much the following year: "You disgraced yourself at the Barry's party, on the yacht at Monte Carlo, at the casino with Gerald and Dotty [Dorothy Parker]. Many nights you didn't come home. You came into my room once the whole summer."[45]

In April 1929, he went on another bender, this time in Cuba, returning home in a distressed condition. Afterward, he went to a hospital to dry out. He became philosophical about the condition in which he found himself. "Back in 1920," he recalled, "I shocked a rising young businessman by suggesting a cocktail before lunch. In 1929 there was liquor in half the downtown offices and a speakeasy in half the large buildings."[46]

He went to Paris at the end of 1929, expecting to pick up with Hemingway where he left off in 1926, but their fortunes had fluctuated in the interim. Hemingway was a major writer now, and Fitzgerald, mightily on the slide. His previous disgraces while under the influence made Hemingway leery about seeing him. Neither were matters helped by the fact that Hemingway's new wife, Pauline Pfeiffer, didn't like him as much as Hadley Richardson had. Hemingway hid his address from Fitzgerald, fearing a drunken arrival into his home, but Fitzgerald managed to track him down nonetheless. When he did, he asked to see the text of *A Farewell to Arms*, the novel on which Hemingway was then working. Hemingway showed it to him reluctantly but ignored most of Fitzgerald's suggestions about improving it.

His respect for him diminished further the day Fitzgerald told him he was worried about—what else?—the size of his penis. "Zelda says it's too small," he informed Hemingway. "Let's see about that," Hemingway replied. He took him into a bathroom and had a look at it. After a few seconds he told him it looked fine to him. He added, "Zelda just wants to destroy you."[47]

Zelda would go on to accuse Fitzgerald of having a homosexual relationship with Hemingway. For Hemingway this confirmed his belief that the woman was insane. It certainly seemed so. One night when Fitzgerald was dining with Gerald Murphy he spotted Isadora Duncan at another table. He went over to her and started tussling her hair. When Zelda saw what was happening she put down a drink she was holding, stood up, and threw herself headfirst down a flight of stone steps. Amazingly, she only bruised her arms and legs.[48]

Zelda was deteriorating just as much as Scott by now. Drink hadn't got a hold of her, but nerves had. A gifted ballerina, she had always wanted to dance professionally. Fitzgerald had always been ambivalent about such a possibility. The chance of it coming about seemed more remote with each passing year. Her dreams of being a successful writer also died. Worn down by life's pressures, she had a nervous breakdown in April 1930 and spent the rest of the year in a hospital in Switzerland.[49]

Many of Fitzgerald's friends thought his drinking drove Zelda mad. Others thought her madness drove him to drink.[50] Maybe the truth was somewhere in the middle.

Fitzgerald told his doctor one of the main reasons he drank was because of Zelda. She had been writing fiction that seemed unnervingly similar to his own, he said, and he was worried that this could compromise his career. Zelda was also beginning to bore him with her ballerina dreams. He couldn't have taken all this without the help of wine. It was almost a necessity for him, he insisted. He said he didn't think he'd have a problem giving up "strong drink," but he drew the line at wine. (Apparently, he saw this as light drinking.) He admitted he had abused liquor in the past. He accepted the fact that this was something to be paid for with suffering and maybe even death, but not with renunciation. For him to forswear alcohol would be "as illogical as permanently giving up sex because I caught a disease."[51]

He wrote a letter to Zelda's parents at the end of 1930. In it he said: "Humpty Dumpty fell off a wall." But not to worry. He was hoping all the king's horses would be able to put the "delicate eggshell" together again.[52] Though the tone may have been sympathetic, the fairy-tale overtones hardly impressed the Sayres—who didn't like Fitzgerald much anyway.[53]

Zelda began to recover in the spring of 1931. In September, she went home. Fitzgerald now journeyed to Hollywood again, this time to write the screenplay for Katharine Brush's *Red Headed Woman*. Zelda was progressing nicely until her father died the following year, whereupon she broke down again. As her moods fluctuated, Fitzgerald struggled with his new book, *Tender Is the Night*.

After Zelda became hospitalized for the second time he was wracked with guilt, a fact he wouldn't admit to himself. He went into denial about it just as he'd gone into denial about his alcoholism. She'd brought destruction on herself, he claimed. She was even responsible for his drinking. "During the first seven years of our marriage" he told a doctor, "it was she who wanted to drink."[54] This was nonsense. He was engaging in rationalization, transference of blame—*anything* that would palliate his sense of responsibility over her fate.

He even used Zelda as an excuse to continue drinking. If he stopped now, he argued, her friends and relatives would accuse him of having been the cause of her "calamity."⁵⁵ It was tortured logic, but it worked for him. He used any argument he could think of to continue the lifestyle that had got him this far. It would, he insisted, have been a bad time to stop drinking. He was at his lowest ebb, financially and emotionally. His wife was gone, his creativity in abeyance, his friends fleeing. But the bottle would never walk out on him. That was a constant ally.

Early in 1933 he wrote to Maxwell Perkins, "Am going on the water wagon from the first of February to the first of April."⁵⁶ The last part of the sentence is more interesting than the first: He's careful to leave the door open for a return to his vice, like a self-imposed Lenten fast. The jug was only half plugged.

He was admitted to the hospital for two drying-out spells that year, and six more in the next three. This prevented his finishing *Tender Is the Night* as quickly as he wanted to and also curtailed his ability to write the stories that were his meal tickets when his health was better.

Prohibition was repealed that year, on December 5, but the U.S. was in the throes of the Depression. People were allowed to drink now; they just couldn't afford to. Fitzgerald didn't lose much money in the Wall Street crash, but its ripple effect on the economy reduced his earning power. The grim atmosphere generated by the economic downturn also made his romantic vision of life seem somehow passé. The Flapper era was over, and austerity was in. Enter Ernest Hemingway with his angst, exit the Party Society (and, by extension, Fitzgerald). As one writer put it, "He became a symbol of the time and was crucified when people became disenchanted with their own excesses. The gin-swilling golden boy morphed into the apocryphal stockbroker jumping out the window."⁵⁷

Tender Is the Night was published in 1934. It had fine passages, but the concept and tone seemed to be relics of another era. It was like a 1920s book being released into an irrelevant decade. How could he halt the slide? In the '20s he hadn't drunk much while he wrote, but in the following decade he lost such discipline. This was first evident during the writing of *Tender Is the Night*, a novel that took longer than his previous ones for that reason.

His modus operandi now was to start his sessions with beer and then segue into gin. If he found himself unable to limit his intake of the latter, he allowed the nurses to dole them out to him in hourly quantities.

Zelda had her third major breakdown in 1934. She never really came back to herself afterward, which caused Fitzgerald to go into another decline. Financial stress added to his depression. When his short stories stopped earning the income of yore he still had large overheads: hospital bills for Zelda, and private school tuition for Scottie. Arnold Gingrich continued to publish him in *Esquire*, but this was only a drop in the ocean when his novels and story collections weren't selling. Or when the big advances weren't coming.

He looked to Hollywood to get him out of a pickle, but this wasn't automatic. Film contracts were difficult to come by, especially at MGM, as tales of his wild behavior became commonplace.

Fitzgerald mocked Hollywood, wrote Nancy Milford. She thought he never got over the feeling that there was something demeaning about going there to write. "But it intrigued him as a place of false glamour against which a part of him competed for attention. He went to the parties and allowed his charm to dissolve in alcohol."[58]

Success was like a bucking bronco to him. He was able to ride it for a while, but then came the diminishing returns. "There are no second acts in American lives," he famously said, and how true it was for him.[59] All he could do now was reminisce.

Where did it all go wrong? Maybe he became famous too soon. When his talent began to slip he needed more and more gin to fill the empty spaces—or to tell himself things would go his way again. If Hemingway drank to reward himself for work well done, Fitzgerald did to convince himself that the work might be so. It was like an IOU he wrote to himself. But he failed to deliver on it as he fell into bad habits, borne of desperation.

A recurrent fear that he would never again be sufficiently in funds caused him to collapse emotionally. One night he wrote a postcard to himself. It read, "Dear Scott—How are you? Have been meaning to come and see you. I have [been] living at the Garden of Allah. Yours, Scott Fitzgerald."[60]

Such dark moods impacted his relationship with his beloved Scottie. One day he hit her for interrupting his writing. Another day he threw an inkwell at her, narrowly missing her ear.[61]

Alcohol made him forget the most basic activities. When he landed an offer to adapt one of his novels as a screenplay, he got drunk in his hotel room and left the bath water on, flooding the whole room.[62]

Fitzgerald was such a hardened drunk he saw himself as being effectively "on the dry" when he came off whiskey for a time in 1935. "I'm on the wagon," he said that year. "No hard liquor, only beer."[63]

His behavior grew increasingly unpredictable, even by his standards. In the summer of 1935 he conducted a mock court case in which, adopting the role of prosecutor, he tried half a dozen men for being Southerners. Another day he walked up to a stranger at a railway station in Norfolk, Virginia, and made derogatory remarks to him about the size of his stomach.[64]

In the mid–1930s he took to carrying around a collection of photographs showing the corrosive effects of alcohol on the body's organs. He did this with a certain amount of black humor. Maybe it was his way of whistling in the graveyard, of trying to confront his fear of self-destruction by hitting himself over the head with it. His consumption was now frightening. When he was hospitalized in September 1935 he was reputed to be drinking up to thirty bottles of beer a day.

The following year he tore his shoulder muscles badly in a diving accident and was laid up for ten weeks. He began to drink from boredom—and the knowledge that he couldn't earn money from his sick bed. Then his mother died. He received a small inheritance from her, which kept the wolf from the door. He now began a series of autobiographical articles for *Esquire*, the most memorable of which was an extended one called "The Crack-Up," in which he laid all his demons bare.

By the end of 1936 he was at his lowest ebb. The story market had all but dried up for him and the prospect of producing another novel was daunting. Once again, he turned to Hollywood. He made many frantic phone calls to producers, most of which weren't returned. There were too many drinking stories about him, and the confessional nature of his *Esquire* articles only solidified the rumors about his undependability. His agent told him he might be able to get him a job if he promised to stay off the hard stuff. Could he guarantee that? He didn't know, but he said he would try.

A picture deal with RKO was delayed because a friend of one of the production team had seen him drinking.[65] He vehemently denied the story, but he still didn't get the contract. It was a heavy blow. Once again he returned to writing stories to try and absorb it. Just when everything seemed lost, his friend Edwin H. Knopf brokered a deal for him at MGM that netted him $1,000 a week for six months, beginning the following July. Fitzgerald contributed to the script of *Three Comrades* in 1937. He regarded it as some of his best work, but much of it was rewritten by the studio. Once again his pride took a tumble.

Ernest Hemingway went to Hollywood in 1937 to raise money for the Loyalists who were fighting Franco in the Spanish Civil War. He had narrated a documentary called *The Spanish Earth* and was using it as a fundraiser. Lillian Hellman was also involved with it. Fitzgerald attended the screening with Hellman. Afterward he drove her over to Dorothy

Parker's house. Hemingway was in attendance. Fitzgerald was so nervous about meeting him that he drove at a snail's pace, crouched over the wheel as adjoining cars honked at him and drivers yelled at him through their windows. His hands were trembling.

Hellman asked him why he was so nervous. "I'm on the wagon," he replied. That made it harder for him to face his old friend. "I'm scared," he told her. "Scared of being sober." When they got to Parker's house he said he didn't want to go in. Hellman took him by the hand and led him inside. When Hemingway saw him he threw a glass of liquor into the fireplace. Fitzgerald's unsteady hold on himself seemed to shatter with the crystal. He only stayed a few minutes and then went off, driving home at ten miles an hour.[66]

If he had indeed "cracked up," he actually thought Hemingway had too, in a different way. Hemingway's inclination was towards megalomania; Fitzgerald's towards melancholia. "He speaks with the authority of success and I with the authority of failure," he said. "We can never sit across the same table again."[67] They were both drinking to excess at this point, albeit with one essential difference: Hemingway was able to work off his hangovers in athletic exploits whereas Fitzgerald spent the mornings after the nights before in slumps of self-loathing.

It was around this time that he met Sheilah Graham, a woman who had a major effect on his life. A former chorus girl and actress, she was currently a gossip columnist. He was immediately drawn to her and they began an affair. She replaced Zelda in his affections and also tried to wean him off the sauce. In this, she partly succeeded.

Despite his sobriety, his health was ruined: his liver was in bits, his head all over the place. The main addresses in his little red book, he estimated, were those of shrinks and liquor salesmen. Graham tried her best to persuade him to go to a meeting for Alcoholic Anonymous, but he refused. "I was never a joiner," he said, adding that AA was only for weak people who received strength from a group.[68]

Graham had a theory that Fitzgerald abused alcohol as fodder for his books. In his eyes, she said, the moods the abuse called up led to dramas he was able to encapsulate in his fiction. She thought he had a complex about the fact that he hadn't done much living by the time he became famous and was trying to make up for that by his adolescent antics while drunk. It was an interesting theory, but as she said later, "What a terrible price to pay for feeding the imagination." And what a terrible price she also paid, watching his grotesqueries from the sidelines. She compared her life with him to "jumping over a cliff with my eyes closed."[69]

Graham signed up for a radio series about movies in 1937. Fitzgerald offered to help her with it. The couple flew to Chicago for a trial broadcast, but he drank so much gin on the flight, Graham told him to get off at Albuquerque. He did, but re-boarded without her knowing it—with an armful of gin. In the studio he punched one of the sponsors and was thrown out. When she returned to their hotel room that evening she found Arnold Gingrich with him. Gingrich was the Chicago-based editor of *Esquire*. He was trying to sober him up by giving him food on a spoon, much as one would to a baby.

Fitzgerald wasn't enjoying this. He spent most of his time spitting the food out—at least when he wasn't biting Gingrich on the hand. When they attempted to board the return flight, the airhostess refused him admission because of his condition. Graham put him into a taxi. She had him driven around and around the same streets for hours until he sobered up. He was then allowed to fly. After they got back to California she employed nurses to keep an eye on him around the clock. They also fed him intravenously. (This worked better than Gingrich's well-intentioned spoonfeeding.)

One day soon afterward Graham found a gun in his dresser drawer. She tried to dispose of it, but he stopped her. In the ensuing struggle her fingers became caught in the trigger guard. He pried them loose with such violence that her flesh tore. Her anger at the wound gave her strength. She managed to wrest the gun away from him and fling it at a wall. "Take it!" she screamed at him. "Shoot yourself, you son of a bitch, I didn't pull myself out of the gutter to waste my life on a drunk like you."[70]

She wasn't altogether surprised that he had sunk so low, seeing him as one of a large bank of Hollywood screenwriters who liked to drink. She believed part of the reason was the intense pressure the studios put on them. It was Irving Thalberg, the boy genius, who started the policy of writers working in tandem, then another couple riding piggyback and then another couple, all working towards the final script. Those who survived such a rigorous process received the vital screen credit. It was a discouraging process.[71]

Apart from Fitzgerald she remembered John O'Hara, Dashiell Hammett, and Robert Benchley as being big drinkers. O'Hara and Hammett lived until their mid-sixties. Benchley died at fifty-six. How long would her man go on? It was anyone's guess. A more pressing problem was wondering if the studios found out how many martinis he generally had before noon.

Fitzgerald once wrote a story called "Crazy Sunday," about a screenwriter who made a fool of himself at a Hollywood party and thereby jeopardized his career. He had many such crazy Sundays himself and was well aware his tenure at film studios hung by a very slender thread.[72] To deflect attention from what was in his tumblers, he stocked up on cases of Coca-Cola for "thirst quenching and work stimulation."[73] He'd like to have been able to work from home but that was a courtesy extended to a select few, like William Faulkner. (Faulkner worked for Warner Bros., which had different policies than MGM.)

Fitzgerald wrote the screenplay for the movie *A Yank at Oxford* in 1938. It starred Robert Taylor and Vivien Leigh. Walter Wanger hired him to work with Budd Schulberg that year on a film called *Winter Carnival*, but he got so drunk on a trip to Dartmouth to see the carnival featured in the film that Wanger fired him on the spot. He spent two weeks in a New York hospital recovering from his binge—and his humiliation. When he got out, his contract wasn't renewed.[74]

He thought he might be on a blacklist now, but that proved not to be the case. MGM asked him to write a screenplay for a Joan Crawford movie, *Infidelity*. It was a tough assignment, not only because the subject was

Robert Young and Vivien Leigh in *A Yank at Oxford* (1938), one of Fitzgerald's few screenwriting credits.

virtually taboo in films at the time but also because of Crawford's tendency to overact.

If Fitzgerald felt Crawford was not up to the job, she thought likewise about him. Looking into his bleary eyes the first day on the set she blurted out, "Write hard, Mr. Fitzgerald, write hard!"[75] Fitzgerald thought he delivered a quality screenplay for *Infidelity*, but it didn't pass the eagle eye of censor Joseph Breen, who found all sorts of controversial material in it. (Breen even objected to the title of the movie.)

Fitzgerald crumbled at this reaction. He was working on the screenplay for three months and was proud of what he'd written. "I've been taken off the story," he told Graham. To cheer him up she suggested they throw a party. It was like something Zelda would have done in the good old days. He jumped at the idea. A few hours later he was happily performing card tricks for all and sundry. Better still, he was only drinking water. Or so it seemed. When Graham looked closer she realized his glass held gin. It was too good to be true.[76]

The screenwriter Nunnally Johnson was one of the guests at the party. His presence seemed to rankle Fitzgerald, perhaps because he was doing something Fitzgerald couldn't, i.e., temper his writing to the film world's dictates. At a certain point in the evening he challenged Johnson to a fight, something he was prone to do when the gin took effect. Johnson demurred and decided to leave the party. Fitzgerald shouted after him, "You probably won't speak to me again because I'm living here with my paramour."[77] It sounded like he had a guilt complex about his lifestyle. If he was divorced from Zelda it would have been different, but he wasn't. Even though she was in an asylum, she was still a part of his life. The situation between them was anomalous. At times it seemed like the story of Rochester and Jane Eyre. A part of him felt Zelda should have been released from care. (Her parents believed he had her put away so he could gallivant with other women.)

Fitzgerald regretted not having had the experience of working with Crawford, despite his misgivings about her acting ability. Crawford herself had no such regrets. Asked once how she felt about him, she said, "I remember him coming to my house in California with Helen Hayes and Charlie MacArthur and all he did was stand in my kitchen near where the liquor was and get very drunk."[78]

Graham did her best to keep him on the straight and narrow after the *Infidelity* disappointment, but it was a full-time job. She wrote about this in her memoir, *Beloved Infidel*. It would be made into a film in 1959 starring Gregory Peck and Deborah Kerr.

F. Scott Fitzgerald (1896–1940)

Gregory Peck and Deborah Kerr in *Beloved Infidel* (1959), the story of Fitzgerald's last desperate days trying to stay on the dry with Sheilah Graham.

Every day was a different type of struggle. In March 1938, he wrote to Maxwell Perkins of a recent fall from the wagon:

> My little binge lasted only three days and I haven't had a drop since. There was one other in September, likewise three days. Save for that I haven't had a drop since a year ago last January. Isn't it awful how reformed alcoholics have to preface everything by explaining clearly how we stand on that question?[79]

Once again, he was protesting too much.

Such lapses became more prevalent in 1939. Graham now seriously believed he was trying to drink himself to death. She knew he felt finished in Hollywood. Maybe finished as a writer, period. His books were all in print that year but only sold a combined total of 114 copies, netting him royalties of no more than $33. The previous year they'd only sold a total of ninety-six. He felt exhausted from his labors and spent much of his time in bed.

He hated nights because he couldn't sleep, and days because "they go towards night." He was heading towards that phase of his life where it was "always three o'clock in the morning all day every day."[80]

By the end of the 1930s he was finding it difficult to keep food down. He was in chronic withdrawal. Nurses fed him glucose intravenously to provide him with the nutrients his body needed to sustain him. No longer was he saying things like, "My name is F. Scott Fitzgerald, the well-known alcoholic." The joke wasn't funny anymore. His ambition was to conceal his drinking from friends. When he employed Frances Kroll as his secretary in 1939 in L.A., one of the first things he asked her to do was to put all the gin bottles she could see into a gunny sack and drop them over the side of a canyon.[81] Kroll liked him. So did the nurses. They did what he asked them, even when they disapproved of what he was asking. He became a very childish patient.

Graham occasionally suspected him of having affairs with his nurses. In 1939, she recalled seeing him with one who gave off a suspiciously proprietary air. "When he was drunk," she growled, "he would have had an affair with a tree."[82]

Fumbled flirtations took his mind off the tensions that were threatening to take him over. He worried about his health, his future, his finances. Scottie was still at Vassar. This was expensive and so was Zelda's continual hospital treatment. He needed money fast, but it was nowhere to be found. Wherever he went, his reputation preceded him.

Life became complicated. He knew Graham was his future, but Zelda was like an anchor dragging him back. He tried to keep both women happy, or at least content. But how could he keep *himself* that way? On a trip to Cuba with Zelda he showed how vulnerable he still was. They went to a cockfight and he became outraged at the blood being shed. He tried to stop it and was beaten up. Why had he done this? Drunken pity for the cocks.[83] He continued to write but the words could only be summoned with more and more alcohol.

The last royalty check Fitzgerald received totaled just $3.13. It was for some books he'd bought himself. "My God," he said upon viewing it. "I'm a forgotten man."[84] At least he was aware of it. There was some salvation in this. He felt like an anachronism. What had it all been about—all the parties and the jollity? He'd once seen himself as someone who could push back the boundaries of literature, but now he felt like a has-been. Hemingway put it best: "All Scott ever got out of writing was a few bottles of whiskey and a few hotel rooms."[85]

The only thing left now was his unfinished novel, *The Last Tycoon*.

Robert de Niro and Theresa Russell appeared in *The Last Tycoon* (1976), based on Fitzgerald's unfinished novel of the same name.

It was based on the life of Irving Thalberg, but one can also see Fitzgerald himself in it as Monroe Stahr, the "Beautiful Dreamer." *Collier's* magazine expressed an interest in it, but they couldn't make a final decision as regards serializing it. Then one day he received a letter from them. It said Fitzgerald needed to send them some extra text.

He balked at this reaction, seeing it as a rejection rather than anything else. In frustration, he started to lay into the drink. It went down the wrong way and he became frustrated. Over the next few nights his mood darkened even more. One night he invited some "deadbeats" to the house to help him drown his sorrows. When Graham came home she threw them out. Fitzgerald went into a rage, picking up a bowl of soup she'd made for him and flinging it against the wall. There was a nurse in the room. She went to Graham's rescue. Fitzgerald kicked her in the legs. Graham tried to leave the room. "You're not going," Fitzgerald told her. "I'm going to kill you." The situation now became comic. "Where's my gun?" he said to her. He was asking her to find the weapon that was going to mean the end of her life. Instead of answering, she called the police.[86]

They took him to the hospital instead of jail. After he was dried out he apologized to Graham and asked her to take him back. Always ready to forgive him, she did just that. He made another effort to go on the dry at the beginning of 1940. This time, against all the odds, it succeeded. Graham never saw him take another drink after that.

One day while they were sitting around she showed him an article from a trade paper. It described a Hollywood intellectual as "a fugitive from the Scott Fitzgerald era."

"You see," she said to him admiringly, "you are now an era."[87]

But he wasn't impressed. It made him feel like an anachronism.

One morning shortly before he died he woke up with a strange sensation. He found he wasn't able to move his arms. He thought he'd had a stroke but the reason proved more innocuous: he'd tangled himself up in his pajamas. He was in the grip of a gin hangover on the morning in question. His doctor, concerned about his future, tried to frighten him. Continued drinking, he warned, could well paralyze him for real. If that happened, Fitzgerald told the doctor, he'd blow his brains out. The doctor said, "Who would hold the gun?"[88]

He died in 1940 at the age of forty-four. "All drunks," he said once, "die between thirty-eight and forty-eight."[89] He was as right about this as he was about most of his pronouncements on alcohol. For his epitaph he suggested: "I was drunk for too many years and then I died."[90]

He once envisaged two life scenarios for an alcoholic. The first was "Drunk at twenty, wrecked at thirty, dead at forty." The other was, "Drunk at twenty-one, human at thirty-one, mellow at forty-one."[91] Fitzgerald's own predicament straddled both trajectories. When he died—the interim between the two predictions—he was both wrecked *and* mellow.

The novelist Joseph Hergesheimer said of him, "Scott could write and didn't; couldn't drink but did." It was a succinct distillation of his tragedy. Raymond Chandler said he "just missed" being a great writer but did well to produce such a solid body of work considering he'd been abusing alcohol since his college days.[92]

The heart attack that killed him might well have been for the best, as it freed his tortured sprit from its frenzied moorings.

What did he leave behind? In essence, the message he gave his readers was that idealists were punished, life was cruel, and time eventually crushed us all. Or, as he put it: "Show me a hero and I'll write you a tragedy."[93]

William Faulkner

(1897–1962)

Faulkner grew up in a culture that revered alcohol. It was as much a part of turn-of-the-century life in the Deep South, wrote Donald Goodwin, "as were the spinning of yarns and whittling on the courthouse lawn."[1] Whiskey was freely available on the hunting trips Faulkner took when men sat around campfires swapping tales about the day's kills. Storytelling was unimaginable without drink in such a setting. The two activities were as inseparable as Rolls and Royce for the young writer.

Alcohol was in his genes, going all the way back to his great-grandfather. Both his father and grandfather were hospitalized after drinking bouts. Faulkner would also be hospitalized for this reason many times in his life.

He had a huge tolerance for alcohol from his early years and this led him to increase his intake. Apart from whiskey he found himself partial to homemade Pernod and doctored Cuban brews. A man with a pronounced distrust of physicians, he drank to cure anything, from a sore throat to his "bad back." He often went for months without a drink, and then the warning signs would appear: "Drumming fingers, evasive looks, monosyllabic replies to questions—then he'd disappear."[2]

His first drinks, he told an editor once, were given to him by his grandfather. He always got the last precious drops from his glass. He started drinking heavily from about the age of fifteen but it wasn't until his early twenties that stories about drunken antics on his part started to emerge. Many of these were fictional, including a yarn he made up about landing an airplane, upside down, on a hangar.

Liquor helped him deal with embarrassing situations all his life. It helped him overcome his shyness on camping trips. By the spring of his senior year at school he was downing a quart of bourbon a day, stopping only when he was shocked into sobriety as a result of passing out twice.

Loaded with whiskey he shed his inhibitions, and sometimes even his clothes. He became a familiar sight in hotels wandering around without his pajamas if insomnia—a byproduct of his binges—took hold. He also suffered spasms at times, and a blueness of the skin brought on by lack of oxygen. He hated doctors and rarely visited them. On the odd occasion that he did he was prescribed paraldehyde, an alcohol substitute popular in the 1920s.

Faulkner went on the wagon now and again but kept such abstentions at a minimum, he said, "so they wouldn't become a habit."[3] He liked to drink while he wrote, but he didn't let drink influence his writing unduly. It was a catalyst, not the *raison d'être*.

Writing was the thing he did best and also the thing he liked most, at least after drinking. It also meant he never had to get a job. Work was anathema to him. As he explained:

> By temperament I'm a vagabond and a tramp. I don't want money bad enough to work for it. One of the saddest things is that the only thing a man can do for eight hours a day, day after day, is work. You can't eat eight hours a day nor drink for eight hours a day nor make love for eight hours. All you can do for eight hours is work. Which is the reason man makes himself and everyone else so miserable.[4]

Such misery was alleviated by combining work with drinking. When asked if the latter meant bourbon, he replied enigmatically, "I ain't that particular. Between Scotch and nothing, I'll take nothing."[5]

Drink inspired him to write the best he knew how but after he finished a book he usually went through a bout of deflation. He drank

Drinking to excess was a hallowed tradition in the Faulkner family from generations before him. It was a tradition he was more than happy to continue, suffering its often painful accidents and hellacious hangovers with equanimity—and even managing to write some classic novels in the process (*Writer Pictures*).

then for a different reason than inspiration—to prop up his spirits. If he took too much he either had an accident or ended up in the hospital. Sometimes he ended up in the gutter. People would gather round him and wonder who he was, being amazed to learn it was "the great writer William Faulkner."[6]

When he reached his thirties he started experiencing withdrawal symptoms as well as episodes of vomiting blood and experiencing blackouts. He stopped for a whole year one time, when he wrote *A Light in August*, but this was rare. (It showed how much reverence he had for that book).

Faulkner married Estelle Oldham when he was thirty-two. They had been childhood sweethearts. She formed the notion that she would marry him from the age of seven but went off with another man when she reached marrying age. That marriage broke down and she came back for Faulkner with two children in tow. His ardor for her appeared to have cooled by now but he married her anyway. He (jokingly?) claimed the reason for this was that one woman was the same as another rather than because he loved her. He liked drinking, he said, because it was mainly something one did with other men.

Like him, Oldham had a drinking problem. But she had no interest in books, even (especially?) her husband's.

Meta Carpenter, a woman with whom he had an affair, remembered him having nightmares when he was in the throes of a bender. He woke up in bed one morning screaming, "They're diving down at me! Swooping! Oh, Lordy!" When she asked him what he was referring to, he replied, "The Jerries. Can't you see them?" He then dove under the sheets for cover as the imaginary bullets pinged around him. "Here they come again!" he screamed. "They're trying to shoot me out of the sky! The goddamn Jerries, they're out to kill me! Oh, merciful Jesus!" Carpenter quieted him, but some days she remembered his trembling so much he wasn't even able to "pour straight."[7]

No matter how many times he was admitted to the hospital in a dreadful condition he received the same treatment. The immediate problem was tackled but not the underlying cause. Neither was he given warnings about what he was doing to his body.

There was no Betty Ford Clinic then, as Maryann Carver would say some decades later when her husband, Raymond, seemed to be given free rein by the establishment to misbehave. There was nobody to comment on the abnormality of it as Susan Cheever would remark about her father John when he was falling down staircases or starting the day with a belt.

Like these men, Faulkner tended to be released "cured." He was sent home to do more damage to himself.

He drank at unusual times and refused drink when one might have expected him to store up. When his child Alabama died in 1931 he refused to indulge, saying defiantly, "This is the one time I'm not going to do it."[8]

Unlike many alcoholics, Faulkner became mellow with drink. Sometimes he quoted poetry to fuel the happy mood in which he found himself. But there were also times when it resulted in traumatic side effects.

He attended a writer's conference at the University of Virginia that year and promptly proceeded to get pie-eyed. Sherwood Anderson described the scene: "From time to time he appeared, got drunk again immediately, and disappeared." When he re-appeared he kept asking everyone for supplementary beverages. "If they didn't give him any, he drank his own."[9]

Faulkner's first three novels didn't sell well so he decided to write a potboiler. This was *Sanctuary*. It had the desired effect and pushed him up the sales scale. (Controversial for its time, *Sanctuary* was later adapted for the screen, first in 1933 as *The Story of Temple Drake*, starring Miriam Hopkins; then, in 1961, under its original title, starring Lee Remick.)

He bought a house with the proceeds, imagining his next books would

Bradford Dillman and Lee Remick in *Sanctuary* (1961). Faulkner wrote it as a potboiler. He achieved that ambition but the writing suffered.

sell as well. Sadly, they didn't. The message was clear. He needed to change his style from the rambling poetic one he treasured to something more commercial. This was easier done in screenplays than novels. That was why he now chose Hollywood for the quick buck.

He went to MGM in 1932 and was immediately informed that if he succumbed to the demon drink he'd be fired on the spot. He failed to take this advice in future years and was dismissed from time to time. When he was too drunk to write he sometimes dictated his scripts to secretaries.

He knew he was writing "down," but he needed the money. He continued to write novels while he was in Hollywood, using the proceeds to fund the kind of books that fulfilled him most, and sold least.

The movie world made him merry and he often acted out of character there. Taciturn by nature, he did things like pose for MGM publicity shots when he had a bag on, surprising even himself.

He also joked about his drinking escapades. He was so drunk at a polo match once, he claimed, he fell off his horse in a stupor and passed out. When he woke up in a hospital, the first thing he saw was Darryl F. Zanuck bending over him. He became shocked by Zanuck's famously protruding teeth. "It was such a feeling of horror," he said, "I became instantly sober."[10]

He found the routines of Hollywood draining. He was away from his comfort zone and, more importantly, had forsworn the privacy he needed to write the way he wanted. Or drink the way he wanted. People were looking at him all the time, so it wasn't enjoyable to indulge. In one comical effort to cut down he hired a male nurse to carry a bottle of bourbon in a bag for him and feed him sips of it from time to time. But, of course, this was never going to work. In no time at all he'd grabbed the bag from him and lashed large gulps of it down his throat. Now, *real* writing could begin.

His intake on an average day was two bourbons at lunch, two more at five, a martini before dinner, a half bottle of wine with it and perhaps two more bourbons during the evening. He was generally content with that amount but, if there was some crisis in his life, he'd "crumble under the chemistry of craving" and increase it dramatically. After that it was "binging toward limbo, the crackup, the hospital."[11]

Being dried out, for Faulkner, was a natural byproduct of drinking rather than a side effect. It was an occupational hazard and one he was more that happy to accept.

He regarded sobriety, not drunkenness, as the unnatural condition. Like his friend Humphrey Bogart, he saw the world as "three drinks behind." When you drank you elevated your consciousness to where it needed to be. It was like insulin to a diabetic.

Faulkner's daughter Jill said he drank mainly as a "safety valve." This was especially apparent when he was nearing the end of a book. Ernest Hemingway talked about a writer's need for "irresponsibility" after the "terrible responsibility" of writing. Faulkner agreed.[12]

Jill worried about his drinking. She implored him to stop for her, if nothing else. She talked to him about the shame it would bring on her in later years because of his high profile. He replied starkly, "Nobody remembers Shakespeare's children." The remark shocked her. She never forgot it.[13]

By the age of thirty-five, he needed a drink first thing in the morning to help him write. This was meant to be a cure for his hangover from the previous night's escapades, but more often than not, it became the start of a new binge. And thus the circle turned.

By 1936 his metabolism had changed. His early morning refreshments, far from being restorative, started to make him aware of just how intense his addiction was. That year his family had him admitted to a sanatorium in Mississippi to have him dried out. Mission accomplished, he went back to his screenwriting job at Twentieth Century–Fox. By now he was under strict observation by the studio. He also had the DTs a lot and was even hallucinating on occasion.

In November 1937 he was found face down on a hotel floor, clad only in shorts and with a third-degree burn in the small of his back. He'd fallen into a steam pipe in the bathroom. A bewildered doctor asked him why he drank so much. With eminent common sense he replied, "Because I like to."[14]

His literary powers diminished in his forties. This was most likely due to his problem. Something similar happened to Hemingway and Scott Fitzgerald. Neither of these writers ever admitted alcohol could have had a part in the decay of their talent. Eugene O'Neill did, as we saw, and prospered afterward. Diagnosis, as always, is half the cure. But denial is much more common than confession for alcoholics, inside literature and outside it.

Faulkner always thought he wrote just as well with drink, if not better. Not many of his readers agreed. John Cheever used to say one could practically "smell" the bourbon off his worst work. Hemingway said, "I can tell right in the middle of a page when he's had his first one."[15] Donald Newlove believed his later books contained "the famous mannered diction, senatorial tone, and a hallucinated rhetoric of alcohol, full of ravishings, musings and empty glory."[16] Faulkner wasn't bothered by criticisms like these. He tended to carry on guzzling regardless of what brickbats were thrown his way. He had a favorite saying: "Civilization begins with distillation."[17]

In 1944, he collaborated on the screenplay of *To Have and Have Not*, one of Ernest Hemingway's worst novels, and made it come alive. It was Lauren Bacall's film debut. She lit up the screen with Humphrey Bogart, whom she would go on to marry in real life. (One particular line of dialogue from the film became her signature. While looking provocatively at her leading man, she purred, "You know how to whistle, don't you, Steve? You just put your lips together... and blow." This notorious *double entendre* was listed as no. 34 on the American Film Institute's Top 100 Most Quoted Lines.)

Faulkner was drinking up to twenty martinis a day in the mid-'40s. The intake led to some incidents that could have had serious consequences. He stopped flying in 1946 after a drunken jape nearly cost him his life. In a burst of bravado, he dipped the plane in which he was flying so close to the ground he might have killed himself if it wasn't for the

Walter Brennan, Lauren Bacall and Humphrey Bogart in *To Have and Have Not* (1944). Faulkner's screenplay made Hemingway's allegedly "unfilmable" novel come alive. The chemistry between Bogart and Bacall wasn't too bad either.

quick thinking of his nephew Jimmy, who was in the cockpit with him. Jimmy wrested control of the steering wheel from him and safely landed the craft.

Three years later Faulkner was awarded the Nobel Prize. Regardless of his mental and physical state, many people still saw him as America's greatest writer. The prize-giving ceremony was held in Sweden. At first he said there was no way he would attend, but Jill finally persuaded him to go. "Just don't drink too much, Daddy," said Shakespeare's daughter. "We don't want you to disgrace us."

Jill wondered how she might avoid disaster. She thought hard and came up with a brainwave. She doctored the calendar, making him think the event was taking place sooner than it was. But the wily author was on to this ruse. When he did so, he looked at it and exclaimed with delight, "I've got three more days to drink!"[18] To everyone's surprise, however, he sobered up the day before he flew to Stockholm. He gave an eloquent acceptance speech at the ceremony, but as soon as it was over he went out and got drunk.

Winning the Nobel made him conscious of his image. He still drank as much, but not as publicly. When he rang for liquor from his home now he ordered it from as far away as Memphis so no connection could be drawn to him from the providers. (Memphis was seventy miles from where he lived.)[19]

In his later years, drinking made him more melancholic. He went to a party thrown by Truman Capote one night and found himself shedding buckets of tears for no apparent reason, in Capote's bathroom. The concerned host joined him in the bathroom and asked what was wrong. Faulkner had no answer. Capote sat on the toilet seat beside him and comforted him.[20]

Faulkner wrote *A Fable* in 1954. He believed it to be his best book, but authors aren't always the best judges of their work; so it proved here. His old rival Ernest Hemingway led the charge in denouncing it. All a writer needed for this kind of work, Hemingway alleged, was "a quart of whiskey, the loft of a barn, and a disregard of syntax."[21] (Hemingway thought Faulkner's incoherent style resulted from his drinking, but we can see this even in the books he wrote sober.)

He was hospitalized for alcohol poisoning in March 1956. When he began to hemorrhage, he was placed in an oxygen tent and given numerous blood transfusions. He pulled through but was told in no uncertain terms that he could never drink again. Once again, the warning fell on deaf ears. A life without drink was no life at all to him.[22] This was how he genuinely

Sharon Farrell and Steve McQueen in *The Reivers* (1969), a later work from Faulkner. He was reading it with a fifth of whiskey by his side just three days before he died.

felt. "When I have one martini," he said, "I feel bigger, wiser, taller. When I have a second I feel superlative, when I have more there's no holding me."[23]

In 1962, he published *The Reivers*, a rollicking yarn that was subsequently made into a 1969 film with Steve McQueen. He had a copy of this book by his side on July 3, 1962, and was enjoying reading it with a fifth of whiskey for company.

Three days later he passed away in a sanitarium, dying the way he lived. He had no regrets. It had been a good inning.

Ernest Hemingway

(1899–1961)

Like most other things he did in his action-packed life—writing, making love, boxing, hunting, etc.—Hemingway regarded drinking as a competition. When he first indulged in it as a boy with his friend Bill Smith in Michigan they had contests to see which of them could take the longest slug from a jug of cider and still remain "reasonably coherent."[1] Hemingway won. It would be the pattern of his future.

He found he was able to out-drink most of his contemporaries from a young age, a very dangerous accreditation. The first public documentation of the habit was when he was hospitalized after being wounded as an ambulance driver during The Great War, in Italy. The injury resulted from his bravely going into the line of fire against the Nazis. He laid into various beverages while recuperating in hospital, either to dull the pain or to increase his good humor as he regaled visitors with details of his experience. He also regaled the nurse, Agnes von Kurowsky, attending him, He developed a huge crush on her. He tried to win her heart by offering her some of his stash.

"Here, have a swig," he said to her, wiping the neck of the bottle on a bed sheet. He then pointed out the empty bottles of vermouth and Cointreau that he'd already finished. (He was waiting to have these smuggled out by the porter, who had brought them in to him for a "small bribe.") Kurowsky didn't snitch on him and he was already a hardened enough drinker not to exhibit the effects of it. The hospital's supervisor, Katherine C. Delong, smelled liquor on his breath; this led to some violent run-ins between them. Under the influence of his various concoctions he held forth to anyone who would listen to his views about the war. Some of the nurses found him rude, but Kurowsky was taken in by his charm.[2] He used his relationship with her as the basis for the love story in *A Farewell to Arms*, wherein his alter ego, Frederic Henry, becomes infatuated with the nurse who tends to his wounds.

Kurowsky eventually broke it off with Hemingway, deeming his feelings for her to be little more than a teenage crush. He was heartbroken and sought to "cauterize" her memory, burning it out of him with "a course of booze and other women."[3]

He eventually got over her, but his fondness for drink remained. His next love interest was Hadley Richardson, the woman who would become his first wife. They were poor but happy during their years in Paris together.

There was a rumor he went there to escape Prohibition, which had just been introduced in the U.S. It's a fanciful notion, but a false one. The reality was that he went there to learn how to write better—and to take advantage of the good exchange rate for the dollar.

He soon made friends with Gertrude Stein, who lived there. "All of you young people who served in the war," she told him, "you are a lost generation. You have no respect for anything. You drink yourselves to death."[4] Hemingway never forgot her words. It was this lost generation who peopled his first novel, *The Sun Also Rises*.

But Hemingway had no intention of drinking himself to death—not yet anyway. When he finished *The Sun Also Rises*, he wrote to his friend Ernest Walsh:

> I want to go on a walking trip and let my head get normal again. It's tired as hell inside and since I finished the book I have been doing a good deal of drinking again. Can drink hells any amount of whiskey getting drunk because my head is so tired.[5]

At times he seemed to see drinking as a talent one developed rather than a vice to which one succumbed. Hadley, he once told John Dos Passos, was "showing a lot of promise as a drinker."[6]

The newlyweds took as much drink as they liked and were young enough to get away with it without too many adverse effects. They often drank a bottle of wine each for lunch, followed by aperitifs before dinner, then another two bottles of wine with their evening meal. They burned it off with vigorous walking so it didn't become a problem. America may have been having its Prohibition but in Paris, drinking was synonymous with adventure and liberation.

The fact that Hemingway had such a huge capacity masked the amount he was consuming. As already mentioned, he was able to drink Scott Fitzgerald under the table whenever they met, though that wasn't saying much. He became friends with James Joyce in Paris as well and got drunk with him more than once, to the frustration of Joyce's wife, Nora. She was all too well aware that "Jimmy" didn't need much encouragement to get sozzled.[7]

Joyce and Fitzgerald were drunks rather than alcoholics for Hemingway, and this lowered them in his estimation. In *For Whom the Bell Tolls*, he has his character Pilar say to her husband, "Of all men, the drunkard is the foulest. The drunkard stinks and vomits in his bed and dissolves his organs in alcohol." But Hemingway was inconsistent on this point. In another mood he said, "I like to see every man drunk. A man does not exist until he is drunk.... To drink is nothing. It is to be drunk, that is important."[8]

The marriage to Hadley eventually collapsed. She gave up drinking when it did so, but Hemingway only increased his intake.

In early 1928, the habit, combined with his customary clumsiness, resulted in his having an accident that could have proved fatal. He'd been at dinner with Pauline Pfeiffer, his second wife, and Archibald McLeish. He came home to the apartment he was sharing with Pauline and went to bed. He woke at two in the morning and went to the bathroom to relieve himself. Afterward he reached up for what he thought was the chain on the flush box but was actually a cord for the skylight window. He yanked it so hard he pulled the whole frame (with its thick glass) down on him. Nine stitches were required to treat the wound. It left a moon-shaped scar on his head.[9]

Undeterred by his pain, he continued along his merry way. He engaged in a drinking competition with Morley Callaghan in Paris in 1929, emptying a glass of beer in a few gulps and then challenging Callaghan to join him in another. Callaghan swallowed three drinks but then asked himself, "Why am I doing this?" and quit. When they left the bar, Hemingway had taken seven drinks to Callaghan's three. This gratified him hugely.[10]

Philip Greene wrote a book solely about Hemingway's drinking habits. In it he tells us about Jake Barnes having a Jack Rose in *The Sun Also Rises*. He describes Frederic Henry having martinis in *A Farewell to Arms* and the lovers in *Across the River and into the Trees* feeling martinis "glow happily through their upper bodies."[11] He also describes Robert Jordan in *For Whom the Bell Tolls* having an absinthe and enjoying its "opaque, bitter, tongue-numbing, brain-warming, stomach-warming, idea-changing liquid alchemy." Greene saw alcohol as being an anesthetic for Hemingway. This is close to the truth. He once referred to whiskey as "my own personal central heating."[12]

His friend Buck Lanham said Hemingway could drink twenty-four hours a day.[13] The bullfighter Dominguin denied that, claiming that after 5 p.m. each day, he was practically insensible.[14] Dominguin was speaking about him towards the end of his life, so there might have been some truth in the allegation. (Or maybe not. The bullfighter didn't like the way Hemingway depicted him in his writing, so he could have been looking for a measure of revenge.)

Hemingway was determined to maintain his dignity regardless of how much he imbibed. "Drink all you want," he used to say, "but don't be a drunken shit. I drink and get drunk every day, but I never bother anyone." (Many people would have refuted this.) He didn't believe in half-measures in the way he drank or the way he lived his life. "The half bottle of champagne," he liked to say, "is the enemy of man."[15]

His mother once asked him if he was an alcoholic. His reply was defensive: "You will hear legends that I am—they're tacked on to everyone that ever wrote about people who drink."[16] This is hardly true. The legends about Hemingway are mainly based on anecdotal evidence from reliable sources.

He called alcohol the "Giant Killer." It killed problems like "storms, wars, and moments of loneliness." The killing, though, was always temporary; he often became belligerent afterward.

Hemingway's boorish behavior reaffirmed the image many people had of him as an arrogant man in love with violence. This is a pity because such an image overlooks the qualities that made him unique—his romantic sense, his ability to plumb the depths of emotional pain, his penchant for subtlety. These were qualities evident in his books, but as the years went by, his brash public persona, and indeed his celluloid characterizations, seemed to belie them.

It was all too easy for him to embody his myth. The world recognized him in Gregory Peck as he lay stricken with gangrene on a mountain peak in *The Snows of Kilimanjaro* (1952). It recognized him in Gary Cooper blowing up a Fascist bridge behind enemy lines in the Spanish Civil War in *For Whom the Bell Tolls* (1943). It recognized him in Rock Hudson making his separate peace with Jennifer Jones in *A Farewell to Arms* (1957). What did it matter that he reviled most of the movies made of his books? He threw his personality at the world and it responded by taking him into its heart. In time he became too fond of his brash image and tried to live up—or even down—to it. Either consciously or unconsciously, he parlayed his fame into his life, and vice versa.

He hunted. He boxed. He fished for marlin. In between such activities he tried to get "the word" down. When work was done he filled his glass, though not always as much as people believed. His biographer Kurt Singer wrote:

> To be sure he drank a lot, but most of the pictures showing him with bottles at the side of his mouth, or an army of "dead soldiers" on the floor, were posed shots to please the photographers. To take a picture of Hemingway without a drink was as unthinkable as a portrait of Marilyn Monroe wearing a Mother Hubbard.[17]

Hemingway went along with this just as he went along with being photographed beside huge fish even if others had caught them. It was too much of a temptation to resist, especially if he was lubricated enough.

Whiskey was one of his favorite drinks. "When you work hard all day," he wrote to his Russian translator Ivan Kashkeen in the mid-1930s, "and know you must work again the next day, what else can change your ideas and make them run on a different plane like whiskey? When you're cold and wet, what else can warm you?" He was also partial to rum: "Before an attack, who can say anything gives you the momentary well-being that rum does?" Wine figured strongly in his list of priorities as well: "I would as soon not eat at night as not have red wine and water. The only time it isn't good for you is when you write or when you fight. You have to do that cold. But it always helps my shooting. Modern life, too, is often an oppression and liquor is the only relief." He ended the letter to Kashkeen by saying: "Let me know if my books make any money and I will come to Moscow and we will find somebody that drinks my royalties up to end the mechanical oppression."[18] He didn't say what he meant by "mechanical oppression." Presumably sobriety.

Hemingway's strong constitution saved him from the terrible hangovers suffered by the likes of Faulkner and Fitzgerald. He worked them off easily by exercise. But maybe if he suffered such hangovers, they would have alerted him earlier to the fact that alcohol was taking over his life. This became more apparent as his reputation grew.

He left Pauline Pfeiffer for Martha Gellhorn when he was writing *For Whom the Bell Tolls*. "Ernest needs a new woman for every novel," F. Scott Fitzgerald derided. "He had Hadley for *The Sun Also Rises*, Pauline for *A Farewell to Arms*, and now Martha."[19] But this wasn't a stable relationship. Gellhorn was tougher than Hemingway's previous wives. She was also a rival to him as a journalist and war reporter, which caused friction between the two. Alcohol fueled their arguments, some of which became comical. He once wrote to Maxwell Perkins about a binge that annoyed her:

> Will have to take Marty to the movies as a present for being drunk Saturday night, I guess. Started out on absinthe, drank a bottle of good red wine with dinner, shifted to vodka in town before the pelota game and then battened it down with whiskeys and soda until 3 A.M.[20]

He often had three Scotches before dinner. His general Saturday night intake was a glass of absinthe followed by a bottle of red wine over dinner, followed by various amounts of vodka and whiskey, drunk in the small hours. He found sleep hard to come by so often washed down these potions with handfuls of pills. His sleep was usually short and fitful. He would be up again at dawn, a pencil in one hand and a drink in the other as a new onslaught on literature—and Dr. Feelgood—began.

Hemingway encouraged his children to drink, either to justify his own behavior or to toughen them up to the levels of his macho credos. In 1943, when his two sons, Patrick and Gregory, visited him at his home in the Finca Vigia in Florida, he plied them with liquor. He also allowed them to indulge in it on their own. Gregory was only eleven at the time. When he told Hemingway he had a hangover one morning, his father advised him to take a Bloody Mary to make it go away.[21]

World War II was raging now. He would dearly like to have fought in it. He'd like to have fought in the First World War as well instead of being "just" an ambulance driver. All his life he found it difficult to square his image as a hard-drinking author with that of a soldier *manqué*.[22]

To give himself the illusion that he was contributing to the war effort, he and some drinking buddies engaged in searching for submarines for Spanish supporters of Franco living in Cuba. For Gellhorn, his U-boat escapades along the Cuban coast were no more than excuses to drink Tom Collins with his friends, or quasi-friends, under the auspices of helping the war effort. This wearing of false hair on his chest—which had angered Zelda Fitzgerald so much in the Paris years—accelerated the demise of his marriage to Gellhorn. When the Allies landed in Paris in 1945, thereby signaling the end of the war, Hemingway's first action was to "liberate" the Hotel Ritz—and then partake of its liquid delights. It became like his private champagne club.[23]

He ran into Mary Welsh there and fell in love with her. She was a war correspondent he had previously met during the London blitz. Currently separated from her husband, she needed to obtain a divorce before she and Hemingway could legally wed.

Meanwhile, Hemingway's latest ex, Gellhorn, had become bitter about the man; she once said she couldn't even talk about him without getting stomach pains.[24] Hemingway shared her bitterness. As he told A. E. Hotchner:

> Only one marriage I regret [was to Martha Gellhorn]. I remember after I got the license I went across from the license bureau to a bar for a drink. The bartender said, "What will you have, sir?" And I said, "Hemlock."[25]

Gellhorn, for her part, suggested some couples would be better off shooting each other.[26]

On June 20, 1945, he drove Mary Welsh to an airport, where she planned to arrange the legal finalities of her divorce, but en route the car skidded on some clay on the motorway. "This is bad, Pickle," he said to her as the vehicle went out of control. "We have to go off." Saying thus, he slammed into a high bank of earth. Mary plunged through the windshield and was lucky she wasn't killed. She had to have plastic surgery on her face afterward to prevent disfigurement. Hemingway had four of his ribs cracked by the steering wheel, and his left knee was damaged by the dashboard. His forehead was also cut by the rear-view mirror. "I was cold sober," he told Maxwell Perkins, as if this was an unusual state for him to be in.[27]

In 1946, he sold the rights to his short story "The Killers" to Universal for $35,000, a decision he would come to regret, as the film went on to gross several million dollars. Having said that, it was one of the few Hollywood adaptations of his work he liked. It was Burt Lancaster's film debut,

The Killers (1946) was one of the few movie adaptations of his work that Hemingway liked. Burt Lancaster and Ava Gardner lit up the screen with atmospheric *noir* potency.

and Ava Gardner's first major role. She went on to become a friend of the writer's, starring in screen adaptations of *The Sun Also Rises* and *The Snows of Kilamanjaro*.

He was interviewed by A.E. Hotchner in Florida in the spring of 1948. He'd arranged to meet him in the Floridita bar. While waiting for him to arrive, Hotchner sampled one of Hemingway's favorite drinks, the Papa Doble. Named after him, it consisted of two and a half jiggers of Bacardi White Label Rum, the juice of half a grapefruit, and six drops of maraschino. When Hemingway arrived, he ordered two frozen daiquiris. These were served in huge vase-like glasses. (He once downed a total of fifteen of these in a night—the house record). Over the next few hours the two men talked about literature while drinking eight Papa Dobles each. It was a miracle Hotchner managed to write up his interview, considering the "rum-mist" that was in his head.[28]

He told Hotchner he gave up smoking once so that he could better smell wine. "Cigarette smoke is the nose's worst enemy," he said, "and how can you enjoy a good wine that you cannot truly smell?"[29] He thought of himself as a connoisseur.

The accidents continued. In the summer of 1950, he slipped on the wet deck of the *Pilar*—his treasured boat—while drinking. He sustained a five-inch cut, as well as severing an artery ("whose name I never caught") and suffering a concussion.[30]

By the early fifties he was drinking up to three bottles of liquor a day, as well as wine with meals. Denis Zaphiro, a ranger with the Kenya Game Department, described him as being "drunk the whole time" he was on safari in the summer of 1953, though not showing it. He just became "merrier, more loveable, more bull-shitty." Without drink, on the contrary, he was "morose, silent and depressed."[31]

His friend Norberto Fuentes documented his daily routine when he was in Cuba. He started with a highball or a Tom Collins, and then graduated to whiskey. At lunch he would have wine. He didn't drink again until dinner, during which he would have wine. If he had visitors, the consumption would increase. Between them they'd knock back three or four bottles of whiskey. Or he might have campari, more wine, or tequila. He liked to serve the wine himself, holding the bottle by the neck. "Bottles by the neck," he'd say, "women by the waist."[32]

Hemingway once went on a binge with a friend in Cuba; it ended only after each man had consumed—standing up—sixteen double frozen daiquiris, each containing four ounces of Bacardi rum. He went home afterward and read all night. "I never felt better," he bragged.[33]

He felt if he could keep his drinking separate from his writing he would be fine, but this eventually proved difficult. A lifelong habit can never be a thing apart.

He regarded himself as an authority on other writers' drinking habits, on how alcohol affected their writing. "When I read Faulkner," he told his friend Harvey Breit, "I can tell exactly when he gets tired and does it on corn." This reminded him of when F. Scott Fitzgerald would "hit it," i.e., around the time he wrote *Tender Is the Night*.[34] He was aware he was "hitting it" too much himself now, to the detriment of his writing. Occasionally, he held off and got his reward on the page.

The fact that he was drinking more than ever was evident in the disjunction between the two books he wrote about his safaris. *Green Hills of Africa*, which chronicled the first one, is the work of a man in total control of his world—and his words—but *True at First Light* betrays the "addled thinking and diminished awareness" of the lush.[35]

Sometimes he drank whiskey prior to hunting big game to steady his nerves. One wouldn't recommend this to everyone—especially the wife of Francis Macomber, who shot her husband on safari instead of a wild animal in one of Hemingway's most famous stories, "The Short Happy Life of Frances Macomber." Hemingway's shooting arm was usually straight with alcohol, but sometimes his judgment was off.

On other occasions he used alcohol as a kind of medicine to inure him to life's pressures, a poultice to place over emotional wounds. In one of his early stories, "The Three-Day Blow," the main character gets over a broken relationship by drinking his way through it with a friend. When Marjorie drops Nick

Hemingway hard at work trying to get down "the one true sentence." Alcohol would guillotine that ambition as it did so many others in his later years.

Adams in the story, Nick is traumatized until he gets drunk. After that, "The Marge business was no longer so tragic. It was not even very important."³⁶ In *The Sun Also Rises*, the characters seem to drink the same way they eat. The activity is like a natural part of their day. This was also true for himself.

Lillian Ross interviewed him in 1949. He had just finished *Across the River and into the Trees*, his last novel. He wrote it against the backdrop of his infatuation with a Venetian woman, Adriana Ivancich. The interview took place over a few days. It was meant to capture the man behind the image but by then, there wasn't much of a difference. Hemingway had become a prisoner of his talent. The action hero, the braggart, the man about town had fed into the writing and dripped out of it. For Ross, he acted out this role and played into its stereotypes. When she met him he drank three double bourbons. Later on at his hotel he downed several bottles of champagne and, at a museum, repeated bracers from a flask. The intense young man of the stories had morphed into "Papa," a giant bear dispensing witticisms and bile.³⁷

"Papa" Hemingway, the paternal figure of later years (Copyright Mary Hunt).

In *Across the River* there's not too much of a difference between Colonel Cantwell, its brash anti-hero, and the man Hemingway had become. It's a thinly disguised autobiography masquerading as fiction. Both men drink Valpolicella and embroider their own mythologies; both men are mini-legends in their own minds. The manager of the Gritti Palace in Venice told Anthony Burgess that Hemingway drank three bottles of Valpolicella in the mornings as a matter of course, followed by Scotch, daiquiris, tequila, bourbon, and vermouth-less martinis.³⁸

The mask has fallen. What we're seeing in this novel is a bumptious *bon viveur* writing about (and as) another bumptious *bon viveur*. Both men are also emotionally broken and evince black humor about that fact.

They've become trivial, more pitiful than tragic, putting themselves on drunken pedestals like tin gods.

Across the River was too stylized by far. Even reaching for the champagne has to be done "accurately and well" by the Colonel. Hemingway claimed the book would outdo *A Farewell to Arms*, but it's more like a satire of it. War becomes an after-dinner story rather than a conflict between countries. The critics noted this and savaged it in their reviews.

Hemingway was shattered. But Raymond Chandler—of all people—came to his defense. Not much happened in the book, he acknowledged, which made the mannerisms of the style "sort of stick out." Still, it was better than most other books being written at the time, even if it wasn't vintage Hemingway. Chandler stuck up for Hemingway just as he had for F. Scott Fitzgerald when the "knife-throwers" were attacking him around the time of "the crack-up." It took one alcoholic to understand another, to empathize with the pressures they were under. But not even Chandler's support could hide the author's decline. From now on, his writing had flabbiness, a sense of the obvious. It seems, too, to be suffused with a "boozy sentimentality."[39] Gone was the old discipline, the laconic tonality, and the second voice burrowing between the lines.

He got himself together for one last work of fiction, a novella. *The Old Man and the Sea* had begun life as a short story years before. He touched it up, transforming a fairly ordinary piece of prose into a semi-Biblical parable. The world sat up and took notice. Was Hemingway back? The answer was yes. Once again he was serenaded by the critics and the public alike.

The Old Man and the Sea was made into a film in 1958. Hemingway, much to everyone's surprise, agreed to work on the script. Though based in Cuba, parts of it were shot in Peru to take advantage of the better location facilities.

He frequented a drinking establishment called the Cabo Blanco Fishing Club, becoming one of its regulars. "His bill kept us operating for a year," the owner happily recalled.[40] Before shooting began, he worried if Spencer Tracy, the actor chosen to play the old man, would be able to remain sober for the duration of the film. Tracy also had a drinking problem, although, at this point, he was between benders. There was a certain irony in the idea of one alcoholic wondering if another one could stay sober. Tracy managed to do so, but Hemingway didn't think much of his performance. He thought he looked like "a fat Hollywood actor pretending to be a poor Cuban fisherman."[41]

Just as Hemingway lost his discipline on the page in his later years, so did he turn from a "good" drunk into a sloppy one, especially after he fell for Adriana Ivancich. He behaved like an adolescent with her. It was almost reminiscent of his "calf love" for Agnes von Kurowsky some thirty years earlier. At that time, drinking was a casual hobby; now, it all but defined him, making the amorous posturings of a middle-aged man all the more disquieting.

Mary said she only saw Hemingway unsteady on his feet once or twice in the seventeen years she knew him. When he contracted hepatitis in the 1950s, she claimed he didn't touch alcohol for a year. Before and after, she admitted, he liked a few martinis each day and "at least a bottle of wine" in the evening, depending on the number of guests they had.[42] This seems to be a watered-down version of the way things really were.

Drinking was starting to show in his features by this time. Gone were the good looks of yore. His skin was raddled, and he was sporting a paunch. When George Plimpton saw him in the early fifties he was shocked to see the bulge of his liver standing out from his body "like a long fat leech."[43]

On a trip to Africa, in the summer of 1953, he got so drunk he fell out of a Land Rover and sprained his shoulder. This was a prelude to something much worse: two plane crashes within two days of each other, the following year. These led to many of the health problems that would haunt him until the day he died. In the first one, his back and shoulder were badly bruised. In the second, he headbutted a door to get out of a burning plane, resulting in a concussion. He also suffered damage to his lower intestine and his eyes and ears. But he was still able to tell reporters—who had actually published his obitu-

Spencer Tracy, another alcoholic, was coming off a bender when he played Santiago in *The Old Man and the Sea*. He managed to stay sober during the shoot but Hemingway still thought he gave a lousy performance.

ary—"My luck, she is running very good."⁴⁴ He talked to them while carrying a bottle of gin in one hand and a bunch of bananas in the other.

The reincarnated Hemingway busied himself reading his obituaries. "Rumors of my death have been exaggerated," he said à la Mark Twain, "but is it not the case that if a man has sought death all his life, he could not have found her before the age of fifty-four?"⁴⁵ It sounded like a plausible point.

A primitive physician in a local bar poured gin into his head to "heal" it, causing Hemingway to scoff, "What a waste." But as his biographer Michael Reynolds noted, "Alcohol, his sovereign, was guaranteed to make the concussion worse."⁴⁶ Further tests revealed he also had a crushed liver, a paralyzed sphincter muscle, and damage to his spleen and vertebrae.

Such injuries were in addition to his other issues of high cholesterol and high blood pressure. He was the proverbial accident waiting to happen. His doctor knew he wouldn't swear off drink completely so he recommended a low alcohol diet: five ounces of whiskey a day and one glass of wine. Hemingway said he would give this a try, but as someone who'd been drinking much larger quantities of wine since his teens, he felt it might be a shock to his system.

Not only did Hemingway practice denial, he wallowed in it. Admitting that one had a drinking problem didn't make you a better person, he believed; it just made you a worse drinker.⁴⁷ When he met the screenwriter Peter Viertel for the first time, he said, "Alcohol is our worst enemy and our best friend" before knocking back a thimble of tequila.⁴⁸ He knew its dangers; he also relished them. Like the corrida and big game hunting, it was just one more challenge to his powers of resistance.

It became both disease and cure for him, staving off the horror of life and then increasing it. It helped him tolerate his enemies and then made them even more intolerable. It helped him sleep and then it caused insomnia. It helped banish fears about his declining creative powers and then it contributed significantly to the decline. It drove away his dark moods and then compounded them.

"Nobody went through the floor of depression like Hemingway did," said Archibald MacLeish.⁴⁹ He didn't talk about this as people like F. Scott Fitzgerald did, preferring to suffer in silence. His wayward drinking was the closest he came to an admission that life was getting to be too much for him. Stephen King saw his logic as being like this: "As a writer I am a very sensitive fellow, but real men don't give into their sensitivities. Only sissy-men do that. Therefore, I drink. How else can I face the existential horror of it all and continue to work?"⁵⁰ This is close to the view expressed by Philip Greene earlier.

By the mid–'50s, A. E. Hotchner wrote, "[Hemingway] drank heavily every night, Scotch or red wine, and he was invariably in bad shape when finally induced to go to his room."[51] Hotchner was with him in Spain now, the country Hemingway loved more than any other.

With the languor induced by alcohol, though, such love dissipated. He couldn't enjoy the bullfights, the cafés, or even the girls. Instead, he sat for hours outside bars with his acolytes, "not really caring who they were, sipping his drinks and talking, first coherently and then, as the alcohol dissolved all continuity, his talk becoming repetitive, his speech slurred and disheveled."[52] On the mornings after such stupors he'd try to pass it all off with his adolescent banter. "Am a little pooped," he'd grin. "Went five rounds with the Demon Rum last night and knocked him on the ass in 1.55 of the sixth."[53] Compensatory potions revived him partially—tequila and vodka, usually—until it came time for the next corrida.[54]

He had a fierce argument with Mary one night in 1956 after having one too many glasses of wine over dinner. He'd been guzzling since early on in the day and they went to his head. Mary went off in a sulk while Hemingway was brought to another bedroom by Hotchner. When he got inside, he turned on the light. After a few seconds, he started glowering at the lampshade. He then went into a boxer's crouch and hit it with a right hook, breaking the bulb and knocking the fixture onto the carpet outside the door. The metal tore a gash in his knuckle. This started to bleed, but he paid no attention to it. The following day he said to Hotchner, "Hotch, I've been drunk 1,547 times in my life but never in the morning."[55]

His logic seemed to be that a man who could be as ridiculous as he liked when the sun went down but different laws applied earlier in the day. The statement made about as much sense as most of his other pronouncements on drunkenness. In fact, it wasn't even true, as is testified to by many people, including his wives. They spoke of the vodkas and tequilas he would have for breakfast, the Bloody Marys at noon, the daiquiris and Scotches slipped in between writing bursts.

But the argument with Mary affected him. Afterward, he cut down his drinking to two glasses of wine a night. He also got his weight down to two hundred pounds, which helped reduce his cholesterol and his blood pressure. Even so, he wasn't happy. Drinking had always cheered him up when things were bad, and nothing could compensate for that. The benefits to his health didn't seem to mean too much to him and he was soon back on the sauce.

Mary was alarmed by the about-face, but took care not to nag him about it. For one thing he wouldn't have taken it from her. For another, she knew he needed it. But, in his last years, the "pleasant medicine" turned toxic, and this caused her deep concern.[56]

"How can you stand by silently while someone you love is destroying himself?" she asked Hotchner frustratedly. "The things that used to sustain him—working, reading, planning, writing and receiving letters—are fading away. He doesn't even have people around him to lean on him and bring him their problems. Now there's just *his* problems and *his* hurts, a day-after-day Black-Ass."[57]

At this point he was on a huge cocktail of medicines, both for his physical and psychological problems. He was taking pills to help him sleep, pills to combat his hyperactivity, pills to treat his damaged liver, and pills for his high blood pressure. Mixed up with the wine and all his other concoctions it was a lethal cocktail. How could he ingest all this and still concentrate on his writing?

In 1959, he traveled to Sapin to cover a *mano a mano* competition between two famous matadors, Antonio Ordonez and Luis Miguel Dominguin. Hemingway wrote a book about this phase of his life called *The Dangerous Summer*. It became this not so much because of the bullfights as the fact that he was drunk most of the time. This, combined with his poor health, meant he struggled with the writing. When he came home he was treated for a kidney disorder.

His liquor bill for 1960 was $1,550, which would be approximately $12,600 in today's currency—the median American national income. He was back to his old habits with a vengeance, but his resistance wasn't what it used to be. Neither, for that matter, was his mental state. He was in and out of psychiatric institutions a lot now, suffering from various forms of paranoia. He worried about things he wouldn't have given a moment's concern to in the past—taxes, passports, travel arrangements. At one stage he developed the notion that people in the street were looking at him. He also thought the government was spying on him.

Hospitals subjected him to electric shock treatments in the belief that they could cure him. Instead, his condition only worsened. They traumatized him and robbed him of his memory. And what was a writer without his memory?[58]

The man who faced down lions in the jungle, who negotiated two world wars in his fashion, and a civil war in Spain, was now afraid to have a meal in a restaurant for fear the FBI was on his case. The man who had tried to drink Spain—and Italy—dry was worried that he would be arrested for having an unopened bottle of wine in the glove compartment of his car. His paranoia was so great he even suspected his friend Bill Davis was planning to murder him.[59]

When we combine this with his physical ailments it's hardly surprising that he frequently contemplated suicide at this time. He was like an animal with his foot caught in a trap, a tethered lion without the ability to roar. The thrills of yesteryear held no allure for him anymore. The intensity with which he had lived his life in the past without discernible ill-effects was now catching up to him. He was entering a surreal vacuum from which there seemed no escape. From his youth he had seen his father unable to deal with the daily stresses and strains. He couldn't understand his weakness, but now such weakness was transplanted into his own head. His father committed suicide when life got to be too much for him. He felt he would, too.

He was admitted to the Mayo Clinic in Minnesota for treatment in 1960, registering under his doctor's name, George Saviers. By now, according to Hotchner, he was washing down pills with vodka to kill the pain of a lifetime of hellraising. Such pills were given to him without any more care than the electric shock treatments that destroyed him. Both of them robbed him of his creative drive. Hemingway joked that his best chance would be a shrink who'd done a creative writing course.[60]

On April 21, 1961, Mary came down the stairs of their Ketchum home to find him in the sitting room with a shotgun in his hand. Two shells stood upright on the windowsill in front of him.

"Honey," she said calmly, "you wouldn't do anything harmful to me as well as yourself, would you?" He put down the gun and a doctor was summoned. When he got to the house he made a half-baked attempt to run to the gun rack, where Mary had placed the shotgun. He was dispossessed easily, but later on, as he took a plane to a hospital in Rochester, he made another attempt to kill himself. They had stopped the plane to refuel and he went for a walk in the car park, allegedly searching the glove compartment of parked cars, looking for firearms. He also tried to walk into the propellers of a plane coming down the runway towards him.[61]

More electric shock therapy was administered after they got to the hospital, but it was as ineffective as previous doses. Hemingway didn't advertise this, fooling the doctors with a carefully contrived calm. So they let him out.[62]

He left the clinic on June 26, 1960. Less than a week later, he woke at dawn on a Sunday morning and made his way down to the basement of his house, where Mary had locked all the guns. He took his favorite double-gauge rifle from a cabinet and loaded it with two shells he had hidden from her. He put the butt of the rifle on the ground and held his forehead against the barrel before tripping the hammers. The sound Mary heard was like a drawer being shut.[63]

"If people bring so much courage to the world," he wrote once, "the world has to kill them to break them so of course it kills them. It kills the very good and the very brave impartially. If you are none of those, you can be sure it will kill you too, but there will be no special hurry."[64]

For Hemingway, it took sixty-one years.

John Cheever
(1912–1982)

Cheever was born in Woolaston, Massachusetts, in 1912, the son of a shoe salesman. He found it difficult to remember a time when he didn't write. He had his first story published in *The New Republic* in 1930. A few years later he joined the Yaddo Writers' Colony and started to become published in the *New Yorker*; in time that publication would become his main meal ticket.

He married Mary Winternitz, an instructor of literature, in 1941. He served in the army line infantry division during World War II and also published his first collection of short stories during the war. He had three children with Mary: Susan, Ben, and Federico. He was a devoted father, but struggled to make a go of things with Mary as their divisions deepened over time.

Cheever's home, like Eugene O'Neill's before him, marched to the beating drum of alcohol. It was the inevitable side order at every meal. It was what everyone sampled at baptisms, weddings, and funerals. People came into the world with it and went out with it. In between, they did their best to deal with the collateral damage. As Susan wrote in a memoir of her youth:

> On Sunday mornings we would have Bloody Marys. In the summer we would stay cool with gins and tonics. In the winter we would drink Manhattans. In the good times we would break out champagne; in bad times we would dull the pain with stingers. My mother dispensed two fingers of whiskey for stomach pain and beer for other digestive problems. Gin was an all-purpose anesthetic.[1]

"Guests were always falling down the stairs," she recalled. "There were scuffmarks on the wall from flying feet. People who came for lunch frequently had to be put to bed during the course of the afternoon." Often there were car accidents. "The family cars made lots of trips to the body shop. In the evenings there were terrible fights. Almost any disagreement quickly escalated into a deadly silence or an apocalyptic rage."[2]

One of the amazing things about Cheever's life was the manner in which he conducted a semi-normal suburban existence with his wife and family while inwardly suffering the tortures of a man who seemed to fantasize about his next tipple from the moment he woke up in the morning to when he went to bed at night. He also harbored homosexual tendencies as well as heterosexual ones. These damaged his marriage beyond repair even if he was never able to walk away from it (*Writer Pictures*).

For Susan, alcoholism was the elephant in the room in her house. Everyone knew her father was an alcoholic; it just wasn't talked about. That's why it went on so long. It was the invisible disease.[3]

She remembered him stumbling upstairs many nights after tea and then hearing a series of crashes and thuds as he tried to get to his bedroom. She didn't see anything too unusual about this at first. She regarded it as normal behavior. There were pre-prandial libations, post-prandial libations, and, eventually, non-stop libations. In time, she came to realize that the reason most of her father's friends drank was because that was *why* they were his friends. Those who didn't drink simply weren't admitted to his circle.

Cheever, she said, judged people primarily by how much they drank and how generously they poured for him when he was a guest in their homes. There were always bottles of gin and whiskey on full view in the pantry in their own house; he also kept bottles in the closet, a bottle in his desk, and even one behind the New York edition of Henry James's works in the library. In warm weather, an extra bottle was placed outside in the hedge near the driveway.[4]

He had a huge thirst even as a young man. He thought nothing of polishing off a dozen Manhattans in one sitting. Some of the motivation for this was escapist. He never faced himself, a friend observed, and when he did he didn't like what he saw.[5]

He went to a party thrown by Malcolm Cowley in 1933 and was offered two drinks. One was a Manhattan, and the other a Pernod. They were both, he deduced, made in a bathtub. He wasted no time in knocking them back. He then had four or five more Manhattans and threw up all over the wallpaper in the hallway afterward. Cowley, he was relieved to note, didn't ask for damages.

He moved to Manhattan the following year to try to earn his living from writing, but it wasn't easy in Depression-struck America. He did some treatments of screenplays for MGM and published the occasional piece of short fiction, but neither paid much. It was only when Cowley suggested he submit stories to the *New Yorker* that his career really took off.

Cheever was unusual in that his drinking was set against the backdrop of a supposedly stable married life in a rambling county house. As Susan mentioned, it was embedded in his life, a life in which he also managed to write, to drive, skate, play backgammon, converse, garden, go on extensive walks—even hikes—and play touch football.

His friend Elizabeth Collins thought he evinced signs of alcoholism from the mid-'40s. He remembered him one night at a party, carrying a woman on his shoulders. He moved around a room like a child, eventually flinging her off when she put a cigarette out in his ear.[6]

Cheever's brother Fred was also an alcoholic. One night Cheever saved his life by having him rushed to hospital when he was threatening to drink himself to death. After he recovered, he continued to over-drink. "Now he is so drunk," Fred wrote of Cheever, "he cannot walk from the chair to the table and when he gets there he cannot eat."[7] It wouldn't be too long before John would emulate such a condition.

He knew he had a problem; this goaded him to seek out others in the same predicament. He was, he said, "one of those men who read the grievous accounts of hard-drinking, self-destructive authors [while] holding a glass of whiskey in our hands."[8]

One of the reasons he drank was to overcome a shyness that hit him at public events. Writing has been described as a self-invasion of privacy. Cheever understood this firsthand. He loved writing, but not its trappings. He drank heavily before readings of his work and then tended to "smile, smile, smile" until his face ached. Afterward, he felt so ashamed of himself he drank even more.[9]

His cravings began as soon as he woke in the morning: "I imagine the water glass on the table beside my bed is filled with whiskey."[10]

"I breakfast on Scotch and Librium," he proclaimed, somewhere between a confession and a boast.[11] One brought him up, and the other brought him down. Beset with everything from vertigo to agoraphobia, he tried to keep his life simple. Words blocked out the world until it came time to do a reading or give a lecture. At this point the two unhappily coalesced.

Mornings were his worst times. His discontent began at seven when light filled his room. "I am unready for the day, unready to face it soberly, that is. Some days I would like to streak down to the pantry and pour a drink." The hours between seven and ten, when he actually did drink, were the worst because he had given in to himself by then.[12] As time went on, his drinking timetable shrunk. His ambition once had been to wait till after 4 p.m. to indulge. Then it became after noon, then after ten. Susan sometimes found him being cranky and wondered at the reason for this. It was only in later years she arrived at the answer. He'd been waiting for her to leave the room so he could dive into the whiskey.[13]

He drank partly from financial pressure, like F. Scott Fitzgerald. It was difficult to run a house on the uncertain income generated by writing, especially when he hadn't established himself in any one genre. He said he wrote stories with one hand and novels with the other as he tried to keep Susie in hairnets and himself in gin.[14]

He moved to Scarborough, New York, in 1950, and was made a Guggenheim Fellow the following year. He won the Benjamin Franklin magazine award in 1955 and the O. Henry one in 1956. That was the year he moved to Ossining, in New York. In time he would inherit the sobriquet "Ovid of Ossining," courtesy of his formidable literary output. His forté was his ability to capture the elegant sadness of so many suburban lives, largely on the edge of quiet desperation. The time would come when he, too, suffered from quiet desperation, mainly due to the breakdown of his marriage to Mary.

He wrote about his drinking routines in 1958, describing alcohol as a painkiller. Mary was depressed, he added. He accepted that her "low spirits" were due to his partaking of different ones. "So the gin flows, and after supper the whiskey. I am even a little shy, keeping my glass on the floor where it might not be seen."[15]

He worked off the effects of these lubricants many mornings by taking long hikes, or by "scything" escapades in his garden. Federico used to be terrified watching him tottering off with the scythe on his shoulder, wondering how much his psychomotor skills would have been impaired by the previous night's drinking. "I was never sure if he was going to come back with all his limbs," he fretted.[16]

The country gentleman surveyed the magnificence of the surrounding hills, the valleys and the skies. But internally he felt like ending it all. He felt like Neddy Merrill, his character in "The Swimmer," a man who had everything and nothing, a man with a hole in his soul.

Cheever liked to debunk the notion that drunkenness could be romantic. "To die of drink is sometimes thought a graceful and natural death," he declared, but that was to overlook the "wet-brains, convulsions, delirium tremens, hallucinations, hideous automobile accidents and botched suicides."[17] Many of his friends, he said, had committed suicide while under the influence: "One of them jumped off a cliff. One of them set fire to his house and incinerated himself and his children. One of them is still in a straitjacket."[18]

Somebody else who'd been important to him shot himself: Ernest Hemingway. Cheever's writing had been influenced by him, as had his drinking. Both influences embarrassed him. Asked once what he'd learned from Hemingway, he droned, "Not to blow my head off with a shotgun."[19]

His problems increased in the '60s. Allied to his alcoholism was the growing knowledge that he had bisexual tendencies. This caused untold damage in the relationship with Mary, as did his flirtations with other women.

He fought with her, and with himself, while trying to kick the drink habit and the gay habit. As his career took off he carried inside himself a dissatisfaction with his circumstances that never quite resolved itself. Desperate to escape the burdens of existence, he became a rabbit trapped in the headlamps of domesticity: a reluctant husband, a latent homosexual, a closet soak.

He considered going to a dry-out farm but preferred to fight the "booze fight" on the battlefield of life. That was where he'd been "advancing and retreating" intermittently since he got married.[20]

He published *The Wapshot Scandal* in 1964. The book garnered the best notices of his career thus far. Suddenly he became a celebrity, of sorts. His picture appeared on the cover of *Time* magazine. It was a watershed for him. People started inviting him places. He bought a car and started traveling. It was enjoyable being cosseted, waited upon. But then reality bit. Back in New York, the problems remained resolutely the same. Mary's moods. His own moods. The drink. The men. Except now he had more to live up to. Scaling the pinnacle of the literary mountain became a poisoned chalice. His writing became more self-conscious as a result.

He met the actress Hope Lange that year and began an extended, if occasional, love affair with her. She was impressed that such an acclaimed writer expressed an interest in her. He, for his part, was over the moon to be seeing "the most beautiful woman in the world," as he put it. He boasted about her even to Mary, who listened to his diatribes in a bored frame of mind. By now she'd grown accustomed to his extramarital dalliances.

Lange was married to the director Alan J. Pakula at this time. Pakula had bought the rights to *The Wapshot Scandal* in conjunction with another director, Robert Mulligan, with a view to filming it. Cheever flew to California to discuss the project with them.

They met in a hotel. Cheever amazed Mulligan with the way he managed to empty two large tumblers that had been filled to the brim with vodka "and then move on to several glasses of wine at lunch, while remaining absolutely sober and lucid."[21] Socializing later with the Pakulas, he drank too much gin in an effort to appear cool. He was smitten with her at first glance and didn't hide this very well.

When she didn't turn up at the airport to say goodbye to him a week later he suspected Pakula had noticed his infatuation with her and forbade her from seeing him. This caused him to retreat to the airplane toilet and imbibe more gin out of fear that he'd wrecked his chances with her—and also the movie deal. He was heartily relieved when this proved not to be the case. His lengthy flirtation with the actress boosted his morale to no end in the years ahead, if not quite managing to obliterate his bisexuality. Lange said he had the sex drive of a "high school quarterback who wants to get his rocks off."[22] She liked him but never considered him seriously as a lover or possible husband.

Cheever, however, had different ideas. He dramatized his relationship with her to friends, telling them not only

Hope Lange, whom Cheever referred to as "the most beautiful woman in the world."

that Pakula was after him with a gun but that Lange had to hide him in a closet one day when Frank Sinatra, another of her paramours, came calling. (This most likely never happened.)

Lange wasn't physically attracted to Cheever, in contrast to his virtually insatiable lusting after her. One night he told her he wanted to make love to her in a hotel, and she refused. He spent the night on the floor outside her room in dejection.[23]

Such excesses continued when he got back to Ossining. Writing alternated with drinking, as before. He made furtive trips to the house pantry after his morning's work was completed. This was usually around 10:30. He kept gin bottles there for emergencies. If Mary or the children were watching him, he preferred to go to a liquor store instead. Neighbors occasionally saw him in his car, spilling bottles over his clothes in his haste to swallow their contents. In later years he dropped the façade, brandishing glasses openly to the family even at breakfast time, his former holy hour.

He went to his doctor, looking for some way to stop. The doctor suggested a course of tranquillizers. These didn't work. They cooled him down but also robbed him of his enthusiasm for life. They seeped his energy from him, giving him no reason to get up in the morning, even if they helped his previous night's sleep.

Cheever convinced himself he drank to escape his problems. A psychiatrist he consulted believed it was the other way around; i.e., that he invented his problems to justify his drinking. Both theories are tenable.

Drink often made him impotent with Mary. Their love life was disturbed by the fact that he was frequently sarcastic with her just as they were about to have sex, which more often than not put a stop to it. (When we factor in his homosexual proclivities, this may have been deliberate).

At times he seemed like a stranger in his own house. He wandered from room to room, checking to see what kind of mood Mary would be in, surprised if she was civil to him and equally surprised by how vindictive he could be to her if she was. The beauty of his surroundings gave him some respite, and of course the gin, or maybe a walk in the woods with Federico. But always there was a gnawing unease eating at him, a feeling of displacement, an unfulfillable yearning for the stability other people seemed to have with their environments, and with themselves.

Mary eventually made him sleep alone. He knew the marriage was dead. He thought about divorcing her, but something always held him back. Elsewhere, he suggested he didn't divorce her because he was afraid of being left alone with his alcoholism, or even afraid of committing suicide.[24] He seemed to prefer being unhappy with Mary than being unhappy on his own. He thought a bad marriage was better than none. Susan said her parents stayed together not so much from love as habit. She always expected Cheever to leave her mother. Nobody ever knew what to expect from him—least of all Mary.

On almost every page of his journals the wonder he describes as enchanting him in the world of nature is underpinned by a deep-seated malaise within himself. It's intensified by Mary's behavior towards him. This grew more hostile towards the end of the 1960s. She seemed like a coiled spring most of the time, waiting to erupt at him at the slightest behest. He became tortured by his desire for Hope Lange, his desire to escape everything he knew. Alongside this was a fear of leaving the comfort of the familiar. Mary wanted to leave him, too, but she knew she couldn't. Both of them were tied to their house, their friends, their surroundings, their children. Such ties became added causes of their hostility towards one another.

Mary slept just a few feet away from him but it could have been as many miles. He asked rhetorically in his journal:

> Are we lying in our separate beds and our separate rooms, only two of millions or billions who wake a little before dawn each morning thinking hopefully that surely there is some man or woman who would be happy to lie at our sides?[25]

At times it seemed as if they didn't so much fall out of love as fail to understand one another. It was as if some indeterminate comment had been passed years ago, leaving a scar that, for some reason, wouldn't heal. Despite having been married a long time and raising three children, they often acted like a couple on a first date, tiptoeing around each other, often trying to score points or put the other one down. It was a subtle war and all the more powerful for that.

They had the formal coldness of many people in Cheever's stories. No doubt Mary was the inspiration (if that's the word) for many of them. One of his shortest stories documents a scenario where the narrator tries to engage a stranger on an airplane in conversation and gets precious little back. Only at the end do we learn that the "stranger" in question is actually his wife, a woman he has "worshipped passionately for nearly thirty years."[26] It's a fascinating concept but, for Cheever, it had a painful autobiographical base.

His children—the innocent victims of their dysfunctionality—suffered too. One day he found a scrap of paper belonging to one of them with these words written on it: "I am miserable and I wish my mummy and daddy would not fite."[27]

By 1967 they were communicating as little as possible. He would say, "Good morning." She would reply faintly, "Good morning." He would say,

"May I have the egg on the stove?" She would reply, "You know I never eat eggs."[28] It was like something out of a Harold Pinter play.

On Susan's wedding day, he sat on Mary's bed. He wanted reconciliation but she was having none of it, climbing out in anger as soon as he did so. Then he drank at the wedding, which irritated her even more. "You are the spectre at the feast," she told him.[29] He didn't argue. After they went home he took solace in his whiskey bottle. Ben put his arm around him. "I'm on your side, Daddy," he said.[30] But he didn't want sides; it only increased the divisiveness between them.

Susan went on to become an alcoholic herself. She also became a writer. One of her books was a memoir about her relationship to her father and his unique secret. She said she was amazed at the fact that he could be an alcoholic and still carry on a normal life, much as Ray Milland did in the movie *The Lost Weekend*. "Most people," she said, "think an alcoholic is someone who drinks a huge amout of liquor and becomes obstreperous or wild as a result. This narrow definition of alcoholism leaves out more alcoholics than it includes."[31]

The situation rumbled on with Mary. For most of the time they lived separate lives, connecting with one another only over domestic trivia. There was an occasional tender word but it was often undercut, or followed, by a barb.

He asked her if she wanted a divorce or a separation. He thought of selling the house and dividing the proceeds between them but he wasn't sure he had the courage to do this and start all over again. "I don't know what to do," he wrote in his journal. "I must sleep with someone. I am so hungry for love I count on touching my younger son at breakfast as a kind of link, a means of staying alive."[32]

The early hours of the day continued to be his most problematic ones. A drink in the morning became *de rigueur* with time. He couldn't pass the whiskey bottle in the pantry without sweating. He fantasized about being a man who could control his drinking, who could "exploit alcohol without having it exploit him," who never drank before noon and after his lunch didn't drink again until five: "At five minutes to five, his hands trembling and his brow soaked with sweat, he would get out the ice, pour the beautiful golden whiskey into a glass and begin the better part of his life." Sadly, that could never be. Instead, he wrote himself a letter: "Dear Myself, I am having a terrible time with the booze. Ride it out."[33]

As the 1960s wound to a close his situation became farcical. He told Frederick Exley—another alcoholic author—in 1968: "The maid is cleaning the carpet. She stands directly between me and the gin bottle in the pantry.

If I ask her to empty the ashtrays in the living room I will be able to sneak into the pantry. Will John Cheever hit the bottle or the Librium or both? Stay tuned."[34]

One of the mysteries of his life is why he made his home life into such a game of cat-and-mouse. If he kept his stash of gin in his bedroom, or some other hiding place away from everyone else, he wouldn't have had to wait for opportunities to make dashes into the pantry to swig back his precious booty. Maybe the writer in him liked the drama of it all.

He often suffered what he called *cafarde*—a melancholy of indistinct cause. *Cafarde* is a condition shared by many people in this book, a kind of abstract gloom. We might call it bi-polar disease today. Mary felt sorry for him on account of this but she didn't know how to deal with it, especially when it rubbed off on her.

Recriminations. Age-old wounds. Senseless insults hurled back and forth as each blamed the other for a loveless marriage. Was alcohol the cause? Was it his bisexuality? Or was it just life, the seven-year itch, or the seventeen-year itch?

Male menopause could be added to that too, and even writer's block. Whatever the cause, he retreated from her to his children for support.

Cheever reached the wider public when his short story "The Swimmer" was made into a movie starring Burt Lancaster in 1968. Shooting had taken place two years earlier. Cheever was nervous meeting the star and drank a pint of whiskey to settle himself. It worked so well he ended up diving into a swimming pool buck-naked after having lunch with Lancaster. He was given a short scene in the film but drank so much Scotch waiting for his cue that he overdid things, kissing Lancaster's pretty costar too vigorously at one point. This annoyed Lancaster so much it ended any possibility the two might have had of becoming friends.[35]

He finished his novel *Bullet Park* in July 1968. He was quite proud of it. Afterward he went to Ireland with Mary for a vacation. It wasn't long before he developed a penchant for Irish coffee—and Irish people.

Bullet Park drew mediocre notices, a fact that shocked him. What went wrong? *Life* magazine sent the author Wilfred Sheed to interview him about it and to take some photographs of him playing touch football on his lawn. Such a clichéd depiction of his life annoyed him. "This is not the way I live," he complained. He would have preferred if *Life* saw him as the boozy recluse he was. Not long into the interview, he started to adhere to that image. He consumed a sizeable number of martinis in the course of it and then got Sheed drunk into the bargain, so much so that he had to come back the following day to finish the interview.[36]

Janet Landgard and Burt Lancaster in *The Swimmer* (1968). Cheever got drunk on the set and made a fool of himself in front of Lancaster instead of impressing him, the reason he imbibed in the first place.

A few months later Cheever's publisher, Alfred A. Knopf, put him up at a hotel to give additional interviews. He overdrank there as well, running up large gin bills as he filled his glasses—and those of his interviewers—with generous measures. "In fighting the hootch I seem to be fighting something much stronger than my own character," he confessed. "I'm overwhelmed by the spirits in the gin bottle. What, under the circumstances, does one do? Pray. Join AA."[37]

He visited Hope Lange in New York in 1969. He still found her astonishingly beautiful but wasn't as electrified by her as he was in previous years. She'd left Alan Pakula by now but didn't show any signs of taking up with Cheever full-time. Their kissing was half-hearted and she demurred when he suggested they make love. After a display of drunken foolishness, they parted. Cheever went home to Mary and talked openly with her about the rendezvous. When she was cool with him, he became surprised. This was where he was at his dimmest, his most naïve. He imagined he could speak to his wife about his infatuation with another woman and expect her to accept this as normal behavior.

Mary told him he was weird. Maybe "misfit" would have been more apt. He was a little man in a big world, both literally and metaphorically. He lived among the country club set but couldn't afford to be a member of one. He listened to the effete chatter of bland souls and felt as removed from them as he could be. Their worlds were narrow, mercenary, crass. Such a dissociation provided him with the tragic irony that lies at the base of so many of his novels and stories.

His bisexuality was gnawing at him amid all of this. The puritanical side of him was repulsed by it whereas his epicurean side embraced it. He drank to try and work out these contradictions. "As long as he was the Ossining squire," said Susan, "the father of three, the dog-loving, horseback-riding, meadow-scything, long-suffering husband, there could be no doubt in the public mind about his sexual preferences, and perhaps less doubt in his own."[38]

By now, Susan recalled, his "first drink of the day" was coming earlier and earlier. In time it blended with the last drink of the evening before, the one at midnight or 3 a.m. There was always an excuse for him to drink, she said. He needed one to drive to New York, to sleep, to get through a party Mary was dragging him to, to work. Even one to "dull the disappointment he felt in his children."[39]

The new decade was ushered in with very little writing. Concerned suddenly about his drinking, he asked his friend Malcolm Cowley for advice. Cowley told him he allowed himself just "one big slug of bourbon" at sundown each day.[40] But that was never going to work for Cheever.

In April 1971, he was arrested for drunk driving. He disputed the charge, insisting that his speed was moderate. "Put me in jail," he said to the arresting office, "if it's a crime to drive carefully."[41] What he didn't realize was that driving too slowly could be as dangerous as driving too fast. When one was over the limit, it could cause undue caution.

Sing Sing prison was located close to Cheever's home and he taught creative writing to the prisoners there in 1971. The experience gave him the raw material for his novel *Falconer*. "I get along wonderfully with murderers," he told a friend.[42] He became sociable with the people he taught, never talking down to them. They appreciated that. One of them even visited him at his house upon his release.

He partied hard at this time but in his private moments he thought of ending his life. He was written out and lived out, he told people. He didn't feel there was any point in going on, especially as Mary was being so horrible to him. "I am not allowed a kiss," he told Dr. Silverberg, the psychiatrist he was seeing. "I am barely granted good morning."[43] He told Silverberg this was one of the reasons he drank so much, but the psychiatrist knew it was a convenient excuse, every alcoholic needing a "reason" to drink. The reality, he surmised, was that Cheever was now incapable of loving anyone but himself.[44]

He reached a kind of meltdown in the spring of 1972 when everyday activities started to become arduous. His speech was slurred and he became dizzy to the point of fainting. He also had a sense of otherness, the feeling that he was in two places at the one time, making him wonder if he was losing his mind.

In desperation he decided to go to an Alcoholics Anonymous meeting at a local church, but it didn't do anything for him. The egoist in him wanted to tell people he was a famous author, but the dictates of AA, by definition, insist on anonymity. This appeared ridiculous to him when he heard people around him saying, "Hey, there's John Cheever!" Everyone knew who he was so why wasn't he allowed say it himself? He may have been an alcoholic but he could never be anonymous.[45]

He was invited to the Soviet Union that year for a commemoration of Dostoevski's 150th birthday. He brought Federico, his younger son, with him to take care of him. It wasn't an easy task. The plane had hardly landed when he started his binging and it got worse when he met the other writers. Pretty soon he was drinking Yevtuskenko, the famous Russian poet, under the table.

After one bout he lost control of his bowels and Federico had to wash his trousers out in the bathtub of their hotel room. The rest of the trip saw him ducking in everywhere he could find to imbibe, including closets and toilets. "Glug, Glug," he wrote to a friend, "even in the Kremlin."[46] When he returned to the U.S., Federico continued his caretaking duties. (One of these was to make sure his father never used his chainsaw while drunk: the dangers were too horrific to contemplate.)

Cheever was given a job at Iowa University in the fall of 1973, teaching creative writing at a workshop there. One of his students, Allan Gurganos, remembered his being drunk most of the time. But Cheever liked the mess. It allied with the way he felt inside. A bigger problem was that Iowa was a dry state. (We'll see how he got around that in the Raymond Carver chapter.)

He allowed his students to smoke in class, which was against university policy. He was rapped over the knuckles for this and for other breaches of discipline. His superiors knew he was too familiar with his students, that his methods were direly unorthodox. It was perhaps for these reasons that his classes were always over-subscribed: Cheever's waywardness was the price one paid for his genius. As was the case with John Berryman and Raymond Carver, two other lecturers who liked the bottle, people came to see him "in performance." It hardly seemed to matter what he said, or if they learned anything from him. They would have hung on his every word even if he was only describing the weather.

He nearly died of heart failure in May 1973 when he exhibited symptoms of suffocating. He attempted to alleviate them by smoking and taking alternate belts of Scotch, which was like trying to put out a forest fire by dousing it with kerosene. Sanity finally prevailed and he had himself admitted to the Intensive Care Unit of his local hospital. There, he hallucinated for five days with the ravages of *delirium tremens*.[47]

When he started to recover he asked his son Ben to get him a pack of cigarettes and a double martini. Ben refused, which caused Cheever to leap up from his bed and try to yank his oxygen tubes off himself. He hit Ben in the chest then, telling him, "You've always been a disappointment as a son."[48] Afterward he was put in a straitjacket. He managed to wangle his way out of this by courtesy of a razor he'd smuggled from his bedside table. The police were called and he was put into a second straitjacket, this time with brass bindings and padlocks.

During one of his hallucinations he came to believe he was being held in a Russian concentration camp. Soon afterward Susan came to visit him. She had a review of his new book of stories, *The World of Apples*, with her. She was looking forward to showing it to him as it was a very enthusiastic one from the *New York Times*, but when he saw it he panicked. For reasons best known to himself he got it into his head that it wasn't a review at all but rather a confession he was being made sign by the Russian authorities. In anger he swore at her and threw it on the floor.[49] As if this wasn't bad enough, he went on to tell her that the hospital food carts were vehicles that were being used to transport prisoners to jail.

Ben was able to laugh about these episodes in time, and even laugh about his father's hallucinations. He decided to look on the positive side of it all. The consoling thing about an alcoholic having a heart attack, he said, was that when he was in hospital he wasn't allowed to drink.

After three weeks in the ICU, he was released. How would he live the rest of his life? He didn't know. On his sixty-first birthday he visited a psychiatrist, telling him the main reason he drank so much was from fear of homosexuality. The psychiatrist took him at his word but Cheever later revealed to his family that he'd merely been baiting him. "I guess I just don't like psychiatrists," he chortled.[50]

He went on the wagon for a while now, and his health began to improve. Then he reverted to it, gingerly at first, with a tablespoon of whiskey a day. Soon he was back to his old habits. Federico pleaded with him to stop, and he promised he would. The two of them went swimming together, but, afterward, Cheever sneaked out to the liquor store and bought some gin, hiding it under his car seat. "I wonder how I will get the bottle from the car to the house," he wrote in his journals. "I read while brooding on this problem. When I think that my beloved son has gone upstairs, I hide the bottle by the side of the house and lace my iced tea."[51]

As he grew older he felt he needed to drink more to achieve the sensory freshness that came naturally with youth. Age brought "a subtle distance between you and the smell of wood smoke."[52] But alcohol revived such sensations for him.

Like many writers, Cheever was a child at heart. His body may have become older with the years but his mind didn't. As Susan said, "It took three heart attacks and a dozen hospitalizations to teach him he couldn't just dive into a cold swimming pool, or tear down the dunes into the surf, or stay up all night reading and drinking."[53]

He told his family he thought he was dying in 1974. By now he was stuffing bottles of gin into every available hiding place in his house, including his boots. His ankles had also swollen ominously. Federico insisted he go to a drying-out clinic, and he reluctantly agreed. He was treated there with vitamins and Valium. Within five days he was deemed sufficiently withdrawn to be released. After he got home he did what most alcoholics do—resumed drinking.

Under such circumstances it was nothing short of amazing that he managed to hold down a lecturing post at Boston University. He drank before classes if not during them, choosing vodka as his tipple now because it didn't smell. A colleague who accompanied him to a hotel bar on the way to the campus one day remembered him trembling so much with the DTs that he needed thirty matches to light just one cigarette. His clothes were frequently ragged and the kitchen of his living quarters covered with empty bottles. "In the final judgment," he said, "it will be discovered that I eat my peas off a knife and there is a hole in the seat of my pants."[54]

Cheever lived a double life in Boston, just as he did in Ossining. He lectured by day and at night sought out call girls. "I divide my time," he said, "between the most disreputable hookers, the Harvard English Department and the highest realms of Boston society."[55]

He befriended the poet Anne Sexton while he was there. Like him, she was an alcoholic trying to deal with a dead marriage and a disastrous home life. They filled one another's glasses and cried on one another's shoulders, two misunderstood children at large in the groves of academe. But soon afterward Sexton killed herself and he was shocked beyond words. Would he be the next fatality?

His brother Fred—who'd conquered his own drinking problem by now—visited him and tried to take care of him but it was nearly impossible to do so. When the Boston contract expired, he went home. There he stared into space with a glass of whiskey by his side, waiting for death.

Mary hid liquor from him, but he found ways around this, either by furtive drives to the liquor store or more mischievous ploys. One day he called on their neighbors the Dirkses. He said to Mary Dirks, "We're having company and the liquor cabinet is empty." He was stinking of booze at the time but she took him at his word and gave him some bourbon. When she learned the truth some days later she was livid with him. "Do you realize what a mess you are?" she shrieked. "You look like a Bowery bum."[56] He knew she was right, but felt he couldn't do anything about it.

He was so addicted at this point he even refused to go to his doctor with physical ailments in case he was put on medication that might clash with the alcohol. Money was becoming a problem now as well. A friend recalled him scrambling around in a gutter one day, looking for a coin. Another day he sat beside a hobo on a park bench drinking wine out of a brown paper bag. When a policeman threatened to arrest him for vagrancy he said, "Don't be ridiculous, my name is John Cheever."[57] This didn't cut any ice with the policeman. Guzzling wine on a park bench made everyone equal. Down-and-outness was the great leveler.

Everyone who liked him thought he was dying, he said to Susan one day. His attitude was, "So what?"[58] In desperation he allowed himself to be admitted to the Smithers Alcoholism Center on East 93rd Street in New York. It was one of the first of the low-cost alcoholic care centers in the country. It contained, as Cheever put it, "freaks, cons, Irish policemen, whores, dismal gays, sand-hogs and seamen."[59]

Before he entered Smithers, he rang Susan to ask her if the program there had any affiliation with AA. She told him it hadn't. It was a lie, but one that probably saved his life.

It was a grim establishment. Not long beforehand a man had jumped out the window in the ward where Cheever slept. He told Susan he didn't think he'd be able to stick it out for any length of time, but she prevailed upon him to stay. There was no alternative, she said. It was either this or the slow suicide of drink.

One of his roommates spent most of his time crocheting a hat.

Another said he'd leave if he was strong enough to carry his suitcase down the stairs. Cheever offered to carry it for him, but the man didn't take him up on it.

While he was there he entered the AA program, despite his previous assertion that he didn't want to have anything to do with that organization. He found it difficult to relate to the other drinkers, feeling he had nothing in common with them beyond that very fact. They found him superior in his attitudes and so did the people running the program. He had to resist the temptation to be sarcastic towards them, to look down on them.[60]

He resisted the regimen at first, still preserving the bravado he'd exhibited on the park bench, but when a psychologist told him he needed to drop his "John Cheeverdom," he listened. When he said he thought he wrote better with drink, the psychologist countered, "But can you make sense of it the next day?" He had to think about that.[61]

The treatment cycle ran to twenty-eight days. By the end of the third week he told the staff he was going to stay on the dry. They were only cautiously optimistic about his keeping to his promise when they released him the following week, an understandable reaction considering his history of setbacks. But he was determined to make a go of it this time.

After he came home, Susan said, he was a different man. "He seemed to notice that the world worked in a certain way; that the house wasn't cleaned by gremlins, that dishes weren't just magically washed, that someone had to cook the dinner for it to be served."[62]

He transformed himself completely in the following weeks. He even bought a bicycle. The next challenge was to get off pills. After a few more weeks he wound down on the tablets that had been part of his daily diet for more years than he could remember: Valium and Seconal.[63] Some people weren't supportive of Cheever's bid to stay sober. Hayden Carruth, a poet he knew, said to him, "At your age I think I'd have gone out loaded." Cheever replied gamely, "You mean puking over someone else's furniture?"[64]

It wasn't easy to carry out his plan, especially when he was in company of old friends. The man who once loved parties now totally despised them. If he went to them at all he tended to leave early to put himself out of the way of temptation. This was the point Susan often made: drinking wasn't just about that simple act—it informed one's whole lifestyle.

In time he became a *habitué* of AA meetings, foregoing the superior attitude he'd once had to the "Christers" who attended them. The more meetings he went to, the more comfortable he became at them. Sometimes he even set up the chairs or brewed the coffee. After a while his attention shifted from himself to others. He went to their houses and talked to them, listening to the stories they told which struck a chord with his own life. He heard about the way they hid the empties, the way they used mints and grape-flavored chewing gum to hide the smell of the booze—all things he might have done himself.

The erstwhile poacher would go on to become a pro-active gamekeeper. When Hope Lange told him her brother had a problem, he rang him and ordered him to attend AA. He even told Truman Capote to follow his path to Smithers. Capote did, eventually, but resisted its program. He appeared on *The Tonight Show Starring Johnny Carson* after coming out, insisting he was cured, but he was holding a drink during the show.

Cheever's sex drive increased when he was on the dry, especially with regard to other men. It was as if he was permitting himself a kind of carnal reward for his self-denial in other ways. Mary turned a blind eye to this just as she'd done throughout the marriage.

In 1978, he took another significant step towards cleaning himself up by attending a course at Smokenders, to get off cigarettes. He succeeded at that, too. In three years he'd gone from being a man who smoked two packs of Marlboros a day (and drank God knows how many glasses of gin) to someone whose main indulgences now were coffee and iced tea.

But life was cruel to Cheever in the same way it would be to his drinking buddy Raymond Carver some years on. No sooner had he conquered his drinking than he contracted prostate cancer. He underwent treatment for it but it proved more aggressive than he, or his doctors, expected.

He knew he was seriously ill but refused to admit it to himself, much as he'd refused to admit his alcoholism for so many years. "I've kicked it," he told people. "I'm getting better."[65]

His sickness brought comfort to him in other ways. Mary grew kinder to him and he to her. What a pity they couldn't have been like this when it might have brought them real happiness. Or was it more precious now?

Marital stability replaced the mad happiness of alcohol. He wrote in his journal in 1980: "I miss drinking. That's the simplest way of putting it."[66] He admitted his new life brought his wife back to him, but his sorrow was still bewildering: "I seek some familiarity that eludes me. I want to go home and I have no home."[67] It's interesting that he equates alcohol, rather than sobriety, with "home." Being out of control for so many years meant normality became almost anomalous to him.

Mary didn't really understand this but Susan did. He said to her one day when the craving became more than he could bear: "I really want a drink sometimes." She replied, "I understand, Daddy."[68]

He died peacefully at the age of seventy, surrounded by his loved ones. It had been a life of frustration and ecstasy, desire and fulfillment, beauty and decay. He tried to capture it through his books and sometimes succeeded, in a career that combined years of neglect with uncomfortable fame. "I just saw him on the *Cavett* show," said the coroner as he prepared his body for burial.[69]

It was a different kind of recognition to that which Ossining's Ovid was generally accustomed.

John Berryman
(1914–1972)

Berryman was born John Allyn Smith in Oklahoma. He wasn't attractive as a young boy, wearing thick-lensed eyeglasses, which led to his being given the nickname "Bleers."[1] His parents didn't have a happy marriage, bickering constantly. At night he listened to them arguing in their bedroom as he tossed and turned in his bed. His mother claimed her husband had raped her when they were dating and then blackmailed her into marrying him.[2]

His father was also called John Allyn Smith. He worked in a bank for years but suffered severe emotional problems and finally lost his job. He and his wife, Martha, afterward moved to Florida, where there was said to be a land boom. They left John junior and his younger brother, Robert, behind in Oklahoma. John was bullied at school because of his appearance and inhibited personality. His mother eventually rescued him, bringing both he and Robert to Florida. There, John senior and Martha opened a restaurant. But it didn't fare well and they had to sell it at a loss.

He now went through a nervous breakdown, wondering what he would do next. He felt he had burned his bridges. The move to Florida had been more Martha's idea than his. When it didn't bear fruit, he panicked.

His moods darkened. When they sold the restaurant they moved to an apartment with John junior and Robert. Their landlords were John Angus and Ethel Berryman. Martha began an affair with Angus, causing her already fragile husband even more distress. In anger, he started seeing a Cuban woman. When Martha heard about this, she sued for divorce.

Smith became unhinged at the whole train of events and took to walking the local beach with a gun, threatening to shoot himself. To prevent this from happening, Martha took five bullets out of it and buried them. (Nobody knows why she didn't remove the sixth one.)

Smith soon shot himself, fatally. A few months later, Martha married

Angus. She always claimed she never loved him, that she was marrying him merely to give her sons a new father. And a new name. But the point was that she'd been seeing him while her husband was alive. There was even a rumor that Martha and Angus had conspired to murder Smith. There were no powder burns on his gun, which was well-nigh impossible in the case of a self-inflicted wound. This wasn't followed up by the Florida police when they heard about Smith's depression.[3]

Martha reinvented herself as Mrs. Berryman. New name, new life. She even changed her Christian name, substituting Martha for Jill. It was like someone in a crime film assuming a new identity. But she insisted she had done nothing wrong. John junior

Berryman was a manic depressive as well as an alcoholic. His life, like that of his father, seemed to be one long journey towards self-destruction. He completed that journey in 1972 by jumping off the Washington Avenue Bridge in Minneapolis (*Writer Pictures*).

cross-examined her more than any court ever did in the years to come, asking her to account for her mysterious actions prior to his father's alleged suicide. She appeared very convincing in her replies to him, but many of her comments had contradictory elements in them.

In one letter to him she said her husband only carried his gun for purposes of self-defense, but this was unlikely considering his depression. She also said she believed he didn't know there was a sixth bullet in the gun and that he pulled the trigger by accident. This was difficult to accept as well. She said she didn't think he committed suicide because "he didn't care about life enough to take it."[4] But, surely, it was those who didn't care about life who *did* "take" it.

Whether Jill had anything to do with the immediate circumstances of her husband's death or not, her personality seems to have pushed him over the edge. She continued to deny he committed suicide, preferring to tell people it was simply an accident with his gun. "Allyn was a weak man," she said. "He wouldn't have had the courage to kill himself."[5]

In a sense he was reminiscent of Ernest Hemingway's father, another henpecked husband who shot himself in retirement when a move to Florida fell flat and his finances failed. Jill dominated John junior in a different way. In youth he lived in her shadow, which compounded an already deep-seated sense of insecurity.

Berryman once told his friend Saul Bellow that his father's death gave his mother a "disproportionate and crippling" role in his life.[6] In a way, she took his place. In later years, other women seemed to displace her. But they never did, much as he would have liked them to.

His greatest love of all was literature, especially the Bard. He was fascinated by Shakespeare and lectured frequently on him. The relationship between Hamlet and his mother was of particular interest to him. Like Hamlet, his father died suspiciously and his mother married with undue haste thereafter. Was Jill his Gertrude? He never said as much to her, but she appeared to inhabit that guise after her spouse died.

Berryman never recovered from the suicide. "I spit upon this dreadful banker's grave," he wrote in a poem.[7] In another sense he believed he could have been partly responsible for his father's death, either through his negative feelings about him or as a result of his mother loving her sons more than she did her husband.[8] The fact that a twelve-year-old boy could have such an impact on a man's psyche, or such Oedipal feelings about him, hints at an already developing mental illness.

The controversial suicide acted like a marker for him for how his own life could—and would—end. "He felt it as a kind of undertow," his first wife, Eileen Simpson (*née* Mulligan), contended, "sucking at him, sometimes feebly, sometimes with a terrifying strength, but always, always, there."[9]

He met Simpson at a New Year's Eve party in 1940 when he was an instructor in English literature at Harvard. They kissed under the mistletoe. Two years later, they married.

Life with her was bumpy. He was unemployed for a time, even selling encyclopedias door to door. He told his friend Milt Halliday he didn't even get "one goddamned order" in all his peregrinations.[10]

He had amassed debts in college as well, many of which he didn't tell her about. She was to learn he had an unhappy knack of spending more money than he had—yet another secret. His extravagant nature, she said, was "as cleverly disguised as a monk's gluttony by loose brown robes."[11]

He sent out job applications for tutoring, editing and library posts.

They all drew blanks. Perhaps his heart wasn't in them, particularly the tutoring. "I'm a writer, for God's sake," he used to say, "not a damn nursemaid."[12]

Simpson was a trained psychologist but he resented her applying for jobs in this field, even though it would have eased their financial burden. He was also against her getting pregnant. He exerted almost total control over her.

Simpson certainly did. Berryman was a full-time job to her. He worried about everything—his poetry, his research, making it in the university world, and so on. He even worried about losing his hair. He saw it as the sign of a lack of potency, both sexual and creative. She tried to reassure him that he wasn't losing it, but Berryman wasn't one to listen. (He still had a full head of hair when he died.)

Eventually he landed an instructorship at Princeton. It became home to him for a decade, but his gloomy cast of mind prevented him from appreciating it as much as he should have. "Each year," he said in 1943, "I hope that next year will find me dead, and, so far, I have been disappointed."[13]

His mind was a cauldron. Teaching drained him, making it difficult for him to concentrate on his academic work. Trying to write poetry was almost out of the question. Money was also a worry. When all these concerns were put into a blender with his nascent depression it was hardly surprising he drank. Simpson fretted about his lunchtime daiquiris, his martinis before dinner, his late-night stingers. He also used martinis as a cure for hangovers, and to help him sleep.

A different kind of problem surfaced in 1947, when he began an affair with a woman called Lise at Princeton. She wasn't the first female who caught his eye. He frequently made passes at women, "often successful."[14]

Lise was married with a son. She fascinated Berryman so much he ended up putting her into his poetry. Maybe he enjoyed writing about her more than making love to her. He saw a similarity between them and the relationship between W. B. Yeats—a poetic hero of his—and Maud Gonne MacBride, the woman who rejected all of his amorous advances in life and thereby bequeathed a huge legacy of poetry to posterity by dint of the elegiac recreation of his pain.

He was contrite to Simpson when she got wind of his duplicity. "It's a disease I have," he said—conveniently. When she threatened to leave him he begged her not to, promising to kill himself if she did. "As long as you do not give up on me," he pleaded, "I am not lost."[15] She stayed, albeit reluctantly.

Berryman harbored suicidal thoughts from early on in life. He called the suicidal instinct his subtle foe. It attacked him as depression did, making him do things like stand on balconies, willing himself to jump. Simpson usually talked him out of these dramatic flurries, but she dreaded them.

"The job of net holder exhausted me," she said. "More importantly, I realized that by making myself available in this way I had been encouraging him to be more and more incautious, less vigilant against the current that was always threatening to suck him under."[16]

He was offered a lectureship in creative writing at the University of Cincinnati in the spring of 1952. He moved to an apartment off campus, with Simpson. The landladies, who were sisters, were officious. They asked for an undertaking that the tenants wouldn't smoke, make noise, or keep late nights. Berryman was aghast. "Not smoke?" the three-pack-a-day man exclaimed to Simpson. "Are they crazy? Tell the dear ladies that what poets *do* is smoke. Only very occasionally do they write verse."[17]

Simpson left him in 1953, unable to accept his drinking—or womanizing—any more. His life was chaotic. He put it down to his multiple addictions. These were, in his words, "Cigarettes, alcohol, women. Need, need, need."[18] Simpson once wrote a *roman à clef* about her life with him. In it, she had a character say of her relationship to her husband, "If only she had been more successful at growing a skin against his infidelities."[19] Simpson worked hard at growing that skin and it finally gave her the courage to leave him.

Berryman couldn't deal with her absence. He wrote to her saying he was contemplating throwing himself off the George Washington Bridge in New York if she didn't come back to him. That way, he reasoned, he'd save her the cost of burying him.[20] But this time she wasn't buying his emotional bribery. She stayed away.

Afterward, he moved into the Chelsea Hotel. Dylan Thomas was staying there at the time. They'd known one another from years before, when Berryman was at Cambridge. They used to drink together then. Now they took up where they left off. Berryman had arranged to meet no less a luminary than W. B. Yeats after one of their sessions. Thomas disapproved of this—he didn't like Yeats as much as Berryman did—and detained him so long in the hotel that he missed the meeting. For the record, Berryman admitted that Thomas was able to outdrink him. Not many people could do that.[21]

Towards the end of 1953, after an especially wild bender, even by his standards—"I've just drunk eighteen straight whiskeys," he's alleged to have said[22]—Thomas collapsed and was taken to a hospital. Berryman was devastated. "Dylan *is* poetry," he often liked to say. If he died, he wailed drunkenly, the form would die with him.[23] Now it was threatened.

He went into a coma and didn't emerge from it. This was perhaps just as well, as his brain was badly damaged, but Berryman was heartbroken when he died. "Dylan murdered himself w. liquor,"[24] he wrote to Robert Lowell, apparently unaware he wasn't far from doing that himself.

It was actually Berryman who discovered Thomas's dead body. He went into the hospital on a visit one day and saw him lying on the bed, as cold as ice. He was shocked that the poet was allowed to die alone and untended. He berated the nursing staff and John Malcolm Brinnin, the man who had organized Thomas's original tour, for their laxity. Afterward in the hospital Thomas's wife, Caitlin, became hysterical. She was completely out of control in her grief and it made her do strange things. She even made a pass at Berryman. He wasn't sure how to relate to this. Did she know what she was doing? He knew she'd been drinking, but that didn't justify it. He behaved discreetly towards her, and the moment passed, to the relief of all.

The following year he went to Iowa to teach creative writing at the university there. Shortly after arriving, he got drunk. He then fell down the stairs of his apartment building and crashed through a glass door. To everyone's amazement, all he injured was his left wrist.

A later incident proved more traumatic. After a workshop finished one night, he went to a bar. He started drinking heavily and abusing everyone in sight. Afterward he staggered back to his apartment and rapped on the door, demanding to be let in. He badly needed to go to the bathroom so he tried to force the door. When the landlord saw his condition he refused to let him in. Berryman squatted on the front porch and defecated on it in protest. The landlord called the police and he was locked up for disorderly conduct. Things went from bad to worse as some of the police officers started to make fun of him, and even to expose themselves to him. Berryman could do nothing about this except glare at them in a cold rage. The newspapers got wind of the story and printed it. Berryman's position at the university suddenly became untenable and he was fired.[25]

Nobody ever knew what to expect from him if he had enough to drink. One night at a party he put his shoes in a fireplace and walked home in his socks. Another night he walked into the sea fully clothed after an argument with the poet Delmore Schwartz. His mind always seemed to be on the edge of an explosion. Sometimes he channeled that energy into his work. Otherwise, it just reflected itself in zany behavior. Sensitivity caused his inspiration but also the destruction of that inspiration because it made him too emotionally wrecked to express it a lot of the time. It was both a blessing and a curse.

He wrote prolifically in the 1950s, publishing a biography of Stephen Crane and also his first collection of poetry, *Homage to Mistress Bradstreet*. He often wrote while drinking, and he drank almost non-stop between books.

After becoming divorced from Simpson, he married Ann Levine, but that marriage also ran into trouble, mainly due to his irrational behavior. One night in 1956 he was at a party with her when he suddenly developed a fear that the sitter with whom they'd left the baby might be hurting the child. Levine couldn't disabuse him of this fantastic notion, and he ended up hitting her. He then blamed her for his action. When his mother heard about the incident she advised Levine to leave him if it happened again. This resulted in a stand-off between Berryman and his mother, one of the many they had throughout their lives, but which always resolved themselves. In a way, they were like lovers' tiffs.

Other women may have appeared to replace Martha—or rather Jill—in his affections, but they never could. His letters to his mother, an incredible output, manifest his passion for her and likewise hers for him. He often referred to her as "darling." They shared almost every thought, desire, and pang. At times Jill appeared almost Medea-like in her emotion, and Berryman shared it. They exchanged mutual anguish over his entire lifetime. There were gaps, to be sure, and tensions—many of them over Jill asking him for loans of money—but they always reconciled.

This didn't mean that they couldn't recognize each other's faults: indeed, their relationship was stronger for the fact that they did. Jill knew her son was ruining himself with alcohol, but she didn't lecture him too much about this, choosing instead to focus on how strong he must be to withstand the pummeling to which he was subjecting his body. At the beginning of 1957 he wrote a letter to her saying, "I'm in my fifth day of severe withdrawal symptoms for a simultaneous cutting-to-the-bone of cigarettes & alcohol; I hear it gets less awful later."[26]

Many of the letters had melodramatic elements as mother and son both appeared to ramp up their angst. "This is what it is to be a parent," she wrote to him at one point, "to suffer inconsolably in the anguish or travail of the child.... Not for one instant since I knew you were to come to this earth have I been me, alone, myself."[27]

Jill, like her son, was a writer, albeit not a published one. Her missives showed a marked literary ability. Did they both have an eye toward posterity with their ramblings? Perhaps. Whatever their motivation, they prove that Jill had much more of an impact on Berryman's life than his father, even if his temperament owed more to him than her. Both of their shadows loomed large over his life, arguably even engulfing it. What chance did his wives have to compete for his love? When he wrote to Jill about being in love, as Richard J. Kelly observed, he sounded apologetic, "almost as if he were breaking off a romance."[28]

Jill was his prime arbiter, his preeminent touchstone. At times they appeared to be clairvoyant, to be seeing into each other's souls. The experience of every aspect of Berryman's life, every last detail of the development of his literary and academic career, was transmitted to her forthwith. His excitement over the publication of his books, or a university promotion, was shared with her immediately. So was his disappointment over being rejected for publication, or being poorly reviewed, or being passed over for tenure. These were the milestones of his life, presented regularly for her reaction.

Even as a middle-aged man he submitted himself to her for approval, just as he had as an adolescent. Theirs was a truly Oedipal relationship, a quasi-sexual bonding. If either of them was remiss about answering a letter, or failing to honor a loan, it was a cause for deep pain. "Your marriage is the important thing," she wrote after Berryman married Ann Levine, "and it may well be that continuing a relationship with me may be a hindrance to your marriage's success. If this is a decision you came or come to, I accept it with all good will."[29] This was gracious, but by then her influence was overpowering. She didn't need to do anything except let the circumstances play themselves out.

The memory of his father was triggered only occasionally. When Ernest Hemingway committed suicide in 1961 it hit him hard, bringing his death back to him. (Hemingway's father had, of course, also committed suicide.) "Save us from shotguns & fathers' suicides," he wrote. "My father, do not pull the trigger or all my life I'll suffer from your anger, killing what you began."[30]

Kate Donahue became his third wife the same year. Berryman tanked himself up with booze before the ceremony, as he did on all big occasions. In fact, his hands shook so much he had difficulty signing the register. The clerk made him practice writing his name several times before allowing him to do so.[31]

In November 1962, he went to McLean's Hospital, outside Boston, to be dried out. He stayed there a week. Donahue gave birth to a daughter the day after he came out. He then started drinking again, celebrating the event on a night out with friends. On the way home a cab ran over his foot and broke his ankle. When it started to fester he looked at it firmly and muttered, "I feel like a minor character in a bad Scott Fitzgerald novel."[32]

After his ankle healed up, he returned to work with renewed energy. He threw himself into lecturing just as he had into writing or drinking, becoming as much workaholic as alcoholic. Simpson said of him, "I sometimes think that if he felt he wasn't paying a high enough price for his gift he would get panicky, afraid that it might dry up. So he keeps the turbulence going all the time."[33]

Mary Ann Wilson was a student of Berryman's in the early 1960s. There was nobody better than he when sober, she said, but when he was drunk it was embarrassing. One day he gave a lecture on Cervantes's *Don Quixote* which he'd already given, word for word, two days before. Everybody sat motionless as they listened to him, painfully aware that he was completely oblivious to the repetition of the material: "It would have been unthinkable to interrupt him," Wilson said. "There was too much dignity and bombast in him to allow for such a thing. It was very sad."[34] His lectures were like stage performances. He sweated and swore as he immersed himself in the texts he discussed, his beard jutting out in all directions.

Between lectures he was restless. A university colleague, Alexander Rose, remembered him having attacks that caused him to crash to the floor in an unconscious state. These occurred with such frequency they were almost taken as common behavior. One day, Rose saw him lying on the floor with his eyes closed. He wanted to get by him so he walked around him to get where he was going. Only later did he discover that Berryman had actually fainted and was quite ill.[35]

His drinking was so bad by now he feared he might die from it. He was frequently admitted to the hospital and treated for exhaustion, a euphemism for alcoholic poisoning. It was a diagnosis he was happy to go along with, unwilling to confront the severity of the problem in his hunger to become America's best writer.

He became a major league poet after the publication of *77 Dream Songs* in 1964. It won the Pulitzer Prize the following year. Suddenly, he was a household name. President Johnson even invited him to dinner at the White House in 1966. Unfortunately, he couldn't accept this as he was in Ireland at the time, spending a year there courtesy of the money he earned from a Guggenheim.

Berryman liked living in Ireland. He and Donahue rented a semi-detached house in Ballsbridge, Dublin, and made it into a home away from home. She shopped for him and washed his clothes by hand, as the words flowed out of him. The poet John Montague, who became a friend, was amazed at the way he seemed to live life on fast-forward. "He appeared to me positively happy," he said. "A man who was engaged in completing his life's work, with a wife and child he adored."[36] He remembered Berryman being excited as he discussed books in the bars he frequented with such enthusiasm, his elbow sending drinks flying as he became carried away with a point, or the way he leapt out of his seat to shake hands with someone.[37]

He enjoyed Dublin's bar culture for its joviality. "Everybody sings," he chortled. "They do not sing well, but they sing together."[38] Berryman preferred to just drink. As ever, he did too much of this for his own good. Towards the end of his Irish sojourn, Donahue had to have him placed in a psychiatric unit in Grangegorman to have him dried out.

Back in the U.S., his career continued to flourish. In May 1967, he went to New York to collect a literary award. Again, he stayed at the Chelsea Hotel, his old stomping ground with Dylan Thomas. Saluting Thomas's memory one night, he overdid the drinking and started vomiting blood. He was taken to the hospital in a condition that was deemed life threatening. As he was being treated he kept a half pint of whiskey by his bed.

Berryman may have feared alcoholism but in some ways he feared sobriety more, imagining it would dry up his creative juices. The nightmares and the "dark attitude" to life they called up he saw as feeding much of his inspiration.[39] It is no accident that he wrote his masterpiece, *The Dream Songs* (not to be confused with *77 Dream Songs*), during one of the worst drinking spells of his life. He was also taking cocktails of pills now to help him sleep and to combat his depression.

He fell in his bathroom in November 1969, the effects of his various medications (Thorinal, Tuinal, etc.) making him drowsy. He was taken to Hazelden, a Minneapolis rehabilitation center, and diagnosed as being both an alcoholic and a drug abuser. There was nothing too surprising in that, but it was the first time the words had been used by the establishment, as it were.

He told the staff he'd been drinking heavily since his twenties, that the longest dry spell he'd had since then was four months from September to December the previous year. He admitted he was an alcoholic and that he had an unstable personality, which veered between arrogance and insecurity. He stayed there six weeks and came out feeling better, but was back on the bottle in no time.

The next few months saw him in and out of the hospital. All the doctors could do was advise him and prescribe medication; they couldn't handcuff him every time he reached for a drink. Healing had to come from within, and he didn't have the willpower for that. The following February he was back in the hospital again, this time with his shins black and blue.[40]

In May, he entered the Intensive Treatment Centre at St. Mary's Hospital, in Minneapolis. He devoutly promised his loved ones he'd give sobriety his best shot. He went through the familiar detox and suffered the sweats and shivers, the DTs, the nausea, and the anxiety. He told doctors he had a fear of insanity as well as suicide; indeed, one might cause the other. He irritated some of the other patients with his overbearing personality, but was equally likely to break down in tears. In his raw state, he ran the gamut of emotions, reaching down into the core of himself in an effort to exorcise his demons.

He told his fellow inmates his life was a catalogue of disasters as he tried to negotiate Step One (i.e., one's powerlessness) of the Twelve-Step Program. He hallucinated a few times; he heard voices; he suffered memory loss; he didn't know who he was. Two wives had left him as a result of his drinking; he'd lost jobs due to it; propositioned men and women when he'd had one too many. He'd even called up one of his students one night when he was drunk and threatened to kill her.

On his trip to Dublin, he said, he'd downed a quart of whiskey a day for two months while working on a poem. He hid bottles wherever he could. He wet beds in hotels while drunk and once even defecated in a university corridor. He only gave himself a few more years to live.[41]

He was discharged with a severe injunction by the staff never to drink again. He said he'd try, but a week later he was on a new rampage. He went back to the hospital as an outpatient and asked the chairman, Ken Stevens, if he could help him. The following week he went to Mexico for a short holiday with Donahue. He said he had two ideas for the trip. One was Plan A, which was "Drink." Plan B was "Don't Drink." Pretty soon he decided, "Fuck Plan B."[42]

He reported the grim news back to Stevens, who asked him if he drank to help his writing. He showed him two examples of his work, one done sober and one drunk. He asked him if he could tell the difference. Said Stevens, "I can't understand a damn think you write anyway, drunk or sober." This caused Berryman to burst out into hysterics.[43]

He was asked to do a poetry reading at the University of Chicago in June 1970. Allen Tate criticized his work the day before it was due to take place and this sent him into a tailspin. An interviewer from the *Chicago Daily News* found him roaring drunk in his hotel room later in the day.

He was chain-smoking and drinking whiskey as the interview took place. It was an angry interview, Berryman lambasting everything from the "atrocious" American government to the lifestyle of the youth. He admitted he was a male chauvinist and that he'd shamed the notion of the American poet. When the time came for the reading he was too drunk to do it justice. His voice was frail and he coughed up phlegm. People found it difficult to hear him. Afterward, he passed out in his room. He slept through a party given in his honor, but the following morning he was full of cheer, telling everyone it had been "a great evening."[44]

As if things weren't bad enough, a new tragedy now unfolded as Jill started to develop dementia. When she wrote Berryman a letter she baked it so it wouldn't carry germs. She insisted on mailing her letters while wearing gloves, for the same reason. When he visited her, she screamed at him, accusing him off ruining her life. He was both shocked and saddened by this turn of events. He realized she needed constant medical attention so he arranged to have her move closer to where he lived, in Minneapolis. Grudgingly, she agreed to this.

The worry over his mother seemed to shake him into a new discipline. He made a serious effort to stay dry and to attend AA meetings. At one of them he said the catalyst for much of his drinking was exhaustion. He would work until he dropped and then reward himself with a whiskey—which then became two whiskeys, and then twenty-two. As he got older it was harder to contact his muse, so such rewards became more prevalent.

A year before he died he sent Simpson a letter in which he stated that he was "writing lyrics like a maniac, 2 or 3 a week, but very calm, oddly." He was also exercising strenuously, "4 barbells, 10 each, hopping and running in place until I drop. Recommend it, dear. Twice a day.... I plan to die healthy."[45]

The sterling efforts he made to wean himself off drink from 1968–1971 drained him creatively, causing a different kind of depression to a whiskey-soaked one. He was writing more prose than poetry now, which was like going from steak to hamburger meat for him. Neither could he finish anything, his mind ablaze with confusion and self-doubt.

With drink, life was unlivable; without it, unbearable. The horrors of excess became replaced by the inanity of deprivation. If he didn't like himself drunk, he liked himself even less sober. Others agreed with this estimation.

In July 1971, he received a sobriety pin for having been six months on the dry. Such an achievement, he was informed, was akin to having climbed a mountain. He accepted it with grim humor. He may have climbed a metaphorical mountain, but it felt more to him like he was "in the Colosseum with lionesses."[46]

Things were going badly with Donahue now too, and his smoker's cough was also worse. He was twenty pounds overweight and up every night with insomnia and/or nightmares. In the mornings he had difficulty getting out of bed. Sometimes he took a knife into his bedroom and looked at it longingly. He had an idea of standing on a bridge and stabbing himself so that he'd lean forward and fall. That would save him from the horrible burden of having to jump. Hadn't Hart Crane done something like that?

He couldn't eat, sleep, or create magic on the page anymore. He couldn't even rage against the death of his old friend Dylan Thomas. The gloom gathered anew. He was written out, burned out, lived out. All that remained was for Henry, his poetic alter ego, to exit gracefully.

On January 6, 1972, after being sober for almost a year, he bought a bottle of whiskey and drank half of it. The following morning, he got up, as was his routine, and told Donahue he was going to the office. His last words to her were, "You won't have to worry about me anymore."[47] She didn't read anything into them; he'd made such threats to her before. What she didn't know was that this time it wasn't an idle threat. He'd made up his mind to kill himself. All his life he'd been pushing himself beyond his limits. There remained just one push left—to eternity.

He took a bus to the Washington Avenue Bridge. When he got there he walked along a ridge and climbed a barrier. He waved at some students who stood there looking at him. Without turning around, he jumped to his death. If he had a hat, one imagines, he might well have tipped it to them.

He was identified by a blank check in his pocket that was made out in his name. How ironic, Donahue thought, for someone who'd been dogged by money worries all his life. The following day she looked in the garbage and found the following words scribbled on the back of an envelope: "O my love Kate, you did all you could. I'm unemployable and a nuisance. Forget me, re-marry and be happy."[48]

His friend Katharine Fraser said Berryman had basically three moods: "Hysterical joy, deep depression, and obvious boredom."[49] His main problem was that he had too much intensity. One might say he was born drunk. So why did he need to continue topping up on that condition?

There was no alcohol in his bloodstream at the time of his death.

Carson McCullers

(1917–1967)

From her early twenties, Carson McCullers was drinking straight gin out of water glasses at all hours of the day and night. Her mentor Louis Untermeyer predicted she would die young as a result of this.[1]

Like many of the people profiled in this book, she came from a drinking family. When some ladies from the Woman's Christian Temperance Union visited her house when she was a child, her mother said to her husband, "Is it time for my toddy, yet, Lamar?" This sent them fleeing in horror.[2] Women weren't supposed to drink at this time, and certainly not to advertise the fact.

Born Lula Carson Smith in Columbus, Georgia, on February 19, 1917, she always felt different from everyone else. "I was born a man," she said once.[3] This became more apparent when she dropped "Lula" and started going by the name Carson. She also had a boyish look when she was young. She exaggerated this by keeping her hair straight and dressing in sagging sweaters and tennis shoes. Her height (five feet eight-and-a-half inches) also made her feel unfeminine. She was as much a tomboy as Frankie, the main character in *The Member of the Wedding*, her most autobiographical book.

Her gangling frame and withdrawn personality made her retire into an inner world from a young age. "I cut myself off from my family when I was six," she told a friend.[4] This withdrawal made her a target for bullies at school. Girls sometimes threw rocks at her, making her aware early on how it felt to be an outcast.

She cared little about what people thought of her. As she grew she continued to dress in offbeat clothes, oblivious to the dictates of fashion. Humanity was what interested in her, especially eccentric humanity. She found a kinship in anyone who, like herself, stood far from the madding throng. "Nothing human is alien to me," she liked to say, after the Latin poet Terence.[5]

Her childhood was plagued with health problems. She suffered from pernicious anemia, pleurisy and, at fifteen, rheumatic fever. This was incorrectly diagnosed, which could well have contributed to many of the ailments she suffered in later years. All of these, like her androgynous appearance, made her see the world differently than others, giving rise to a cast of characters in her fiction that were distinctly at odds with the rest of society.

Her first love was the piano. It was said she could play a tune straight through after hearing it just once.[6] Her mother had great faith in her. She was, she boasted, "trained to be a genius."[7] She had ambitions to be a concert pianist but changed her mind about this, regarding it as too expensive for her family to fund. She decided on a career in writing instead. This was something that could be done just as easily at home.[8]

She studied creative writing at Washington Square College in New York in 1936, publishing her first work, *Wunderkind*, the same year. The following year she married Reeves McCullers, an army corporal. He was, she announced, "the best looking man I had ever seen."[9] He later bought his way out of the army to become a credit manager.

Reeves had an engaging manner. He made friends easily, in contrast to his socially awkward wife who was cautious with people at first and then often became too touchy-feely with them. He saw it as his mission in life to take care of Carson.

Their first days of marriage were happy. Even though they lived in near-poverty they managed to entertain themselves—and one another—by

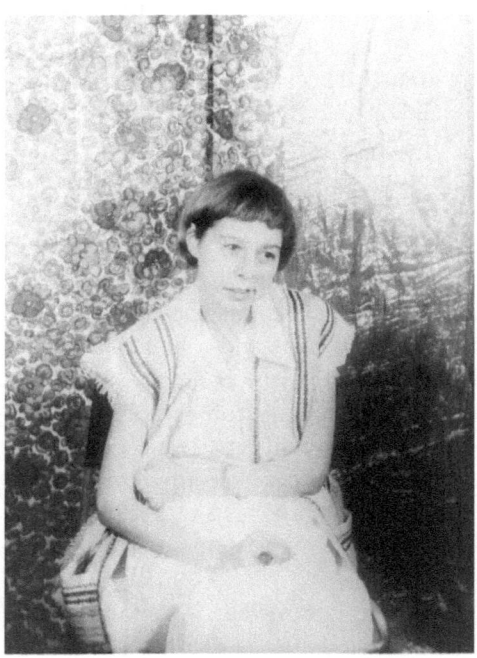

For McCullers, drink was the potion that released her from her native bashfulness. It also opened some magical worlds to her and to that extent it alchemized her writing. But being married to another alcoholic proved a bridge too far for her in the long run (*Writer Pictures*).

playing chess, the piano, and classical music on their turntable. When Reeves was out at work, Carson wrote. He offered interesting opinions on her jottings and promised to get down to some of his own when time permitted. There's no indication he would have thrived in this area, though she believed the letters he sent her during the war were worthy of publication.[10]

Carson wrote with the help of wine and Thermos flasks filled with "hot sherry tea." Such flasks generally contained more sherry than tea.[11] The tea warmed her; the sherry got her creative juices flowing.

At this time Reeves was in the superior position in the relationship. He was the breadwinner and he'd given Carson—a girl who'd hardly been on a date before he came into her life—stability and a measure of social standing. More importantly, he gave her love. But he had insecurities of his own which would come to the fore in dramatic fashion after she became famous.

When she was taking her first steps as a writer she had an arrangement with him that each of them would take turns writing while the other one worked. After the sensational success of *The Heart Is a Lonely Hunter*, however, such an arrangement proved unworkable. Carson's career went on in leaps and bounds while that of Reeves lingered in dry dock. Her fame was so sudden it inhibited him. For the rest of his life he would live in its shadow, whatever glory he enjoyed being that reflected from it.

The Heart Is a Lonely Hunter was a stunning achievement. The publishing world was amazed that a twenty-two-year-old girl could "probe at such depth the passionate idealism of a half dozen characters."[12] She was also praised particularly for the "ease and justice" with which she depicted black people.[13] But her success came at a price. During the winter of 1940 she was diagnosed as being mildly tubercular and also to be suffering from dormant grippe. She was advised to take better care of herself—and to cut down on her wine intake—if she didn't want to end up an invalid.

Her next book, *Reflections in a Golden Eye*, was a tale of repressed homosexual desire set in an army camp in Georgia. It dealt with the attraction of a military officer, Major Penderton, to an enlisted man who's infatuated with Penderton's wife. Penderton is impotent, which causes his wife to have an affair with a neighbor. His wife is repulsed by sex and has amputated her nipples with a pair of garden shears because of this.

Carson dedicated the book to her friend Annemarie Clarac-Schwarzenbach, a Swiss writer who fascinated her. But this woman was psychologically disturbed and addicted to morphine. They were rumored to have had a lesbian relationship but Carson discounted this, claiming they didn't go any further than kiss.[14]

The book cemented her reputation. It was viewed as an amalgam of the styles of everyone from Chekhov to Eudora Welty in a genre that came to be known as "Southern gothic." Certain aspects of it irritated narrow-minded members of the public. There were even threats from the Ku Klux Klan to kill her. If she'd shown herself to be a "nigger lover" in *The Heart Is a Lonely Hunter*, now she was coming across as a "fairy" as well.[15] One critic dismissed the book as "nothing more than nutty people and pseudo porn."[16] When Carson's father read it he threw it across the room in disgust. After the threat came from the Ku Klux Klan he spent the night sitting on his porch with a loaded gun, nervously awaiting their attack.

Clarac-Schwarzenbach went back to Europe after the book was published. Carson was overcome with loneliness and hit the bottle with a vengeance, swapping sherry for bourbon in an effort to find relief from her pain. Sometimes she prowled the bars in search of companionship with other women. She became even more distraught when she learned that Clarac-Schwarzenbach had been hospitalized in a psychiatric institution after attempting suicide. Neither was it her first attempt. Clarac-Schwarzenbach would die soon afterward in a freak bicycle accident.

Her health issues continued to torment her. In February 1941, she was beset with stabbing pains in her temples, as well as blinding headaches. It turned out to be the first of many strokes. Later such episodes would be accompanied by paralysis. If she didn't have her writing, she thought, she might well have gone mad.

Carson and Reeves were sleeping in separate beds by now. Her fame had overshadowed him completely, and he was drinking more than ever. Carson was drinking more, too, but not as much with him. She saw him more as a brother than a husband now. She felt sorry for him—and for herself.

In April of that year she was invited to Yaddo, an artist's colony in Saratoga. While there, she developed a fascination for the writer Katharine Anne Porter, but Porter didn't reciprocate her feelings.[17] She began to write her next book there, *The Ballad of the Sad Café*. She also met the composer David Diamond. For a while, Diamond seemed to fill the gap in her life created by her alienation from Reeves. The three of them spent many nights together, where the boundaries between friendship and romance seemed tenuous. Carson cavorted with both men, and Diamond seemed attractive to Reeves as well as to Carson.

Her first meetings with him were characterized by profuse amounts of alcohol. Diamond was fascinated by Carson's enormous capacity. She never seemed *not* to be drinking, he thought, and yet she rarely showed its effects. By now she was finding it difficult to write without drinking. She usually started the day with a beer, then shifted to sherry or whiskey on the rocks, polishing things off with a few cocktails over dinner.[18] She was slow to go to a doctor, which would probably have meant cutting down.[19]

She argued frequently with Reeves and there were occasional outbursts of violence.

Their relationship with Diamond continued to be a three-way one. Everything in her life, she said, eventually found its way into her books.[20] This situation actually harked back to the unique love triangle depicted in *Reflections in a Golden Eye*. It was also reminiscent of her relationship with Annemarie Clarac-Schwarzenbach from the previous summer. Reeves was like the third party on the sidelines of Carson's infatuations. Diamond was warned away from her, but he couldn't help being drawn to her unique charms.

Reeves told Diamond that Carson had gone off him sexually and was sleeping with whomever she wanted, both men and women. His own relationship deepened with him now. But Diamond feared being sucked into Reeves's drinking lifestyle.

Reeves now started forging Carson's name on checks and cashing them, using the money for drink, as his life spiraled out of control. Carson put up with this for a while but then told him she had no option but to divorce him.

After the divorce came through, she moved to New York. There, she lived with George Davis, the editor of *Harper's Bazaar*. He shared Carson's love of alcohol. Their indulgences were free of the tensions that accompanied her drinking sessions with Reeves. He took her to the home of his friend Lotte Lenya, who played hostess to the pair as they "sipped their way to a giggling incoherence" on many afternoons.[21] She fed them hot dogs and refilled their glasses with iced tea, leaving plenty of room in Carson's glass for her customary sherry or gin.[22]

Carson and Davis lived at 7 Middagh Street, in Brooklyn Heights. That address became more famously known as February House. It was so named because many of its boarders were born in February. These included W. H. Auden, Gypsy Rose Lee, Benjamin Brittin, Christopher Isherwood, and Thomas Mann's son Golo. Carson—another February baby—spent five years there in all, enjoying its bohemian ambience.

Reeves now re-enlisted in the army. Though Carson felt the marriage was over, she worried about him. She thought his state of mind was fragile. Meanwhile, the writing went on, fueled by "gin and cigarettes."[23] She was awarded a Guggenheim Fellowship in 1942.

She met Reeves off and on over the next few years when he had furloughs from the army but didn't see re-marriage as being on the cards. He conducted himself well in the army, being wounded both at Normandy on D–Day and, later, in another offensive in Germany. He told Carson he had cut down on his drinking and she felt heartened by this. Occasionally, they discussed getting back together. He applied for discharge from the army and considered going to medical school.

Absence definitely made the heart grow fonder with this pair. The letters they exchanged during the war years were like lovesick missives of two teenagers who were head over heels about one another. It was as if the past never happened. They both accepted that the marriage was a disaster but believed they could now experience even greater happiness together. She used terms like "Precious," "My dearest one" and wrote "I adore you" frequently in such missives; he was equally uxorious.[24]

People don't generally suffer from depression in times of war: they're too busy trying to stay alive. Reeves's mental health was never better than when his physical health was threatened. He learned to treasure the small things in life, like a pack of cigarettes sent by Carson, or a kind word from her. And there were many of these.

When he returned from the war it was as a hero. He had some injuries, but nothing significant. Carson wrote the following to him when he was recuperating in hospital:

My blessed Reeves,
   There are no words tender enough for me to call you. Take care of yourself. Drink very little, as I plan to do. Too much drinking is very bad for both of us.[25]

Reeves, for his part, had written to her shortly before: "For our sake and for our future happiness I beg of you not to drink too much."[26] Each knew the other was a temptation in this department. Each was hoping the other could be strong enough to keep their temptation under wraps. If they could, they held high hopes of their future together.

In a letter she wrote to him in July 1944, she said she was at a party the night before and over-indulged: "This morning I felt completely crushed. You know that ghastly feeling that comes after too much drinking, the guilty and hopeless penitence."[27] She wrote in May 1945: "Dear darling, I'm being very good. Only two jiggers of whiskey a day."[28] A few months later he wrote back, "I made an agreement with myself last week to not have another drink until I see you next."[29] They remarried in 1945, planning to move to Europe, where Reeves had spent much time during the war.

The Member of the Wedding was published in March 1946. The following month she was awarded a second Guggenheim. Tennessee Williams loved the book and wrote to tell her so. She was so impressed by his letter she decided to meet him. He was living in Nantucket at that time. She traveled there on a ferry. She was dressed in beatnik gear: slacks and a baseball cap. She greeted him with her crooked-toothed grin and they bonded immediately. She lived with him for several weeks and put his house in order, cooking and cleaning for him—something she rarely did in her own abode. Williams suggested she turn *The Member of the Wedding* into a play and she set about doing this. Dialogue was never one of her strong points but she managed it, with a little help from Williams.

The two writers often got drunk together on wine. One night there was a thunderstorm and all the windows on one side of the house were broken. A pregnant cat climbed in one of them. A friend of Williams acted as her midwife, serving her up teaspoonfuls of whiskey to keep her energy levels up for the birth. It was the only time he'd ever seen a cat drink whiskey. It had a huge litter, eight or nine kittens, according to Williams' recollection. In the following days it brought fish-heads in through the (still broken) windows to feed them. Carson took all this in her stride.[30]

Tennessee Williams became a close friend of Carson McCullers after the war. The two of them often disgraced themselves with drink—together or alone.

Williams regarded her as a kind of surrogate sister to him. The same didn't apply to his actual sister, Rose. Rose was discommoded by Carson's drinking and her buoyant personality. When they first met, Carson threw her arms open and bellowed, "Kiss me, Miss Rose!" Rose withdrew from the offered embrace, pleading, "No thank you, I have halitosis." Later that day, Carson and "Tenn" got down to the serious business of imbibing. Rose spent the evening standing in a corner, praying for "drinking sinners."[31]

The problems with

Reeves continued. Even though they were more mature now, the issues that dogged their relationship before the war continued to rear their ugly heads. One of these was Carson's inability to forget the way Reeves had robbed her of so much money. She was never comfortable with checks afterward and took to pinning them onto her blouse where he couldn't get at them. This became a source of some amusement to those who'd always seen her as flat-chested. She was now, they noticed, sporting something of a bosom.[32]

Carson also became friendly with Truman Capote at this time. She accused him of plagiarizing her style, but this was said mainly in jest. They enjoyed one another's company when both of them were in their cups. Capote did a good imitation of a drunken McCullers trying to find a script she'd written, as David O. Selznick stood outside her door, demanding she find it. "Just a minute," he'd say, mimicking her Georgia accent. "Ah'll hunt under the bed.... It's around heah somewhere ... daggone if ah know where that script is."[33]

When she went to Paris with Reeves in 1946 they decided to switch from bourbon to brandy as that beverage was cheaper there. Both of them astounded the French by being able to knock back a bottle a day each and still not show the effects of it. It was too much for them to be able to resist the temptation of cafés and bars that were open until the wee hours of the morning.[34] Doctors told her she could have two cans of beer every evening as well as one large cocktail or two small ones, but they didn't define large or small.[35] Her own definition of such terms was always, to say the least, generous.

She suffered a second stroke in August 1947. When she was released from the hospital, she was advised to quit drinking altogether. She ignored this dictate, continuing to have beer in the afternoons and cognac at night. Part of the drinking was from stress. As well as her health problems she was having difficulty finding a producer for the play version of *The Member of the Wedding*. One night she invited her friend Natalia Murray to dinner. She claimed to be "off the sauce." She held a teacup in her hand the whole evening but was drinking its contents through a funnel. Murray suspected there was alcohol in it. She waited for ages for the dinner to be ready. When it was finally served it was burned to a cinder. Murray later learned the cook was drunk too![36]

Such a lifestyle couldn't go on indefinitely. A third stroke followed in December, which caused her to fall to the floor. She lay there conscious but unable to move for eight hours. She suffered a loss of lateral vision to the right eye and the right side of her face was numb. The left side of her body was also paralyzed. She was flown home from Paris on a stretcher. Reeves was placed on one, too. He had the DTs. He was drinking heavily again and suffering from deep-seated depression, the problems that had beset him before the war re-surfacing with a vengeance. He was finding it more difficult than ever to cope with Carson's success, and with his identity as Mr. Carson McCullers.[37]

She separated from him at the beginning of 1948 and he moved to New York. Afterward, unable to deal with the split, she attempted suicide. She was hospitalized in a psychiatric clinic at this time. When she was discharged she reconciled with him. Their relationship, again, went into the familiar pattern of crisis followed by recrimination, followed by another crisis. He was like alcohol to her: yet another addiction for which she couldn't find the cure. She spent most of 1949 with him.

Considering both she and Reeves drank so much, it's surprising more scenes of them misbehaving together didn't find their way into her fiction. She only wrote two stories in which marital disharmony is attributed to alcohol: "A Domestic Dilemma" and "Instant of the Hour After." In the second of these it's the sherry-tippling housewife who precipitates the conflict.[38]

Albert Einstein once defined madness as the practice of doing the same thing over and over and expecting to get a different result. Carson's problem with people was that she could never fully let go of anyone who came into her life for however brief a time, no matter how they behaved—or misbehaved—towards her. She went back to Reeves once too often and very nearly paid for that mistake with her life.

Her psychiatrist William Mayer told her, "Men don't change essentially because of a war," but Carson didn't listen to him. Because of his heroic conduct in battle, she expected a "miraculous" change to have taken place in his character. In so doing, she forgot the reasons she had divorced him in the first place.[39]

A producer was found for *The Member of the Wedding* in 1949, but she still kept fretting about it. Her main worry was about cast member Ethel Waters. She was terrified she'd ruin the production because of her unique acting style. Waters refused to take direction, claiming she only took direction from God. As the production date neared, Waters tried to reassure Carson that she knew her lines. She steadily drank whiskey as rehearsals progressed, terrified everything would go pear-shaped, but Waters managed to remember her lines in the end and the production became a sensation, playing 501 performances in all. Waters would also go on to star in the 1952 film version, with Julie Harris and Brandon de

Julie Harris, Ethel Waters and Brandon de Wilde in *The Member of the Wedding* (1952), arguably McCullers' greatest novel.

Wilde. It was produced by Stanley Kramer, and directed by Fred Zinnemann.

Buoyed by the success of the play, Houghton Mifflin now published a bumper edition of all of Carson's published work to date. She was regarded by many as the outstanding Southern writer of her time on the strength of this. But her chances of outshining her contemporaries—Eudora Welty, Flannery O'Connor, and Katharine Anne Porter—were dashed by the health problems that plagued her. From 1950 on, her story became "the history of declining health and talent."[40]

Carson was still on and off with Reeves. Every time she tried to draw away from him, he pursued her all the more avidly. When she sailed for England aboard the *Queen Elizabeth* in the summer, he stowed away without her knowing. He finally revealed himself, threatening to throw himself overboard unless she made up with him. "I had to handle him like a spoilt brat," she said, "conceding to everything, but the dignity of our marriage was quickly being destroyed."[41] She finally relented and asked him to dinner. She traveled to Italy with him the following year and they hooked up with David Diamond again in Rome. As was the case with this strange threesome in the past, there were many drinks consumed in these assignations.

Carson was now having highballs before dinner and a bottle of wine or two after it. She was still in denial about her problem, insisting to people that she only drank to assuage the pain of her various health maladies. Reeves was working in a bank now and promising to kick the habit—again. He even attended AA meetings for a time. This made it sound like he meant it, but then he left his job, upset at not having been promoted, and went on a binge. He signed himself into the Doctor's Hospital afterward to dry out. He told David Diamond he was thinking of killing himself by washing down a fifth of whiskey with Antabuse. (This was a pill given to alcoholics which was never to be taken with drink for fear of bringing on a coronary.)

They bought a home outside Paris in 1952. He promised her he was going to reform, and she believed him. He even told her he was writing a book, which delighted her. She had a studio built for him beside their house to help this come about. But below it was a wine cellar. He used his hands more for raising glasses to his lips here than forming words upstairs.

The drinking caused his moods to fluctuate and gave rise to violent episodes. One night Carson felt his hands around her neck "and I knew he was going to choke me." He only stopped when she bit his thumb and blood spurted out.[42] She blamed herself for not realizing how dangerous his alcoholism made him, but it was often concealed behind his "splendid constitution" and his amazing recuperative powers.[43]

Throughout the summer of 1953 he often talked about doing himself in. He told Carson he thought they should engage in a suicide pact. If he died alone, he argued, who would take care of her? She went along with this to placate him, realizing he was deluded at this point, his mind destroyed by all the years of indulgence.

One day he tried to hang himself from a pear tree in their orchard, but the limb broke under his weight. Carson didn't believe the attempt was serious. "Please, Reeves," she said, "if you *must* commit suicide, do it somewhere else. Just look what you did to my favorite pear tree."[44]

Another day he brought her out to their barn and picked up a piece of rope from the ground. Looking up at a beam overhead he said, "See that rafter? It's a good sturdy one. You know what we're going to do? Hang ourselves from it." She passed the incident off as ineffectual rambling, but a few days later she was in the car with him on the way to the hospital for a checkup when he veered off course. She then saw a piece of rope on the floor and panicked. As she said to Tennessee Williams when telling the story later, "Tenn, honey, it made me right nervous looking down at that rope."[45]

Her worst suspicions were confirmed when he told her he was driving her to a forest where they were both going to hang themselves. "But first," he exhorted, "we'll stop and buy a bottle of brandy. We'll drink it for old time's sake ... one last fling."[46] He stopped the car a few minutes later and went into a roadside tavern to buy it. Seizing her opportunity, Carson fled from the car when he was out of sight. She then hitched a ride to a friend's house, where she hid from him.[47] This account of the events is from Virginia Spencer Carr's biography of Carson. In his memoirs, Tennessee Williams says Carson came up with the idea of the liquor as a decoy to get Reeves out of the car so she could clamber out.[48]

She fled to the U.S. to escape him. He kept forging her checks and drinking himself into oblivion with the proceeds. Towards the end of the year he rang a friend, Simone Brown, and told her he was "going west." This was military parlance for committing suicide. She tried to talk him out of it, to no avail. His body was found on November 19 of that year in a hotel. He died from a combination of alcohol and barbiturates, choking on his vomit.

Reeves wasn't the only member of his family to kill himself. His sister Marguerite had died of an overdose of sleeping pills in 1946 when she was just thirty-two. Wiley Mae, another sister, overdosed in 1961. Four years later, his brother Tommy threw himself from a window in Greenwich Village. These events served to convince Carson that there was nothing she could have done to save Reeves. She saw his problem as a kind of genetic malfunction.

At his funeral, she downed a fifth of whiskey. Though in deep shock, she was aware of a serenity enwreathing her. She knew this outcome was best for all of them. The man she loved but couldn't live with was finally out of his pain. She'd tried to make it work between them, but it was impossible. The writing had been on the wall almost from the moment her first book was published. He had tried his best to enjoy her career at first but as time went on it became too much for him. "Reeves died of his love for Carson," Tennessee Williams reflected. "Without her he was as empty as a shell."[49]

Carson went downhill in the following years. She became bloated from drink and increasingly irascible with other people. Some saw her as a glory-seeker behind the surface shyness. They referred to her as "an iron butterfly."[50] She may have parlayed her sensitivity into her writing, but there was true grit there as well. There had to be. How else could a body cope with her inventory of afflictions? She could only walk with a cane now. Her hand was withered; her speech, slurred. Neither could she control her tongue. She had difficulty making it form words and, when she did, they could be devastating in their impact.

She was asked to give a lecture on writing at the Poetry Center of the 92nd Street YMHA in 1954. She invited Tennessee Williams to speak as well, feeling he'd be better at that kind of thing than she. He agreed on condition that a pitcher of martinis be perched at his elbow. Carson thought this was a good idea, and decided she'd have one as well. As the evening went on, the two of them became more interested in the martinis than the lecture. Donald Spoto captured the scene:

> Two of America's most famous writers sat for the evening interrupting one another, stumbling and slurring over their words, perversely relishing one another's boozy humor as much as they were oblivious to the uncomfortable audience.[51]

Her mother died in 1955. Combined with the shock of Reeves's death, this led to one of her darkest works, a play called *The Square Root of Wonderful*. Not being a natural dramatist, she struggled to write it. Maybe she was too close to the material.

She signed herself into the Doctor's Hospital soon afterward to recover from the stress of trying to get the play onto the stage. Reeves had stayed in this hospital in the past when he was drying out. Carson insisted her motives were more general. When her director, Albert Marre, visited her, he found her sitting up in bed with a tumbler full of bourbon in her hand. It was early in the day. He said, "What in the hell is that?" She replied, "The people in here think I'm some sort of wild drinker so they bring me a drink at nine in the morning and then again at two and six. I'm getting absolutely stoned sipping like this."[52] Her reputation had preceded her—but she still didn't refuse the bourbon.

The Square Root of Wonderful was staged on Broadway in 1957, but it wasn't a success, closing after forty-five performances. Carson went into depression as a result, not knowing what had gone wrong. She consulted a psychiatrist to try and deal with her disappointment. He helped her recover some self-belief, but she seemed to know her most creative years were behind her. Her activities now were peripheral to creativity: lecturing, writing prefaces, engaging in panel discussions, reading publicly from her past work. After *The Square Root of Wonderful* failed, she said, "I felt that God had turned his back on me."[53]

By the end of the '50s, money had become a major worry because of all her medical expenses. She sought grants to ease this burden, but they were refused. She was the beneficiary of so many of them in the past she felt she had exhausted this avenue of income. Her sight was poor as well now and her arms weak. Her joints were so swollen that she could barely hold a pen now. Such problems caused her to become testy with people. They were always surprised when her generally sweet disposition failed her. Her writing ability was more depleted than ever, reduced to a page a day. She could only type with one hand, sitting up in bed.[54]

She realized she was trying too hard to recapture the glory of the past against insuperable odds and became philosophical, giving this summation of her life:

> I became an established literary figure overnight and I was much too young to understand what happened to me or the responsibility it entailed. I was a bit of a holy terror. That, combined with all my illnesses, nearly destroyed me.[55]

Her last novel, *Clock Without Hands*, came out in 1961. It was one of her most challenging efforts as well as one of her most fulfilling, perhaps for that reason. Her friend Jordan Masse helped her correct the proofs. Such work, as ever, was combined with liquid refreshments. Whenever he filled her glass with bourbon it was never high enough. When he would go to refill it, she'd say, "No honey, just leave the glass there and bring the bottle." She liked to drink it virtually neat. If he started to put water in it she'd say, "Don't drown it, darling."[56]

She broke her hip one night in 1964 after getting out of bed to go to the toilet. She experienced much pain after this which she couldn't account for. It was eventually traced to a pin that slipped from the hip after the operation and was wandering inside her body, pinching her. A subsequent operation relieved this, but she needed a lot of physiotherapy too. She was barely eating by this time, nor was she drinking much. The surgery had robbed her of her taste for rum. She occasionally drank Coca-Cola instead, something which would have been unthinkable before.

Carson was almost totally bedridden in her final years. Her withered arm meant she couldn't dress without help, and the pain of trying to move her legs just wasn't worth the effort any longer. She had enormous trouble trying to type, even from her bed, so she usually just wrote in longhand or dictated.[57]

She still smoked a lot of cigarettes, or at least lit quite a few. (She was notorious for lighting up and then stubbing them out, or forgetting where she left them.) Her main drinking now was done just before bedtime. It was fortified by an assortment of pills.

She received an unexpected bounty towards the end of her life when

John Huston said he wanted to film *Reflections in a Golden Eye*. Montgomery Clift was originally slated for the role of the homosexual Major Penderton, despite his aversion to Huston (who'd been so cruel to him while directing him in *Freud* some years before). Clift was virtually uninsurable for big-budget movies because of his chronic drinking, but his friend Elizabeth Taylor, contracted to play Penderton's wife, agreed to put up her salary to get him on board.[58] But then Clift died and Marlon Brando slipped into the breach. One of his main reasons for doing the film, he said, was because he admired Carson's writing so much.[59]

Huston tried to normalize the nightmarish events of the novel into a more manageable melodrama.[60] Many people found Penderton's bisexuality difficult to understand, but this was a scenario Carson experienced with her own husband.[61] As shooting progressed, Huston invited Carson to visit him in his ancestral home in Ireland. Much to his amazement, she jumped at the opportunity.

The difficulty of getting her on a plane seemed insurmountable at first, but, somehow, it was achieved. Huston worried about whether her health would stand up to the trip. She had been in Ireland once before, in

Julie Harris and Elizabeth Taylor in *Reflections in a Golden Eye* (1967), McCullers' explosively gothic novel which resulted in death threats from the Ku Klux Klan.

1950, and loved it then. She also loved Irish writers. She'd visited Elizabeth Bowen on her 1950 trip. Another favorite was James Joyce, especially because of his book *Dubliners*. (Huston's final film would be an adaptation of the last story in this book, "The Dead").

She went into a deep sleep on the third day of her visit. A coma was feared but it turned out to be mere exhaustion from the long journey. After she woke up she was back to her old self. When a doctor called to examine her, he found her sitting up with a cigarette in one hand and a drink in the other. "You'd be much better if you gave up smoking and drinking," he admonished. Carson, looked up at a crucifix that was on the wall above her head and said, "I will when He comes down off that wall." It was an amusing answer, but the doctor had a good response to it: "He has been known to do so."[62]

Two weeks after she returned to America, Carson suffered another stroke. She lingered in a coma and died two months later. The iron butterfly had finally shed it wings.

Charles Bukowski

(1920–1994)

Charles Henry Bukowski—his friends called him "Hank"—was born in Germany, but grew up in Los Angeles. His mother was German; his father, American with a Polish background. He was a cruel man who beat his son relentlessly with a razor strop for even the smallest infraction.[1]

He was also beaten at school by his classmates because of his German heritage, but in time he learned how to stand up to bullies. His appearance helped in this regard. He wasn't a pretty child, being afflicted with a condition called *acne vulgaris*, which caused him to break out in boils and scars all over his body. It worsened an already considerable tension in his life.[2]

When he started drinking he discovered a new side to himself, a side that made the world a tranquil place. It was escapism, but a beautiful one. He saw alcohol as the happy drug. To some extent it would always remain so for him—if not for those who were watching him. Every time he had a problem in later life he drank his way through it.

His induction to liquor took place in the cellar of a friend's house where barrels of wine were stacked. The first swallow made him feel sick but by the second one he started to enjoy it: "I went from barrel to barrel. It was magic. Why hadn't someone told me? With this, life was great, a man was perfect, nothing could touch him."[3] The wine didn't just taste good in itself; it gave him the kind of ammunition he needed to confront the obstacles that had inhibited him up to now. He sat on a park bench with his friend afterward and thought,

> I have found something that is going to help me for a long time to come. The park grass looked greener, the park benches looked better and the flowers were trying harder. Maybe that stuff wasn't good for surgeons but anybody who wanted to be a surgeon, there was something wrong with them in the first place.[4]

His parents went to bed at 8 p.m. most nights. Bukowski pretended to turn in at that time as well, but he usually climbed out his bedroom window afterward and made his way to the local bar. Though he was under the official drinking age his acne made him look older, enabling him to be served.

One night he got so drunk he wasn't able to climb up to his window, so he knocked on the front door instead. When his father went to answer it he was shocked at his condition and refused to let him in. Bukowski heaved the door in and staggered across the living room, where he proceeded to throw up on the rug. When he stood up, his father grabbed him by the neck and pushed him down on the floor again. "Do you know what we do with a dog when it shits on the rug?" he said. "We put his nose in it."[5] Bukowski wasn't having this and punched his father in the face. His mother couldn't believe what she was seeing. "You hit your father!" she screamed. It was all right for his father to physically abuse him, but not vice versa.[6] This was the first time he ever stood up to this bully. It was a seminal moment for him. His father never raised a hand to him again.

Drink also helped Bukowski stop his father from beating his mother. One night, he even threatened to kill him. He meant it, and his father knew this. Drink freed him from the shell of the troubled adolescent who'd been steadily thrashed by a coward wielding a razor strop. When the beatings stopped, his life began.

When Bukowski was drunk he found he was more at home in the world. It was like a journey to his inner self. When he drank he didn't seem to mind that he came from a loveless home, that his life would probably go on to be loveless as well. He didn't seem to mind that the world wasn't his oyster, that he was born ugly, poor, hated. The bottle was a substitute for all of those things. It was his friend. It brought him into a comfort zone, a harmony with himself and his surroundings.

Once the magic juice kicked in he became another person, relieved temporarily of all his inhibitions, ready to take the world on. It was an escape from the straitjacket of home, school, life.

After graduating from high school, Bukowski spent two years at Los Angeles City College, studying journalism and literature. When World War II broke out, he moved to New York. He espoused some pro–Nazi sympathies at this time, not so much because he believed them, but to be controversial. And, as he joked, it was easier to scrounge free drinks off right-wingers in bars than left-wingers.[7]

He moved to New Orleans after leaving New York. Then he went to Atlanta. There, he experienced the first of his bad depressions, most brought on by his failure to get anywhere with his writing. He considered suicide in a tar shack, but wrote his way out of it. He scribbled poems on the margins of old newspapers, the only writing material he could find there.[8]

He went to Philadelphia in the summer of 1944. After he got there he found a bar that opened at 5:30 a.m. The barman served him drinks on the house until the regular customers arrived in at 7. He delivered sandwiches or newspapers to the other customers to earn these drinks.

In July of that year he was arrested on suspicion of avoiding the draft. (When he left Atlanta, he didn't mail a forwarding address—because he didn't have one.) He was held for seventeen days, eventually being released after being deemed mentally unsuitable for military service. This relieved him hugely. Drinking was much more fun than keeping the world free from Hitler.

On his first night in the in the Philadelphia bar a fight had broken out. Bottles had sailed over his head. He thought, *This is my kind of place*.[9] He expected another fight the following night but there wasn't one. In fact, it stayed quiet almost every night for the next year. The reason he knew that was because he was *in* it almost every night for the next year. It was so run down, he said, one night a hooker came in and the patrons felt honored that she would grace it with her presence.[10]

At closing time, he usually lay in a nearby alley to sleep off the effects of the beer before starting again at dawn. Often, he was robbed and beaten here. Children even poked him with sticks. Sometimes he went to churches at midnight to get in from

Bukowski always insisted drink saved his life (Copyright Allen Berlinski).

the cold. If he hadn't any money to drink he might sit on a park bench, or seek shelter from the elements in a library.

In his favorite bar, Bukowski ran into many of the colorful characters who would form the central plank of his writing. He wasn't aware of that then. He wasn't seeking them out as raw material. They merely appeared in his life and then disappeared. If they found their way into his work it was almost by accident. He wrote his poems on the edges of cigarette packs, on stray pieces of paper, on anything, in fact, that was on hand. Many of them he lost. Some he stuffed into pockets that were robbed by people looking for his wallet as he slept. Maybe the biggest surprise is that so much of the writing he did during this period of his life survived in any shape or form.

Bukowski did most of his writing when he was drunk, or at least moderately tipsy. Perhaps this was why he didn't usually bother with capital letters for punctuation—it was too difficult to locate them. (e.e. cummings may have had more artistic reasons for the habit.) He'd churn out poem after poem and story after story and then go off to bed, leaving them all over his floor. The next morning he would be amazed at the near-indecipherable pages laying on the floor in front of him, hardly remembering having written them. Most often he wouldn't be able to remember how or why he'd written what he did. He resolutely refused to edit what he wrote. He submitted poems and short stories to various magazines all over America like messages in a bottle—or from one—usually without even bothering got keep carbons.

There were many days when he did nothing but drink from dawn till dusk. It was almost like a career with him. For variety's sake he might have a fight with another drinker, or with a barman, and then return to his stool, where he would continue where he left off. His big build and great physical strength gave him an enormous capacity and this only increased the more he drank. He seemed to have no goal in life in these years, save to get as drunk as he could, as quickly as he could. Alcohol was his perpetual standby, his inspiration for whatever writing he did. But writing was never the priority—merely getting through the day was.

One night during an argument in a bar, a man put a gun to his head and told him he was going to pull the trigger. "Go on," Bukowski said. "You'd be doing me a favor. You'd be solving my problem," he continued, "but creating one for yourself. You'd probably do life in jail or get the chair." The man dropped the gun when he heard this. He was later put in an asylum. "I was a nut too," Bukowski admitted. "That was what made the incident interesting. But he bit off more that he could chew when he put the gun to my temple because I was ready to go. If I'd said *'Don't* do it,' he might have been more likely to shoot me."¹¹

After he left Philadelphia he went back to his parents. He was now beginning what he would later refer to his "ten-year drunk"—a decade of more or less non-stop drinking.¹² This wasn't quite true, as a photograph from the time shows him looking dapper in a suit and tie, his hair neatly cut.

He was also writing more now. He had a story published in a prestigious magazine called *Portfolio*, which featured works by such luminaries as Jean Genet and Jean-Paul Sartre. Bukowski's father, who shared his son's name, tried to pawn the story off to friends as his own. Bukowski was so enraged at his duplicity he stormed out of the house, going to live in the red-light district of L.A. instead. This suited him better for a number of reasons—the main one being that he could drink there in peace with his fellow dropouts.

One night in 1946 he met a woman in the Glenview Bar on Alvarado Street, one of his favorite haunts. Her name was Jane Cooney Baker. Like him, she was a free spirit, a woman without any visible direction in life, a maverick. She was older than he and looked worse the wear, but she had a kind of class about her that impressed him. She looked like she might have been somebody once. She sat on her own, looking into space. When Bukowski asked the barman why nobody was talking to her, he said, "Because she's crazy."¹³

Bukowski was attracted to craziness. He went over to her, sat down beside her and ordered a drink for her. "I hate people," she said to him. Now he became even more interested in her because he hated people, too. ("I distrust everyone," he once told Neeli Cherkovski.)

"What do you do?" he asked her. Without looking at him, she replied, "I drink." Bukowski smiled. He knew he'd just met his kind of woman.¹⁴

He told her he had no money, so she accompanied him across the road to a liquor store. She ordered two fifths of Scotch and some beer and cigarettes. The clerk made a phone call, which seemed to okay the purchase. When they left the store, she told Bukowski she'd put it on the tab of a real estate broker she knew.

They went to Bukowski's apartment and continued drinking. His bed sagged in the middle. A naked light bulb emanated a sickly yellow glow. A wobbly table stood in the center of the kitchen, looking as if it would fall if anyone breathed near it. "It'll do," she said as she poured two drinks and lit a cigarette. "Let's just forget about everything and get drunk."¹⁵

Jane had been married to an attorney. They lived a life of luxury for a time but both of them were heavy drinkers and the marriage ultimately fell apart. Then he was killed in a car crash. Jane started drinking more heavily as a result. When she met Bukowski, she was a broken woman.

They began living together in one dead-end joint after another. They fought, scavenging drinks from wherever they could. They were often evicted from rooming houses for wrecking them, or for shouting too much. They lived from hand to mouth, not caring which way the wind blew. When times were good, life was one continuous party. They'd sing and dance together with no thought of tomorrow. But the hangovers from their marathon binges were ferocious. Sometimes they'd stay in bed all day just sleeping them off, letting time pass. Jane seemed better at dealing with it all. "Hank could out-drink any three men I know," his childhood friend William Mullinax said, "but he couldn't out-drink Jane."[16]

When he sobered up he went looking for work, so they could begin the madness again that night.

Some of his jobs he lost through drink, some through fighting, some through a combination of both. Whatever money he earned, he drank. One night he was drinking with Jane in a cocktail lounge that had a large window.

"I bet you don't have the guts to break [it]," she said to him.

"I do," he said, "but it wouldn't make any sense."

A few minutes later she took up a glass to throw at it. He stopped her but later in the night, he got drunk and smashed it himself. They ran out of the bar as police sirens screeched around them. "Jane goaded me into doing it," he said. "I guess when I saw her getting ready to smash it herself, it put it into my mind."[17]

Jane drifted into a part of him that he had once been too inhibited to disclose to anyone. He laid bare his insecurities to her, his neuroses and his fears. Because she put up no defenses, he didn't put up any either. There was no game playing in the relationship, no striking of poses, no Thanksgiving promises. They were just two people looking for a shoulder to cry on. It was like two negatives making a positive.

Loving Jane was easier than anything he'd ever done. And she reciprocated. All she asked of him was that he allowed her to drink—an irony, considering his own past.

Drink afforded him a necessary release. It also released his muse. The writers he knew didn't understand that when they nagged him, when they told him booze would kill him at a young age. He felt this wasn't true, that the absence of it would kill him more quickly. Without it, he believed he would have died from apathy. It was the beer that wrote the books. He was merely the funnel through which it operated.

From 1946 to 1955 he drank with more dedication than somebody pursuing a career ambition. The sheer consistency of his intake would have killed lesser men before they reached thirty, but he waltzed through it with equanimity.

He worked mainly in laboring jobs through these years, dropping them—or getting fired—not long after he took them on. Booze helped him maintain his sanity in the face of work he abhorred. It also helped him cope with the depression that hit him when he saw writers he didn't respect becoming successful as he waited to be discovered.

As well as writing poems and short stories, he also managed many letters. In these, we find as much passion as in his fiction. The letters are his postcards from the edge, so many testaments to the savage indignation that lacerated his breast.

He didn't drink because he wanted to, but because he *needed* to. It was like a bulletproof vest he wore to inure him to life's casual cruelties. You worked fourteen hours a day for three bucks an hour and then you entered this special haven. He asked for nothing more. He didn't want warmth, or encouragement, or even a beautiful woman. Just fill up that glass. And then fill it again.

In his dark times he thought about ending it all, but hope and humor kept him going. In one of his early stories he wrote about an attempt to gas himself to death; he failed because he woke up with a headache. "The automatic pilot [light] on the stove wasn't working," he wrote, "or that little flame would have blasted me right out of my precious little season in hell."[18] Another time he was tempted to stab himself to death with a butcher knife. On that occasion he had to grab on to the mattress of his bed with both hands to stop himself.

Bukowski spent ten years living on and off with Jane. When they didn't have enough money to pay the rent they either skipped the premises or propped furniture against the door of their room to keep the landlord—or, as was sometimes the case, the police—out. One night he got so drunk he fell off a couch and lay on the floor, looking up at her.

"Baby," he said, "I'm a genius and nobody knows it."

"Get up off the floor and sit down, you damn fool," she replied.[19]

Bukowski could only laugh.

He woke up many days in L.A.'s drunk tank, usually as a result of being involved in a wild altercation the night before. He retched so hard on these mornings he might well see blood in the toilet. He expected to die young of some drink-related accident.

He was clumsy even when sober. With it, he was the proverbial bull in a china shop. He often knocked things—and even people—over. He also had a habit of walking around without shoes and suffered many injuries as a result of stepping on broken shards of glass. At times his skin seemed to take on the coarseness of a crocodile's. It was scarred so much, eventually he stopped feeling the pain. Alcohol, of course, also acted as a painkiller.

Bukowski didn't usually get aggressive with drink. If a fellow drinker wanted to fight him, he sometimes agreed out of a sense of duty. He might go out to an alleyway with the man and punch his lights out, or have his lights punched out by him, and then return to the bar with his opponent and resume drinking. It was a game of being the hard and frozen man.

He could be revolting while drunk, but we should remember that one of the main reasons he drank was because he found the world itself revolting. Alcohol was his protection against it. He wouldn't have been the first writer who was too sensitive to face the world sober, who used alcohol to burn some iron into his soul. Asked once what the meaning of life was, he replied, "Drink as much as you can."[20] It wasn't a habit—it was a philosophy.

"When things close in too much," he said, "the bottle seems the only thing that seems to ease them. The body must pay, of course, but the mind has to be considered too."[21] Hangovers, car accidents, ruined relationships and even the drunk tanks were small prices to pay for his euphoria. It was a process one could repeat indefinitely. "One of the finest things about it," he wrote, "is you can get very drunk, extremely drunk, and all you have to do is to step outside the door into all that clear cold blue whiteness of oxygen and just breathe it in and you sober up and can get drunk all over again. It's the same with a hangover. You just walk outside, breathe, and the hangover is gobbled up the in whiteness."[22]

In the early 1950s he took a job as a letter carrier with the U.S. postal service in L.A. He stayed at this for three years, an eternity by his standards. After work most evenings, he listened to classical music, another passion of his which kept him sane. He took a hit of whiskey and pulled the drapes down on a world that had failed him and that he had failed. Its only constant was pain. You lived and died with it each day, burning it out of yourself and then becoming strong again. Maybe.

He hated amateur alcoholics. This was a breed that proliferated on special occasions, like birthdays or Christmas or New Year's Eve, when these dilettantes drank themselves senseless and slapped one another on the back at inane parties before slumping off to their well-heeled suburban residences. The true alcoholic didn't advertise his drinking in this manner, he pointed out. Instead, he sat in a lonely room or on a quiet barstool, contemplating the misery that was life. Or maybe cutting his wrists. Or putting his head in the oven. His drinks weren't merry, and neither were his wishes.

Bukowski's drinking caught up to him in the spring of 1955, when he took ill one day at the post office. He started to vomit blood. An ambulance was summoned to the scene and he was taken to the charity ward of Los Angeles's County General Hospital. He had a bleeding ulcer and needed a blood transfusion immediately. He wasn't sure he would be eligible, as he had no health insurance. At this point, he didn't care if he lived or died.

As it happened, he lived—even though his liver was "the size and color of a watermelon."[23] His survival was miraculous. Before he left the hospital a doctor told him that if he even took one more drink he'd die. Bukowski walked out onto the street and went straight to a liquor store for some beers. When he got home, he drank them slowly—for once.

"I didn't die," he said, "and that made me realize how full of crap doctors were." The next day he drank a little whiskey, putting milk in it to weaken it, and still didn't die. After a few days he became brave enough to return to his normal routine.

He didn't drink as heavily after 1955, however, his escape from death giving the "Poet Laureate of Skid Row," as he came to be called, at least the semblance of a will to carry on in the cesspool of life.

One of the problems he encountered now was how to fill his days if he wasn't going to be in bars all the time. Jane suggested he take up gambling on horses, advice he delightedly took. In time, the track became almost as much of a compulsion to him as drink, and it also gave him inspiration for his poems and stories. It wasn't long before he discovered beer was sold there. Now he could merge his two favorite hobbies, if he wished. But, in actual fact, he didn't. "I drink when I write because it makes the world flow," he said, "but at the track I need to concentrate."[24]

Bukowski and Jane drifted apart after 1955. His brush with death had changed his attitude toward her and toward the kind of life they led together. Their arguments now didn't have the humor they used to have. Eventually, they split up.

After he broke with her he started corresponding with a Texan woman, Barbara Frye, the editor of a magazine to which he contributed poetry. One day Frye wrote to him and said, "No man will marry me."

Bukowski wrote back to her saying, "I will." He married her just one day after they met. Not surprisingly, the marriage was a disaster.[25]

She was rich, but Bukowski wasn't interested in her money. They divorced in 1958. Frye died in India some years later under mysterious circumstances. It was rumored she was murdered.

Jane tried to get back with him now, but he wasn't interested. She was drinking more than ever; he, slightly less. He dated her a few times for old time's sake, but there was nothing there now. The magic was gone; they were dancing to a tune that had stopped playing long before.

The time with Frye had made him less self-destructive, more focused on his writing. He decided to go straight for a while and went back to his old job at the post office.

Over the next two years, his parents died. His father left him a house worth $15,000, part of which he drank away, and part of which he invested. (The fact that he didn't drink away all of it was perhaps the biggest surprise.) He went back to L.A. in 1960 to resume work in the post office, this time as a letter filing clerk. He would keep this job for the better part of a decade.

He worked the night shift there, coming in at 6:30 p.m. and leaving at 2:30 a.m. That gave him time to write during the day. He came to work many nights hungover. This would have meant instant dismissal if it was discovered but he was protected by his (mostly black) co-workers. He was one of the few white men who didn't look down on them or patronize them.

Jane died in 1962. He didn't know she was sick until he called to her hotel room one day. There he found her bed empty and a plethora of empty whiskey bottles under it. When he visited her in hospital, she was in a coma. She came out of it when she saw him. "I knew it would be you," she said, words that touched him.[26] They would appear many times in his poems and stories.

Jane had visited him in the charity ward of Los Angeles County Hospital when he hovered between life and death in 1955. Now the roles were reversed. Bukowski survived on that occasion, but there would be no reprieve for Jane. She'd supped too much on Whiskey Hill, and her insides were eaten up. After she spoke to her old love she went back into the coma again and died two days later.

For Bukowski, it was the end of an era. A part of him died with her. He went back to her room like a murderer returning to the scene of a crime. He was shocked by its grottiness, a grottiness of which he had once been a part before a switch clicked on in his brain. There would be no more bunking down in dilapidated hotels, no more nights of wild sex and drinking, no more falling into one another's arms as they laughed at the lousy hand life had dealt them both. She was the only "real" woman he had ever met, he said, and now she was gone.

Seeing her in her casket gave him a shock no doctor could. This was what happened to drinkers, he thought, or at least the ones who didn't get warnings in the form of bleeding ulcers. For over a decade they were united in a journey that went everywhere and nowhere. Now it was over for one of them. How would the survivor fare?

"I cannot hope for many more days," he wrote to his friend Ann Bauman. He said he awaited death "like a plumed falcon with beak and song and talon searching for my blood."[27] Why was one of them spared and not the other?

Was there a plan?

Had she died to save him?

Maybe the main difference between them was that Jane drank because there was nothing else in her life, whereas Bukowski did to find out if there might be.

His first book was published in 1963. Entitled *It Catches My Heart in Its Hands*, it was brought out by Loujon Press, a small company run by his friends Louise and Jon Webb—hence the compound term.

He now began living with a woman named Frances Dean. He had a daughter by her the following year. He called her Marina and became a devoted father to her. Was he going soft?

He became vaguely respectable with Frances, who often had her society friends to dinner. But many of these nights ended with Bukowski becoming so drunk he would insult his guests, prompting them to leave.[28] Part of him was still the old Hank and the relationship collapsed.

He was writing hard, and usually with a bag on. "I don't think I've written a good poem when I was completely sober," he said in 1963, "but I have written a few good ones—and a few bad ones—under the hammer of a bad hangover when I didn't know whether another drink or a blade would be the best thing."[29] The blade was a reference to stabbing himself—something he thought of more than once. Sometimes he was just too drunk to bother.

He talked about the parallels between drinking and killing oneself:

> Alcohol is such a pleasant god. It allows you to commit suicide and awaken and kill yourself again. It's a slow process of dying. In other words, you're not quitting all at once. You're quitting inch by inch instead of quickly giving up. You're waiting around until maybe something might happen a little bit better.[30]

The something "a little bit better" was his career choice. In 1965, Loujon Press published another one of his poetry collections, *Crucifix in a Death-*

hand. This would become a collector's item in time, but few read it when it was first released. He was a fringe poet, the "king of the littles," as he put it, a reference to all the magazines in which he was published. Most of these would surface in future years after he became famous, fetching large sums. A lot of the time he wouldn't have even seen them or received acknowledgment—or payment—from the editors. Doing it was enough for him. He compared writing to sandblasting.[31] Bukowski met the company manager, John Martin, in early 1969. Martin loved his work. He offered him a monthly stipend to write full-time and give up the post office job. Bukowski was interested, but nervous about the unknown.

Neither was he impressed when he offered Martin a drink and he refused. "That kind of put me off right there," he said afterward. "This guy's inhuman," he thought, "he doesn't drink beer." But Bukowski's ears pricked up when Martin said he was thinking of starting a small press. (This would become Black Sparrow.) He said he wanted to reprint some of his chapbooks. This was music to Bukowski's ears, so he decided to go for the gamble. The post office was getting ready to let him go anyway. If he hadn't been dismissed he would have gone crazy there. "I have one of two choices," he wrote to his German translator Carl Weissner. "Stay in the post office and go crazy or play at [being a] writer and starve. I've decided to starve."[32]

There was another reason for leaving the post office: a physical one. His back ached from years of putting letters in cubicles: "I could no longer lift my arms."[33]

It's impossible to overstate how good leaving the post office made him feel. Chucking it meant he could commune with words all day and all night. His deskbound colleagues he viewed as dead—like his father, dead before death itself arrived, clocking in and clocking out like automatons, in love with petty dreams commensurate with their tunnel vision about what constituted happiness or fulfillment.

A month later he completed his first novel, *Post Office*. Written in his trademark lean prose, it was unlike any other novel due to its strong sense of iconoclasm. As Leonard Cohen—an unlikely admirer—put it, "Bukowski brought everyone down to earth, even the angels."[34]

Over the next few years he wrote like a man possessed, mostly poetry but also a number of stories and novels. He also had many affairs with women. They came from far and wide to break bread with the living legend. He was amazed to find them interested in an ugly old hobo like him. (He was no beauty, to be sure, but he was always good company.) He also gave readings of his work, many of which degenerated into comedy shows. Meanwhile, the poetry collections flooded out of him.

He was less receptive to the male fans who showed up at his door with six-packs in hand, anxious to "share a beer" with the great Bukowski. These usually got short shrift, especially if they wanted to talk about writing. People depressed him; he still hated "amateur alcoholics." Give him the ones who took too much, who drank—like him—when it was destroying them. Who woke up in alleyways with the effects of it before getting rolled, or hauled down to the drunk tank. These people were, to him, infinitely preferable to the smooth souls who took just enough to feel mellow.

He was more inclined to talk to those who attended his readings. During one such event, he discussed how he procured wine from local liquor stores: "I usually order by the case, so I'm a very popular boy around my neighborhood. The liquor men love me. Which reminds me: I'm making those bastards rich and I'm killing myself."[35]

Raymond Carver, another hard-drinking poet, invited him to do a reading in Santa Cruz in 1972. Bukowski disgraced himself, perhaps inevitably, and then the two got drunk together. At this point both of them were regarded as being on paths to self-destruction. But when Carver stepped back from the brink and saved himself, Bukowski was glad for him: "Ray gave up drinking and that was fine by me [because] he really started to write then. I'm different. I drink and I write, I write and I drink and there's a rhythm to it."[36]

He did a reading at the City Lights Bookstore in San Francisco that year which was riotous even by his standards. A fridge stacked with beer stood beside the stage; he proceeded to drain its contents. Afterward, he had an argument with his girlfriend of the time, Linda King, which resulted in him falling down a flight of stairs.

He gave one of his wildest poetry readings in San Francisco soon afterward. A refrigerator was positioned behind him on the stage, replete with bottles of wine. As he lifted his glass he said to the packed gathering in a W.C. Fields lilt, "This isn't a prop, it's a necesssssity."[37] The drunker he got, the more he started to abuse his audience, at one point threatening to take them all on in a fight. Some of them started throwing bottles at him, frustrated at the fact that he was rambling instead of reading, and drinking more than talking. At the end of the evening he had to be hustled out the back door for his own safety—probably the first time in history a poet was ever threatened with violence from his audience.

After tales of Bukowski's hellraising became known, people visited him expecting him to misbehave in front of them. Often he obliged, even when it bored him. "I tried to become my image to entertain them," he said. Fights often broke out as a result, his life becoming similar to an extended free-for-all. "I'm the immortal writer Charles Bukowski," he'd scream out in the middle of them, "even greater than Hemingway." He'd built his style on Hemingway, but found "Papa" sorely lacking in humor. And what was a writer without humor?[38]

Bukowski was never short on humor, with or without a drink. One night he told a friend that any writer worth his salt should be prepared to eat his words. Whereupon he put a copy of a newspaper in which he'd written an article into his mouth. He chewed it for a few moments and then threw it up.

As he once said:

> Hemingway can have his wars and his bravery. I have the other things that were happening to me and to everybody around me. Millions of guys and women going mad and being murdered inch by inch every day. That was the real world.[39]

Bukowski captured such a world with his dizzy passion and made Black Sparrow and himself rich in the process. John Martin managed his career carefully, tapping into the cult appeal he had built up during his years on Skid Row, when he was writing for those offbeat literary magazines few people read. His days of penury were over, even if the drinking would continue relatively unabated for the next twenty years.

He was still threatened with jail for being drunk and disorderly, or for driving under the influence, but he usually escaped with a fine and quickly returned to his old ways. At home he kept the drapes drawn as he slept off his hangovers and avoided his disciples.

Alcohol may have landed Bukowski in some jams with women and the law, but he's one of the few writers about whom one can say that, in general, it improved his frame of mind, even over the long term. He didn't have a problem with the fact that it was an escape from reality or a crutch to help him cope. Either therapy was fine for the simple reason that life would have been unbearable to him without it. It was the lesser of many evils for him.

"The longest shot that ever came home," as one writer described him, continued to give readings to the public and to university students. (He also bedded as many co-eds as possible.) People who'd never read poetry before read Bukowski. This included prison inmates. People who'd never attended a poetry reading before came to his. He liked tough crowds. If they heckled him, he heckled them back. The poetry was almost like the subtext to his antics.

He hated the trendy poets, the Beats with their *faux*-hippie auras, their group hugs. Much poetry was little more than self-indulgent preciousness, in his view. People attended their friends' readings and sucked up to them so that such friends would, in turn, suck up to them when it was their night. It was glorified incest. Real art died on the vine as the circle of mutual congratulation kicked in. Bukowski stayed aloof from such cliques, beating his own path to truth down Terror Way. "The reading is over when the wine runs out" was as close as he got to a definition of artistic symmetry.[40]

He had a particular aversion to the Beats. They pretended to espouse a left-wing ethos, he said, but many of them held down white-collar posts and lived with their mothers, who funded their florid expostulations.

It was the blue-collar people who comprised Bukowski's main audience. These were the people who understood his pain, the pain he transmuted into art under the influence of whatever potion was ready at hand. In his own words:

> When you work for a dollar and seventy-five cents an hour, you need something at night to keep yourself sane. You need a fistfight, you need a bitch, you need whiskey. Otherwise you couldn't face it all again the next day. I'm all for alcohol. It's the thing.[41]

These were controversial words, but he was entitled to say them because he *lived* them. He was the Dylan Thomas who survived, the John Berryman who didn't jump from a bridge, the Scott Fitzgerald who chose life over death, the Ernest Hemingway who stared down the barrel of a gun and then guffawed.

But he couldn't have gone on forever like this unless fate took a hand. And it did, though in a different way.

When Bukowski met Linda Lee Beighle in 1976 she tuned his life around, realizing his body needed a break from the four-decade mauling to which he had subjected it in every seedy bar east of the Hollywood Hills. She owned a health food restaurant—irony of ironies. She said he needed to get off beer and whiskey and sample fine wines instead. Over time, he listened to her. (She also stopped his eating red meat.)

As it turned out, he preferred wine for reasons other than health. "I used to drink beer and Scotch together and write, but you can only write for maybe an hour or an hour and a half that way." With beer you also had to go to the bathroom every ten minutes. "It breaks your concentration. So wine is the best for creation. The blood of the gods."[42] The problem with whiskey was that it made him feel too tough. "Then I got to prove it."[43]

By and large, "Hank the Crank," as he came to be called, had been tamed. He also became more conservative. He bought a house in the fashionable suburb of San Pedro and started driving a BMW. Most surprising of all, he bought a computer and typed his poems onto it. No longer would the illegible scribbler have to wade through wads of verbiage on the morning after the night before.[44]

Was this really the former wino who had lived in trashcans while penning his verse after being 86ed from the local gin mill? Had he sold out?

As he grew older, he drank less in bars and more at home. One day, in 1978, he passed a bar with a friend of his, restaurant manager Jane Manhattan. She suggested having a drink, but he refused. "I can't go in there," he said, starting to cry. "So many years were so terrible, all those hours and days I spent in bars drunk out of my mind. I feel sick to the stomach when I even look at a bar like that."[45]

He told his friend A. A. Winans: "The bars finally lose their appeal. I mean, the trouble and the fights, the drunk tanks, the women, the stupid bartenders, the bad conversations, and the bad music. Those places are just full of lonely people and I decided I wasn't lonely, not for that."[46]

But the Poet Laureate of Skid Row wasn't totally gone. "I have always admired the villain," he told Italian author Fernanda Pivano. "I don't like the clean-shaven boy with the necktie and the good job. I like desperate men, men with broken teeth and broken minds and broken ways. I'm more interested in perverts than saints."[47]

He appeared drunk on a French TV show called *Apostrophes* in 1978, creating some consternation. He insisted on having two bottles of wine served to him while he was in make-up, promptly emptying both. When he got on air, he showed more interest in an attractive fellow panelist than he did in the host, Bernard Pivot. A few minutes after the program began, Bukowski said

Bukowski in later years when he cut his drinking down—but not out—under the influence of Linda Lee Beighle.

he wanted to see more of the woman's legs. More specifically, he wanted to examine her ankles. That way he felt he might know how good a writer she was.[48] He then started to abuse Pivot with a string of four-lettered words, which gave the translators of the show a problem—it was broadcast live.

When Pivot tried to shut him up, Bukowski pulled off his earpiece and stumbled toward the exit. When he got to reception he spotted two security guards and thought he was going to be arrested. Instinct kicking in, he reached into his pocket and drew out a small hunting knife. A scuffle ensued, during which he was overpowered. He was allowed back to his hotel afterward. The next morning, he forgot the whole incident, but the newspapers had not. The American hellraiser had roused a literary show from dullness. "What did I do?" he asked a journalist who rang from *Le Monde*. A few hours later, all his books were sold out in Paris. People even bowed to him in the street.[49]

The "big fight atmosphere" continued at the readings. He did one at Redondo Beach in 1980 which had the threat of violence bubbling just beneath the surface. "I'm Humphrey Bogart," he roared at the collected throng. "I'm carrying steel." When a heckler shouted, "Just read your poetry," he threatened to go down to him and lay him out.[50]

In 1981, the Italian director Marco Ferreri directed *Tales of Ordinary Madness*, an adaptation of some of his short stories. It was released by Fred Baker Films. Ben Gazzara played his alter ego. One of the stories dealt with a woman who had sex with a tiger. For a time, Ferreri considered filming it with a real tiger. When Gazzara met Bukowski, he was drinking wine.

"I'm really disappointed you've gone upscale, Buk," he said to him.

Bukowski replied, "Well, I made a little money. I thought I'd live well."[51]

At the premiere, however, he reverted to type. He sat at the back of the theatre, drinking from a bottle he had in a brown paper bag. He hated the film—the "pretty" Gazzara sickened him—and the drunken poet kept yelling derisive comments at the screen. Driving home later he was stopped by the police, whom he also baited. He was forced to lie face down on the road and was handcuffed. For Bukowski, this was the most enjoyable part of the night and much truer to his life than anything he had seen on screen a few hours earlier.

He married Beighle in 1985, dressing himself up in a suit for one of the few times in his life. John Martin was best man. Bukowski insisted he break the habits of a lifetime and have a glass of champagne for the occa-

Bukowski with Fred Baker on the set of *Tales of Ordinary Madness* (1983).

sion. Martin was so unaccustomed to alcohol he became dizzy after just one sip. Bukowski was amazed.

"I don't understand it," he exclaimed as if encountering a strange species of being, "How can you go your whole life without drinking?"

Martin replied with equal befuddlement, "How can you drink all your life?"[52]

Another metamorphosis was to come: Bukowski, the Hollywood star. His name reached a global audience after the filming of *Barfly* in 1987. He wrote the screenplay. The film wasn't so much a biography as ten years drinking microscoped into a few days. It was directed by his friend Barbet Schroeder and starred Mickey Rourke and Faye Dunaway. Dealing with a time when he cavorted with Jane from one seedy dive to another, it was a faithful enough adaptation of a walk on the wild side, even if Rourke was a mite too contrived, and Dunaway (as Jane) too dreamy and glamorous.

Bukowski appeared on set most days and was offered a cameo role as (what else?) a drinker sitting at a bar. He learned a lot about the movie world during the filming and went on to write a novel about it, which he simply called *Hollywood*. He hated it mostly.

There were some exceptions. He befriended Sean Penn at this time

Mickey Rourke getting down to some serious drinking as Bukowski in *Barfly* (1987).

and even let him accompany him to the track one day, a signal honor. He'd have liked Penn to play him in *Barfly*—he had offered to do the part for the proverbial dollar to keep costs down—but it didn't happen. Penn wanted his friend Dennis Hopper to direct the film, but this wasn't possible as it was Schroeder's pet project for years now, and neither did Bukowski like Hopper.[53]

He told Penn in 1987 that alcohol was one of the greatest things to arrive upon the earth "alongside of me." It was ultimately destructive to most people, he agreed, but not him: "I do all of my creative work when I'm intoxicated." It even helped him with women. "I've always been reticent in the love-making act so alcohol has allowed me, sexually, to be more free. It's a release because basically I'm a shy, withdrawn person. Alcohol allows me to be this hero, striding through space and time, doing all of these daring things."[54] It wasn't too unusual to hear drink being talked of as providing Dutch courage, but it *was* unusual for us to hear the catalyst applied to Bukowski, such an allegedly rugged soul.

His life after *Barfly* went on as before. He continued to abuse drink, but never quite saw himself as an alcoholic. Such terms were clichés and his whole life was a war against that. In *Women*, arguably his best novel, he wrote, "If something bad happens, you drink in an attempt to forget it: if something good happens, you drink in order to celebrate: and if nothing happens you drink to make something happen."⁵⁵ Later on he describes himself as a drinker who writes, as opposed to a writer who drinks.

When Henry Miller told him drink was killing his muse, he guffawed. The reality was that it was *summoning* it. If he stopped drinking he would also have stopped writing, he thought—and maybe even living. He'd read Tom Dardis's fascinating *The Thirsty Muse*, a book which investigated the negative aspects of the relationship between writing and drinking. He liked it but he refused to see himself in the same league as the writers Dardis dealt with in this respect, writers who suffered the most horrific hangovers and blackouts, who eventually felt unable to write with drink or without it.

Eugene O'Neill came across as especially pathetic in it, and Scott Fitzgerald wasn't far behind. The other two writers Dardis dealt with were Faulkner and Hemingway, both of them raving alcoholics but somehow able to contain themselves for creative splurges. That, in a nutshell, was the dividing line for Bukowski. It wasn't the damage you did to your body that counted, but whether you could get up the next morning—or evening—to hammer out another novel or poem. Hemingway could because he was such a giant of a man; Faulkner, also, seemed to have miraculous recuperative powers, but Fitzgerald eventually reached a point where alcohol was consuming him rather than the other way around; O'Neill, too, was like that, as we saw, before he gave it up.

No matter what condition Bukowski was in he seemed to be able to get something down on paper. Basically he saw himself as a two-and-a-half bottles of wine kind of writer. The poems written on the third one probably wouldn't have been up to scratch. But that still wasn't bad compared to the writers Dardis studied.

For Bukowski, the destruction of the body was almost worth it for the preservation of one's sanity. Everything had its price. Sobriety exacted a bigger one for this man. Drink saved him from insanity. "I feel perfectly normal," he told Fernanda Pivano, "in my own mad way."⁵⁶ Like Hamlet, he might have said, "I am mad but north by northwest."⁵⁷ Such madness was built into his routines rather than being something that was imposed on it, so he had to be a bit mad to fit into it.

His life would take one more turn towards its end because he contracted tuberculosis in 1988 and went on the dry. He could never have done this without the disease. The point is that drink sickened him now because of the number of antibiotics he was on. "I didn't feel like lifting a bottle," he admitted. "It wasn't a great sacrifice."⁵⁸

Time was closing in on him now, making him think about the big questions: God, eternity, what it was all about. How had he lived this long? He didn't know, but he still wanted to hang on. His ambition was to see in the new millennium. He would have been eighty then.

At seventy, he said, he'd drunk more alcohol than most people had water. More importantly, he was still around. Many of the doctors who told him he was killing himself were dead. He'd supped with the devil, using a short spoon, and survived. Because fame came later, he never grew bored with it. In a way his burnout was in his pre-fame days. One might even say he destroyed himself before he was created. He lived two lives in one, moving from self-destructiveness to a new kind of self-knowledge.

The Irish rock singer Bono from U2 was a great fan of his writing and the band dedicated one of their concerts to him in 1993. Bukowski attended it with Beighle, but it meant little to him. He thought rock singers like Bono pretended to threaten the establishment but behind the rebellious façade they were just millionaires who buttressed the system that created them. He got drunk at the concert and after it was over had to be carried home, collapsing finally on the front steps of his house.

He died in 1994. As a young man he didn't think he'd see thirty but as things worked out he lived to the relatively ripe old age of seventy-three. The gods had smiled on a man his friend Harold Norse once referred to as a "bastard angel."[59]

Buddhist monks conducted the funeral service, which was a subdued affair attended only by close friends. The man who had created minor explosions everywhere he went, bowed out quietly, gone off to whatever hunting ground was reserved for deranged—and very thirsty—poets.

Anne Sexton

(1928–1974)

Sexton was born Anne Gray Harvey in Newton, Massachusetts. She once gave this account of her early days:

> I was the third and last daughter. As a young child I was locked in my room until the age of five. After that, at school, I did not understand the people who were my size or even the larger ones. At home or away from it people seemed out of reach. Thus I hid in fairy tales and read them daily like a prayer book. Any book was closer than a person. I did not even like my dolls because they resembled people. I stepped on their faces because they resembled me.[1]

Here we see the beginning of her escapism, if not her ability to like herself.

She was a needy child, but her needs weren't catered to by either of her parents. Her mother was too absorbed in her own personality to attend properly to her. "She always wanted top billing," was her daughter's way of putting it.[2] She had a strong emotional bond to her great-aunt, "Nana," and was devastated when she died.

There's a possibility her father sexually molested her when he was in his cups. She remembered him doing so, and wrote about such a memory. Was her memory reliable? She left herself open to this charge, saying once, "It doesn't matter who my father was; it matters who I remember he was."[3]

Alcohol was an endemic part of her youth: "My mother drank two drinks every noon and three drinks every night come hell or high water.... She would stand at the sink and—slosh—pour the whiskey right down."[4] Her father was a bigger drinker, but a more secretive one. Sexton was glad to carry on the family tradition: "I still have the glasses they had in the twenties." Replenishing these glasses, she saw as "justice."[5] Her parents drank themselves into stupors and she felt validated to do likewise. "My father was fat on Scotch," she wrote. "It leaked from every orifice."[6]

His personality changed with drink: "He would suddenly become very mean, as if he hated the world. He would sit and look at you as though you had committed some terrible crime."[7] At such times he picked on her for trivial things, like the fact that she had acne. This was something that made him not want to sit at the same table as her. Such abuse left an indelible mark.

She married Alfred Sexton in 1948. From childhood he'd been nicknamed Kayo, after a cartoon character. The name stuck. He dropped out of medical school to become a salesman in a woolen firm after they were married. The Korean War broke out two years later. He joined the Naval Reserves to avoid being drafted.[8]

She had two children. Linda was born in 1953, and Joy, two years later. Both daughters caused her stress, partly due to the fact that she wasn't ready to be a mother when she had them. She had too many needs herself. "I want to be a child and not a mother," she said, "and I feel guilty about this."[9]

Her vulnerability helped her to become a writer but it also stopped her from being an "apron and cookies" type of mom.[10] Linda would go on to decry such a dull stereotype in later years, writing about "the women on our block who sold pies at church socials and brought cupcakes to school for their children's birthdays; the women who wore housedresses and aprons instead of sleek pantsuits; the women who belonged to weekly bridge groups or ran the PTA; the women who

Like William Faulkner, Sexton came from a long line of alcoholics. Like John Cheever, she was able to live a double life with her demons for many years. And like John Berryman, she eventually took herself out of her misery with a kind of ritualized suicide (*Writer Pictures*).

squirreled away 'pin money' for the ice cream truck that clanged down the street on summer nights."[11]

Linda was going through the "terrible twos" when Joy was born. This fact, combined with post-natal depression, led to a nervous breakdown. For a time, it was believed she was schizophrenic. This prognosis was later changed to depression.

Her frayed nerves meant she couldn't be a full-time mother to her children, so Linda and Joy were relegated to the care of their grandmothers instead. Sexton didn't get on with Billie, Kayo's mother. The girls were shuttled between the two women and this caused tension for everyone. Billie was bewildered by Sexton's moods. She got a shock one day shortly into the marriage when she asked her to go out and buy a bottle of milk. Sexton refused point blank, throwing herself on the floor and beating her fists against it in a rage. Linda commuted between the two houses but, for 1957 and half of 1958, Joy stayed with Billie and her husband, George.

On the day before her twenty-eighth birthday, when Kayo was away, Sexton felt she couldn't cope with life anymore and took an overdose of Nembutal. She then panicked and phoned Billie. She underwent a stomach pump and survived, but the incident had ramifications. Her problem had taken on a public dimension. She had crossed a line. From then until the end of her life, she would be seen more as a patient than a mother or wife.

The situation with Billie worsened afterward. She became addled with her, accusing her of trying to usurp Joy's affections. Billie, for her part, saw Sexton as an unfit mother she was bailing out. Tempers flared. Sexton felt undermined, but she knew she had to put up with the unique situation.

Sexton's personality clashed with Billie's. She didn't strike Billie as a homemaker. She slept in late every morning. She liked to talk rather than perform domestic chores. She smoked and drank like a man. And she wrote.

She felt out of her depth in her marital environment, which served as a catalyst to her drinking. She consulted a psychotherapist, Martha Brunner-Orne, to try and alleviate this behavior. Orne had already treated her father—and his sister—for alcoholism.

When Brunner-Orne went on holiday in 1956, Sexton was seen instead by her son Martin, who was a therapist. He put her on a course of anti-depressants. She enjoyed talking to him. She opened up to him in a way she couldn't to her husband. She even joked with him, telling him she thought the job she was best suited to in life was that of a prostitute. She said she'd already practiced this trade by picking up men in parking lots. When she said she also liked writing, Orne suggested this might be a slightly better option than prostitution.[12]

She set to the task with great determination and, by the end of the year, had managed to compose no less than sixty sonnets. She loved showing these to Orne. He became a father figure in the absence of an actual one. Each week she looked forward to presenting him with her latest composition. Her writing was personal and intimate, sometimes too intimate. She set no bounds on what she wrote about, especially in the sexual sphere. She wrote poems that, as she put it, "want to tear their way out of my soul and on to the typewriter keys."[13]

Before she started writing poetry, she was living a comfortable life. She had financial security, a man who loved her, and two daughters. But she felt dead inside. The pressure to conform to what society expected of her made her feel mummified. One could even have taken that term literally. To be a mummy (i.e., a mother) was to be a mummy, i.e., a corpse. If her life was a fairy tale, everything had to be turned back to front to interpret it. The magic castle—in other words, the financial security—was her hell. Getting out of it to trawl humanity's dark underbelly was liberation.

At the age of twenty-nine she realized she could put words together to document her pain. "One can't build little white picket fences," she said, "to keep nightmares out."[14] Dr. Orne was the prince in the fairy tale. She referred to it all as her "rebirth."[15]

She had a catharsis. Her literary muse became her second analyst. It was like a voice speaking to her. Sometimes the poems wrote her instead of her writing them. They gave her legitimacy beyond the picket fence. She was like Ibsen's Nora, breaking out of the doll's house—only she used a pen instead of a gun.

Words held the key to an inner truth. Sometimes she played with them, inverting and subverting them. If she turned the word "rats" back to front, for instance, she got "star." The inversion of "evil" was "live." (One of her collections was called *No Evil Star*. Turned back to front this reads, "Rats live on.") The magic of words released her from captivity. With them she became "a secret beatnik hiding in the suburbs in my square house on a dull street."[16] The poems knew things that she didn't know herself.

By mid-1958 the antidepressants she was taking managed to kick in and she felt able to take Joy back from Billie and George. Her poetic career was also taking off now. But the home tensions went on. Kayo didn't really approve of her new role as poet *extraordinaire* and let her know this in no uncertain terms.

She became friendly with Sylvia Plath that year. They started drinking together, usually in Sexton's car. She used to park in a loading bay outside a hotel. "It's okay," she'd joke to the doorman, "because we're going in to get loaded!"[17]

Drink was a comfort blanket to her. It was her savior, not something to be feared. Sobriety, it turned out, was where insecurity lay.

Linda remembered the drinking routines when she was growing up: "Joy and I would be banished during the cocktail hour while Daddy and Mother absorbed their martinis. By the time dinner was served at eight or nine o'clock they would be sloshed." Food came a poor second to booze. "Mum would gag down a drumstick. She was hardly able to swallow anything solid. She'd often get up from the table and vomit her food."[18]

Alcohol took over the household. The first thing Kayo did after coming home from work was open the liquor cabinet. He mixed martinis "as if he were conducting a symphony." He taught Linda to do likewise before she was twelve. When Sexton partook, the cocktail hour ran into two or three hours. The evenings usually began peaceably enough but as they went on, the arguments began. Voices were raised and nasty things said. Linda and Joy would sit on the staircase, watching the nightly drama unfold as they gazed, transfixed, through the wooden bars. If Sexton annoyed Kayo enough, he might even punch her in the face. At this point the daughters would leave their vantage point on the stairs and try to pull him away from her. Once or twice the police were called. She didn't press charges and things returned to normal—if anything could be called normal in this house. Kayo applied cold compresses to her wounds as if he had no part in their administration. A hurricane had swept through the house "and when it moved out, he simply went to bundle up the branches and rake the leaves."[19]

All this friction makes it hard to understand the fact that Sexton experienced severe separation anxiety any time Kayo was away from home. She went stir crazy in the empty house, combining bursts of cleaning with attempts at reading: "I twirl my hair until it's a mass [of] snarls—then as I pass a mirror I see myself and comb it again."[20]

After he returned, her turmoil failed to abate. She was in and out of the hospital for treatment, almost as a matter of course. Many people thought she was going crazy but Sexton didn't see it like that. Her breakdowns, for her, were tunnels into a different kind of light.

In 1959, she became fascinated with the poetry of James Wright. She wrote to him to praise him for his latest book, *Saint Judas*, and the two became good friends. As time went on, they wrote each other a staggering number of letters. Wright advised her how best to progress her career from where it was. They became lovers in the summer of 1960.

Her poetic career started to take off in earnest now. After her first book was published in 1960, she was appointed a Scholar at the Radcliffe Institute for Independent Study, where she taught poetry. When her second book came out she won the first Traveling Fellowship of the American Academy of Arts and Letters. She also began to lecture and run workshops.

She didn't believe poetry could be taught. What she did in her lectures on the craft was to act it out with her students, using them as guinea pigs for her to revisit the muse's shrine. Her colleague Eric Edwards said she was wonderful to be with when she was sober—and even when she wasn't. "It was as if she would take you down into hell with her."[21]

"I wobble on a drunken sea," Sexton declared, "crawling between pebbles and slow fish, never knowing if anyone will like my poems."[22]

She threw her heart across the page, drawing on imagery that sometimes appeared surreal as she dug up the terrors of her subconscious for similarly pained souls to savor and empathize. She was a poet to be read at three in the morning over Scotch, neat.

Billie didn't like Sexton's confessional poetry, believing it disgraced the family. She came from an era where one suffered in private, not in the full glare of the public, even the poetry-loving public. She believed Sexton traded off the kindness of strangers and milked her afflictions for fame and fortune. This wasn't true, but it's understandable how she might have felt this way considering she was so generous with her time in helping to raise Linda and Joy. "Why isn't it enough to be a wife and mother?" she asked her daughter-in-law.[23]

Her louche lifestyle was light years away from that of Billie. She had hippie-style ideas of free love. She engaged in multiple affairs with both men and women, flirting outrageously with them in front of Kayo. She even asked him to parade about the house naked so Linda and Joy would know what a penis looked like.

Kayo became increasingly dismissive of his wife as her absorption in the world of poetry became more intense. Drinking became a different kind of absorption. It wasn't only an escape; it was a friend as well. When her husband didn't understand her, a martini did. A martini never argued with you. It didn't tell you you were selfish or a bad mother. It never told you to stop going to lectures or to stop writing poetry.

He told her she was unreasonable. She said that was how she functioned, that was where the magic came from. But the pills she was taking meant she could only work sporadically. "Every letter, every syllable, is a strain. I feel botched up."[24]

Feeling abnormal was her normality. She treasured what she deemed to be her perversions, strip-mining them into the motherlode of her work. Her addictive personality made her as locked into poetry as she was into drink, pills, therapy. "I act rather well for someone who's crazy," she declared.[25]

She found another poetic mentor in the writer Anthony Hecht, whom she befriended after a trip to New York. Hecht was recently separated. Sexton was attracted to him and let this be known. Unfortunately for her, he was not receptive to her advances. He stayed friends with her, but he wasn't interested in having an affair with a married woman.[26]

Sexton's sexual tension was palpable. "The aura of this thing is more strong than alcohol," she said. "Ever since my mother died I want to have the feeling someone's in love with me." It was like a narcotic.[27] But their relationship remained platonic. In a way she was relieved. Lust was inadequate, she averred, but love exhausted her.[28]

Ernest Hemingway committed suicide in 1961. The event both shocked and fascinated her. She'd always been fascinated by suicide. Now America's foremost scribe had done the deed. Might she one day emulate him? She couldn't envisage herself putting a gun in her mouth. Shortly afterward she took an overdose of Nembutal. Again, she survived. After she recovered she admitted it was an exercise in attention grabbing. She had a new collection on the way. How could she have died, she asked, with a book coming out? She called it *All My Pretty Ones*. It was well received.

"Poetry led me by the hand out of madness," she said.[29] But it was leading her into another kind of madness, that of the demented lush. She wrote to Dennis Farrell in 1962:

> I drink quite a bit. I'm not an alcoholic but I seem to rely on drinking too much (my Dr. says). I drink three martinis before dinner. That's really all. I might have a beer with lunch, when I remember to eat lunch. The time I actually drink too much is when I go away to give a reading at a college. Then I drink secretly in my hotel room for I am afraid to meet people, afraid of the deans and instructors etc. and determined to impress them.... If you should meet me I would seem like an extrovert (but I would be so afraid to meet you that I would have four martinis first and that's where the extrovert comes from).[30]

Her comments are interesting not only for the denial of alcoholism but also the drip-feed of information, the casual insertion of the beer, and the increase of the martinis from three to four because of the extenuating circumstances of the readings.

When Sylvia Plath killed herself in 1963, she felt a sense of deprivation. This was different than Hemingway. She knew Plath. The event became worldwide news, and Sexton felt strangely envious. Like her mother, she wanted "top billing." Suicide was one way of achieving that. "She took something that was mine," she snorted with some bitterness. Plath "had the suicide inside her," she told a friend, "as I do. As many of us do. If we're lucky we don't get away with it and something or someone forces us to live."[31]

Marilyn Monroe was another tragic figure who excited her. When she read Arthur Miller's *After the Fall* in 1964, she felt a kinship with Monroe, seeing in her a mirror image of her own anxieties. Shortly afterward she wrote one of her most famous poems, "Waiting to Die," a kind of ode to suicide. She told her friend Anne Clarke that year, "I am becoming a drunk. Not an alcoholic but a drunk."[32]

Dr. Orne put her on Thorazine in the mid-'60s. It was a pill that stabilized her moods. Did she want this? Sometimes. One day she forgot to take it and went cavorting around New York in a state of high good humor, eventually treating herself to the purchase of a four-foot-high stuffed dog.[33] "She laughs at me all the time," she said, "I also laugh."[34] The withdrawal made her elated: "If I can pick, I [will] pick this illness (if it is one)."[35] A side effect of Thorazine was that it made the skin sensitive to sunlight. Sexton came off it to get a suntan one time. She was always engaged in this juggling act between wanting to be well and wanting to be herself.

When she was well, she was a brilliant mother to her children. She played with them at their own level, at times appearing more like an overgrown sister than a mother. But then her career intervened, or her work, or she had an affair, and the distance between them grew again. She became a stranger to them—and to herself.

She loved her children but her maternal instinct didn't extend to wishing to be interrupted by them "every few minutes" when she was writing.[36] It disturbed her when they became needy. Most mothers would have enjoyed catering to such needs, but she regarded them as irritants.

Linda and Joy would come to her room, she said, and "break right into a poem" as they told her their problems: "She hit me. She pinched me."[37] To free herself from them, she used to sit them in front of the TV, using it as a kind of babysitter. Afterward she would begin to feel guilty for her negligence and try to over-compensate by extra bonding. They never knew where they stood in this constant seesaw of love and its withdrawal. When drink was involved, as it often was, such a seesaw became more problematic.

Linda used to serve her mother an iced martini with an olive in it when she was working.[38] Often, Sexton wouldn't even acknowledge this, immersed as she was in her work. One night, however, Linda came in without warning and startled her. She leapt from her chair with the fright and started screaming. Linda jumped, too, and then they both started to laugh. It was a rare moment of levity in a strained relationship.

Her therapist tried to alleviate such strains. She often went into trance-like states in therapy. During such trances, another personality would emerge: She called her "Elizabeth." At such times she felt she was regressing back to her childhood, even pre-birth. She also went into these states when she was writing poetry. In both instances, another identity seemed to take her over. If she was a woman possessed—as she often appeared to be—therapy and poetry seemed to be the twin mechanisms to exorcise her demons. Perhaps that's why so much of her writing reads like an emotional striptease.

It can't have been much fun for Linda or Joy growing up in such an environment. Some of the first words in Linda's vocabulary were "martini," "ambulance," "therapy." Sexton's moodswings were a daily occurrence. But then she'd rally, usually when a lecture or reading was imminent.

At her readings she captivated Boston's literati with her devastating insights and creative flair. None of these people knew what she was like to live with, however. Nor did they know she was an alcoholic.

The public face of Sexton was that of a feminist extrovert. She even had her own rock band, Her Kind, which put her poetry to music. In time she became a performance artist herself, a woman who was like the literary equivalent of Judy Garland, belting out lyrics to the throngs who came to listen to her in the same way as Garland belted out songs—both needing the stimulant of liquor to work up the requisite adrenaline.

In 1966, there was another suicide attempt. Again it preceded the publication of a book. This one was called, significantly, *Live or Die*. (It would win her the Pulitzer Prize the following year.) She went on a reading tour that year, which took in colleges in Pennsylvania, Maryland, and Virginia. The last of these was a dry state, which posed a problem. (One of the conditions of her going there was to make it at least "semi-wet" for her.)

The first thing she did when she got to a hotel room before a reading was search out the ice machine. She would chill the multiple cases of vodka she had brought with her in her suitcase. She usually carried martinis in a Thermos when she was traveling. At home she was more partial to "stingers," i.e., brandy and crème de menthe. She needed extra "juice" in her tank to put her in the mood for a reading. She was aware she turned into a "ham" sometimes as a result, but she was willing to put up with this—anything for her audience.[39]

Linda often came home from school to see Sexton at the kitchen table, a cigarette in one hand—she was a self-confessed "three pack a dayer"[40]—and a stinger in the other. She would then start to read, asking Linda for her views on her latest poem "She loved Linda." But in another mood she would say Joy was her favorite daughter. Joy was a social butterfly. She didn't spend as much time in the house as the more introverted Linda did. That meant she wasn't as influenced by Sexton as Linda was.

Some days Linda would find her mother crying at the table, for no apparent reason. Sexton would run her hands through Linda's hair and ask "Stringbean" (her nickname) to cuddle her. At these times there was a role reversal. Mother was daughter and daughter was mother. Linda never knew what to expect. Who was her mother? America's most lauded confessional poet or a lonely woman crying out for a hug?

Sexton treated Linda like an adult long before she was one. She gave graphic accounts of her periods to her and also discussed subjects like masturbation with her, and what lesbians did in bed. She also touched her inappropriately in sexual areas under the guise of "sex education." This caused Linda immense psychological trauma, which necessitated her having her own therapist as she grew into adolescence. When she told the therapist what was going on she was strongly advised to get away from her mother's clutches, something that outraged Sexton when Linda told her.

If Linda wasn't available to comfort her, Sexton would sometimes run to the other people in her network of acquaintances for succor. Barbara Schwartz, a psychiatric social worker, gave her permission to call her at any hour of the night. She used to sing lullabies to her, and give the repeated assurance of "Anne, you are a good girl," just as Kayo had done when they were first married.[41]

The distance between Linda and Sexton grew as each became more involved with their respective therapists. It broke Sexton's heart to have to keep Linda at arm's length afterward. Sexton knew she had to stop leaning on Linda when she was afraid: "Somehow I must push you away so that you can stand straight and alone and firm and happy."[42] The pain she felt at doing this was akin to what she felt when Nana had died, all those years ago.[43]

Even at arm's length, Linda had a ringside view of her mother's decline. She watched her "slumped at the kitchen table in her coffee-stained bathrobe, her hair tangled from her fingers as they twirled endless knots, her eyes empty."[44] One of the reasons they were empty was because of all the pills she was taking. They were her salvation, the little pellets that would ease her path to eternity—or the lack of it. "Whoever God is," she said, "I keep making telephone calls to Him. I'm not sure that's religion."[45]

In 1969, she wrote an autobiographical play called *Mercy Street*. This was staged Off Broadway. The title was a metaphor she liked to use for a safe haven, the kind of happiness she got from alcohol. "I don't drink martinis anymore," she said that year, but rather "Jack Daniels, Canadian Club or rotgut bourbon. Time passes.... I smoke more and I cough more. I am size 14–16 ... big belly."[46]

Her Smith Corona continued to be her best friend. Sitting in front of it minting sentences from the chaos of her brain made her feel connected with her higher self. Her lower self, meanwhile, sought oblivion. She was afraid to die and yet longed, like some latter day Keats, to "cease upon the midnight with no pain." Her ideal would have been to just die in her mind: "Let the heart-soul shrink like a prune and only to the typewriter let out the truth. That alone deserved it."[47]

Sexton was now drinking all day long, with predictable results: "Alcohol helped generate the curves of feeling on which her poetry lifted its wings but it dropped her into depression, remorse, sleeplessness, paranoia—the normal host of furies that pursue alcoholics."[48] It also deprived her of her talent for editing, the ability to know when she'd written too much, or not enough. "She had the drunk's fluency but not the artist's cunning."[49]

When Linda went to Harvard, Sexton arranged to do a reading there. She wanted Linda to attend it, but Linda begged off, terrified that she'd drink too much and embarrass her in front of her friends:

> I felt unable to deal with Mother in one of her frantic pre-reading states, drinking heavily to escape her anxiety, somewhat hysterical and always on the verge of last-minute collapse. I was done being a nursemaid.[50]

"Linda is just like me," Sexton countered, "which makes me alternately adore and loathe her, depending on which me she seems like (good Anne or bad Anne)."[51] Before another reading—one she did attend—Linda had to witness Sexton being too inebriated to get out of the bathtub. She eventually prevailed upon her to do so, afterward dragging her back to the cheap motel where they were staying, her head lolling on her shoulder.[52]

Kayo wondered where the girl he had married had disappeared to. He knew her literary friends still saw that girl, because she appeared happy when she was discussing poetry with them, but they didn't know what it was like to live with a genius. When he was in the presence of such people he felt at a loss, unable to speak with them on their own terms. Like his wife, many of them may have looked down on him as being just a businessman. Or, when she had readings in the house, a bartender. Sexton was glad he didn't really like poetry. It suited her to have the two sides of her life separate.[53]

One Saturday afternoon she was due to meet her friend Maxine Kumin, another poet, to attend a workshop together. She was going to be away for the whole day, with Billie relegated to child-minding chores as usual. Kayo felt this was unfair. "It's an indulgence," he fumed, "just like all those hours with a psychiatrist are an indulgence. You can't expect my mother to take care of the kids all week long because you're too sick, and then make a miraculous recovery on the weekend when there's something you feel like doing."[54]

He was hitting her at a weak spot here. She retaliated, calling him "a little old maid" who knew nothing about her other life.[55] She then grabbed her typewriter and flung it at the wall. A tussle ensued in which Kayo struck her on the jaw with his fist. A part of her enjoyed this. "Come on," she said, "Do it right." He was astounded, and even more so when she started hitting *herself*. "Kill me," she sobbed. "Please just kill me." She then said, "You win. I won't go to Dr. Orne. I won't go to lunch. I won't write anymore."[56] The incident showed the huge distance that had grown between them as well as the manner in which she liked to dramatize her circumstances.

Dr. Orne felt she used Kayo as a weapon to beat herself. She didn't like herself and needed someone to punish her for being a "bad girl," so she chose him.

Kayo feared Dr. Orne was taking his wife away from him; he asked her to stop the therapy. Sexton likely felt that she'd break down again if she stayed away from him. It was as if he was a gun she held over Kayo's head, sabotaging the stability of the marriage—which was always going to be tenuous anyway because of his inability to appreciate her poetry.

Kayo wasn't a New Man. He didn't like discussing the parabolas of their relationship. Sexton felt she was not reaching him when she told him their marriage was in trouble. She felt he didn't want to hear it, that he was in denial. At this point they weren't sleeping together. (This frustrated Sexton more than Kayo, as she was more highly sexed than he).

They started to drink—and argue—more. When alcohol loosened their tongues, mutual abuse was never far away. The blame game began. Who was responsible for all the things that went wrong? Who defaulted?

One word borrowed another. Occasionally, they ended up wrestling on the floor as they launched physical and verbal assaults at each other.

One day, Sexton told Kayo she was leaving him. Despite all the arguments leading up to this moment, he was shocked. Sexton, on the contrary, was elated and full of bravado. She told him she was going to better things, better men. She went off her Thorazine as if to usher in her new clean life. She was so high on the plan that her hands shook. She didn't realize that she was experiencing withdrawal symptoms from the Thorazine.

By now her fame had made her into something of a diva. "She demanded a particular seat on an airplane," Linda declared, "or in a restaurant. When dining out she ordered the most expensive items on the menu and often sent them back."[57] To sign books after a reading she required a particular brand of pen. One night she lit a $100 bill with her cigarette lighter just because she felt like it.[58]

She also conducted lesbian affairs, sometimes in her own house. And she was drinking more, "from rising to sleeping."[59] She attempted to "self-medicate her depression by imbibing round the clock."[60]

Life without Kayo was a novelty for a time. She enjoyed her identity as a woman about town, soaking up the blandishments of her admirers. But soon the allure wore off. When her old demons re-surfaced she was back to the gloomy midnight suicide calls again. She became demanding with her old friends, expecting them to pander to her every whim. When they didn't, she sought out new ones.

She told Kayo he didn't understand her but often she didn't even understand herself. Poetry may have saved her in the late '50s, but it also took away her secure domestic environment. Her mistake was in thinking she could survive outside that environment. The pen may have been mightier than the sword, but, in Sexton's case, it *was* the sword.

Kayo had provided the base for her to soar. Without that base she was flying blind. She was a poet without a life to underscore the words. She stopped eating. She became cripplingly lonely. Her dark poems of this period reflected a damaged heart.

She started to worry about money now. Though earning a significant amount from readings and teaching fees—not to mention royalties—she spent it lavishly on food, wine, clothes. In letters, she told people she was funding her daughters' education, which was untrue. She also lied to one of her doctors, Dr. Chase, about her financial situation to persuade him to reduce his fees. When he learned the truth, he was outraged.[61]

There was no other man in Sexton's life when she threw Kayo out. This left her exposed to what she called the "madness" of middle-aged dating.⁶² It may have sounded adventurous when she first considered it but when she experienced it head-on she regretted what she had so cavalierly given up.

She confided her regrets to Linda, coming to the conclusion that while her marriage may not have been perfect, it beat loneliness hands down. "A little love is better than no love at all," she pined.⁶³

Her about-face angered Linda, who had done her best to persuade her to stay with Kayo. "Too late now," she reprimanded.⁶⁴

Kayo was with a new woman at this point. That hurt, too.

Sexton wanted Linda to testify in a court hearing that Kayo beat her frequently. Linda was unwilling to do this, reminding her mother that he only did so under severe provocation. Sexton then accused Linda of siding with him.⁶⁵

Linda didn't see it that way. She wanted to paint a true picture of a relationship where nobody was the bad guy. They were just two troubled souls trying to work through difficult circumstances. Linda had almost totally drawn herself away from Sexton by this stage. She had even stopped taking her calls.

Sexton's weight dropped to below 110 pounds. An attempt to get back with Kayo failed. (This, after employing a bodyguard to protect her from him.) In desperation, she joined a computer-dating agency. That didn't work out either.

She had become almost totally alienated from her family and friends. She preferred talking to strangers, people who had no history with her, no significant connection point. No doubt feeling that she was nearing the end of the road, she took religious instruction at an Episcopalian Divinity School. She thought of death as a comfort rather than something to be feared. It was a lush embrace, a sinking into the "great mother arms" she never had.⁶⁶

In the fall of 1974 she found a drinking friend in John Cheever, who was a writing tutor with her at Boston University that year. They behaved more like mischievous students than faculty members, encouraging each other to do childish things. She stuffed her handbag with airline liquor samples to tide her through dreary departmental meetings and shared these with him.⁶⁷

Cheever originally found Sexton aggressive, but their common addiction—and the fact that they were both running away from their families— brought them together.⁶⁸ She spiked his coffee with vodka and a friendship was born, a friendship based on "licensed" premises.⁶⁹

Art had become much more important than life for her now. She wrote to her friend Richard McAdoo: "I fear I sounded a bit drunk on the phone.... I suppose in certain ways I'm cracking up, but don't let anyone know, because until the poems crack, it's all okay."[70]

But the poems *did* crack. Their quality wasn't what it once was. When she realized this, it made her feel even worse. If she couldn't write there was no point in living. It was writing, after all, which had brought her back to life when she was "dead" in 1955.

At one time she imagined her success at writing derailed her death wish. She now realized it had merely postponed it. Suicide wasn't just an escape for her: It was an ambition. By now she was suffering from panic attacks, malnutrition, insomnia. The woman who had so admired Arthur Miller's *After the Fall* shared Marilyn Monroe's fear of going mad, of ending up in a psychiatric institution.

On October 3, 1974, she gave a poetry reading at Goucher College. She seemed upbeat. Afterward she went to a workshop at the university. Nobody noticed anything untoward about her. The next day she had a visit from her friend Louise Conant and they had breakfast together. Afterward she went for her regular therapy with Barbara Schwartz. It was nine months to the day since her first session, a detail that wasn't lost on her. She saw Schwartz as a kind of spiritual midwife. Nine months ago she had implanted a seed in her; now it was seeing the light of day.[71]

She had lunch with Maxine Kumin. They discussed the galleys of a forthcoming book. "We had a wonderfully gay and silly lunch together," Kumin recalled, "and I remember thinking how much better she seemed."[72] After they parted, she drove home. When she reached her house she poured herself a glass of vodka. Then she took all the rings that were on her fingers and placed them in her purse.

She was happy, happy because she'd made up her mind how her life would end. The pain wouldn't be there for much longer.[73] She put on her mother's fur coat and went out to her garage. She had the glass of vodka in her hand. She closed the doors and sat into her bright red Cougar. She turned on the ignition and sipped her drink. Autumn light streamed through the windows as the fumes engulfed her.

This wasn't, like some of her previous suicide attempts, one that would leave anything to chance. It wasn't done in a moment of hysteria, rather a kind of elated tranquility. She knew it was right for her. She wouldn't have had the courage to put a gun to her temple, like Hemingway. This way was cleaner. It left no mess.

She died quickly. There was no suicide note. She'd already written a poem called "Suicide Note" years before on a paper napkin. She later typed it up and worked on it. "If it were a real suicide note," she joked, "there would have been [just] one draft."[74]

Nobody was too shocked when they heard the news, not even her family. Some people felt her demise was even overdue.

John Cheever boycotted her memorial service. He felt many of her problems were caused by the grim atmosphere in the university. He even threatened to resign from it after she died.[75]

Sexton had been envious of the celebrity status given to Sylvia Plath after her suicide. She'd seen it as a good career move. The casualness with which she approached her own death seems to underline the fact that she wanted to emulate Plath. But this didn't happen. Posterity would view her as just another tragic poet haunted by confused ambitions.

After Sexton died, Diane Wood Middlebrook wrote a revelatory biography of her. To help her in her task she was given access to private papers submitted by Linda and also tapes of many of her therapy sessions with Dr. Orne. Both Linda and Dr. Orne became objects of scorn for this. Orne was even cautioned by his superiors for breach of doctor-client confidentiality.

Linda went on to write books about her relationship with her mother. These books helped her work out her anger towards her for leaving her in the way she did, for not being there for her even when she was alive.

Like her mother, Linda suffered from depression for a long time. She went into therapy to try and deal with this. At her lowest points she attempted suicide, both by cutting her wrists and taking an overdose of pills. "My mother's suicide," she wrote, "solidified inside me like rebar under concrete."[76]

Joy believed that the moment their mother died, Linda began to "slide into her shoes."[77] Linda's son said he used to come home every day "not knowing if I was going to find you dead in your bed."[78] For a time Joy believed Linda exploited her mother's life—and death—for her own ends by writing about it in such painstaking detail. This led to years of alienation between them before they reached a tentative détente.

The legacy of dysfunction, then, continued from one generation to the next. But Linda came out the other end. When she did, it was with an added understanding of her mother. Sympathy became empathy, as was evidenced by her best-known book, *Searching for Mercy Street: My Journey Back to My Mother*.

It wasn't a *Mommie Dearest* style tome, though some sections of it— like her mentions of Sexton masturbating herself against her, or feeling her breasts, and even her vagina—crossed the boundaries of good taste in many people's minds. Linda said she depicted these scenes not to portray Sexton as a bad person but rather a tortured one, a woman who couldn't cope with the way her life had spiraled out of control. The book depicted her as a kind of masochist, an emotional wreck spinning on the edges of her damaged nerve ends in a vortex of alcohol.

Linda believed that if her mother had been born some years later, different pills like Prozac or Zoloft (which have since gone mainstream) might have helped her. This is debatable. Sexton's refusal to stop drinking while taking pills would have reduced the impact of these medications, however effective they may have otherwise been. (This happened towards the end of her life when she was put on lithium for a brief time.) We also have to face the fact that she regarded her topsy-turvy emotions as part of her. Being neurotic, she once said, was normal to her.

Her basic philosophy, quoting Saul Bellow, was, "Live or die, but don't poison everything."[79] She abided by this precept to the letter, except when it came to her health. In that respect, liquor proved to be the rotten apple in her self-styled Garden of Eden.

Raymond Carver

(1938–1988)

Many people hold with the theory that alcoholism is inherited from a parent, either through genetic or behavioral channels. Raymond Carver's father was a heavy, sporadic drinker. He didn't drink all the time but, when he did, he didn't know when, or how, to stop. He never hit his children when drunk, but his personality changed. Quite simply, he became another person.[1] Some of these qualities transmitted themselves to his son. Carver thought his drinking problem was largely caused by circumstance.

He became engaged to Maryann Burk when he was seventeen, marrying her two years later. Children arrived very soon in the marriage. Their daughter, Christine, was born within six months—Maryann had been pregnant while walking down the aisle. Carver wrote in a story once, "Wasn't *everybody* pregnant in those days?"[2] Their son, Vance, arrived a year later. Carver wasn't yet twenty and often complained that he'd become a father too soon. The new identity upset his equilibrium; nor was the routine of domesticity conducive to inspiration. It was the pram in the hallway syndrome.

Maryann was a bright girl who put her career on hold for him time and again when he was a struggling writer. She was a teacher for many years and also temped at everything from cocktail waitress to telephone sales person. She even sold encyclopedias door to door at one point. Carver had many casual jobs, too. At various times he worked as a janitor, a deliveryman, a library assistant and a sawmill laborer. He refused many academic posts over the years to concentrate on his writing.

No matter how many jobs they held, however, money continued to be a problem. Friends were generous to them, but there was always the threat of being removed from the various homes in which they lived due to an inability to pay the rent. There were also frequent threats of having the phone and the electricity cut off. Despite this, the couple seemed content to roll with the punches in the hope that, one day, Carver would make it with his writing. Maryann was content to sacrifice everything she had for a man she believed in dearly. Her priority was always Carver's scribbling with a pen.

"More than anything," she often said, "I wished I could go to college."[3] This, unfortunately, was out of the question, with two small babies to contend with and a full-time job. As the man of the house, Ray should come first, she believed. He was the one with the talent, the one destined to become a major author. Writers' wives, she knew, were only accorded secondary status. Uncharacteristically, she showed both sarcasm and anger in elaborating women's place in this arrangement:

> They worked so their husbands could write. They kept the children quiet. They edited and suggested and consoled their Great Men through years of rejection slips and meager income. When and if the good times arrived, they could only watch as superficial friends surrounded the newly acknowledged Great Man, eager to take him away to bigger and better things.

Carver had his first story published in 1961. Entitled "The Furious Seasons," it owed a debt to Faulkner in its style. Two years later he graduated from Humboldt State College in Arcata, California, with a B.A. In the mid-sixties he and Maryann moved to Sacramento. He worked as a night custodian at a hospital there, writing *Near Klamath*, his first book of poetry.

By this time, Maryann and he were arguing a great deal and engaging in prolific drinking sprees. Alcohol occupied a central part of every day. They drank to get drunk, having beer by day and wine at night, sometimes followed by cocktails. Christine likened her parents' marriage to a rudderless ship. There was nobody at the wheel. How could two deeply intelligent people throw their lives away on drink? It was unfathomable to her young mind. (In years to come, she would go on to have a drinking problem herself.)

Carver had a high tolerance for alcohol. Over time, he became physically and psychologically dependent on it. He used to say that there were really two people inside him: Good Ray and Bad Ray. The good one was sweet, wholesome, and unselfish. He didn't drink. The bad one was moody and cantankerous. He was selfish. He lied and cheated. He even hit Maryann when he was frustrated. He skipped writing assignments. He drove drunk and ordered his children around. And he wrote badly.

Carver openly admitted he couldn't write with a drink in his hand. Nothing good ever came of it. "I never so much as wrote a line worth a nickel when I was under the influence of alcohol."[4] Even still, he continued to do so. Meanwhile, the bills piled up. He filed for bankruptcy in 1967. It was one of the lowest points of his life, but he continued to write his way through it, determinedly submitting his stories to literary magazines.

As the years went on, more and more of them were accepted. When he got into *Esquire*, it was a benchmark. A man called Gordon Lish was one of the editors there. He struck up a significant relationship with Carver, advising him on ways to improve his work. Carver didn't always agree with his views but he went along with them because Lish was connected. He knew he could bring him where he needed to be. Maryann disapproved of some of his editing choices.

Carver almost destroyed himself with vodka before he became famous.

In 1967, his story "Will You Please Be Quiet, Please?" was included in a *Best American Short Stories* anthology. That made his name. Money started to come in, which made it possible for Maryann, at long last, to go to college.

Unfortunately, as their income increased, so did their drinking. There were beers in the daytime and wine at night as before, but added to this were an inordinate number of parties and book signings. Both usually tanked up for these occasions.

They drank much more than their non-bookish friends but didn't really notice—or didn't want to. It was as if literary folk had a license to drink more than others. According to Maryann: "Writers needed to drink. The muse wasn't going to bestow her favors on any teetotalling namby-pamby son-of-a-bitch excuse for a real man of talent."[5]

One day a teaching friend of Maryann's came up to her and said, "You might think about watching your drink[ing] a little bit. It seems as if you and Ray have really gotten into the fast lane. Just be careful, that's all. Do you realize that alcohol is a drug?"

A miffed Maryann replied, "No, it's perfectly legal. It's not like taking prescription narcotics or shooting dope in your arm, for God's sake."

But it was. The next morning Maryanne had a "monster" hangover as well as dehydration. She considered her friend's words. Carver was hungover as well. Had they cause for worry? "Come to think of it," she said to herself, "we both never stopped drinking until we were drunk."[6]

She graduated from San Jose State College in 1970. She had postponed this for so many years her accomplishment was all the sweeter now. At last she could get a job where she used her mind. She taught English at Los Altos High School from then until 1977. In 1971, Carver started teaching at the University of California, in Santa Cruz.

As already mentioned, he invited Charles Bukowski to read his work there in 1972. Bukowski was his hero. Carver knew he drank, but didn't realize how much. As things worked out, Bukowski's intake made Carver look like a teetotaler. Like Dylan Thomas, he seemed to take a special delight in disgracing himself at literary gatherings. It was a kind of inverted snobbery he practiced at prestigious locales, and Santa Cruz was no exception.

Bukowski was already drunk when Carver met him at the airport. At dinner he kept pawing Maryann. When it came time for the reading he discovered that he had forgotten his poems. He had to be given a copy of one of his books. As he read from it, he started to verbally abuse the students who had come to listen to him. This was standard behavior from Bukowski, but Carver wasn't accustomed to it. He saw his credibility with his superiors at the university slipping with "every syllable Bukowski growled."[7]

At a party afterward, Carver adopted an "If you can't beat 'em, join 'em" attitude. Bukowski started to drink more—and faster. It was as if he saw in him his worst self and rushed to embrace it. The two writers drank all night and continued into the next day. It was a minor miracle Carver managed to get Bukowski on a plane back to L.A. in one piece. This was Bad Ray, back with a vengeance.

Carver's marital problems started to worsen at this time. As well as arguing fiercely with Maryann, he also began an affair with a woman named Diane Cecily. He even told her his marriage to Maryann was over. This wasn't true, but Cecily chose to believe it.

Carver was drinking so heavily by now that he had lost any genuine sense of perspective about his life. He told people he drank because he couldn't choose between Maryann and Cecily. Maryann drank heavily at this time, too, perhaps to try and block out the fact that her husband was drifting away from her. The marriage stumbled onto very rocky ground. Maryann tried to keep the ship together as her husband drowned himself in drink and knocked out stories between—or during—binges. He crafted miniaturist tableaus about domestic disharmony that mirrored his own circumstances. Such tableaus were captured to perfection in Robert Altman's 1993 film *Short Cuts*, which merged a number of them. Maryann marveled at their genius while simultaneously weeping at the craziness that inspired them.

She served cocktails to earn extra income. At home, meanwhile, her husband emptied their own private supply of liquor. He wrote thumbnail sketches that would become iconic emblems of *anomie* as she worked the red-eye shifts. She tried to juggle the demands of work and home as he drew inspiration from the pedantic parameters of his life, a life that was both feeding his muse and destroying his body.

He sought escape from Maryann—and from himself—in alcohol. He went off it now and again, but only for short periods. He loved Maryann, at least in his way, but when "Mr. Whiskey" arrived, such love came to an abrupt end, because Mr. Whiskey always brought Bad Ray with him.

Maryann took a graduate course in English literature at Stanford University in 1972. One day she came home in a brown wool miniskirt and

Matthew Modine and Julianne Moore in *Short Cuts* (1993), Robert Altman's melange of Carver's stories concerning a cross-section of people in Southern California living lives of quiet—and sometimes vocal—desperation.

found him sitting in the living room, "drunk as usual." He told her she looked sexy. "Maybe we could just step into the bedroom," he suggested.

At that moment all the frustrations of the previous months seemed to collide in her mind. "I want a divorce," she said, the words coming out almost without her being aware of having said them. "I can't live in this limbo."

Carver started to cry. "Please, please," he begged her, "don't leave me. Just bear with me and help me get through this. You are my real lady. You are my wife." She was so touched by his words she told him she'd give him another chance. When the kids came home from school that day they all sat at dinner together, clinging to the illusion of being a happy family "for one more evening."[8]

The next morning, however, the chaos began again. She went into the bathroom and found him breakfasting on vodka. She said, "Ray, you are going to have to leave and let us settle down and get some peace of mind."[9] When she saw he wasn't taking her seriously she went out to the kitchen and got a butcher knife. She had no intention of using it. She just wanted to let him know she meant business. He panicked when he saw it and lunged at her. She dropped the knife. He grabbed her around the waist from behind and rammed her head against the wall, cracking her skull. Christine (who was too young to have a driver's license) drove her to the hospital. She was lucky her injuries weren't serious. So was Carver.

She forgave him, as she always did, and life returned to semi-normality. Shortly afterward, he told her he loved her so much he would die for her. "That's what I'm afraid of," she said, "with all this drinking." It was now a round-the-clock preoccupation with him. "You're slowly committing suicide," she said. "I want you alive."

Carver then said, "Whatever you do, don't find someone else."[10] (This was ironic, considering *he* was the one with "someone else." He wanted to keep both Maryann *and* Diane Cecily.)

When Maryann started to drink less, Carver didn't drink with her anymore. It was more fun, he discovered, to imbibe with his male friends. One of these was Dan Domench, a confirmed alcoholic. Carver and he would go on road trips together. They had a fatalistic attitude toward life. Domench firmly believed that he and Carver would ultimately drink themselves into the grave.

"Death becomes a choice," Carver said in 1973. "Death looks pretty good. You can't imagine a life without it." Sobriety was very much a long shot for him. "The miracle either happens or it doesn't. You get clean or you die."[11]

The highlight of their road trips was locating liquor stores. Carver, according to Domench, was like a medium in this respect. He had the alcoholic's instinct for where such stores might be, even if they were in the middle of nowhere. If they were locked or boarded up, he would wait until he saw signs of life. Drink was his viaticum for these trips. It was his adrenaline, gas, and life-blood. Driving was unthinkable without it.[12]

Carver was appointed visiting lecturer at the Iowa Writers' Workshop in the fall of 1973. There he met John Cheever. Pretty soon they were spending time together, trying to find the best ways to get around the liquor laws in a dry state.

Together the "Mutt and Jeff of literature,"[13] as Maryann described them, drove through the snow and ice to get to the local liquor store, Carver picking up where he left off with Domench. As soon as it opened, they would stock up on Scotch, the fuel of choice.

Meanwhile, Maryann was at home, trying to raise her children and hold down a teaching job. For her husband, she thought, alcohol provided "a daily blackout that somewhat eased the pain of the limbo his life was heading into. He couldn't seem to go forward and he couldn't go back." By now he was drinking until he fell asleep, and even afterward. "If he woke up in the middle of the night he drank vodka. For a long time, I think he never went more than two hours without it."[14]

One day, Carver and Cheever delayed going to the liquor store; they arrived just as it was closing. They started to panic in case they were too late to be served. Cheever raced from the car before Cheever had even turned off the engine. By the time he got inside, Cheever was already at the checkout stand.

They drank so much it was surprising any teaching at all got done. Frequently, it didn't. Carver went AWOL many days, either sleeping off hangovers or being too sick to appear. One of his students who missed the first few classes never saw him the whole term. He was eventually fired for absenteeism.

He was too "pickled" to write at this point, but the stories and poems that were already "out there" were gaining more and more attention, so his inactivity was not yet apparent. Maryann didn't know what to do, whether to leave with Cecily or try to rake up their marriage from the ashes. "I couldn't let go of him and he couldn't let go of the bottle," she said.[15]

The idea of entering a treatment program didn't strike him. He was living in a culture where excessive drinking was permitted, even joked about. There was no Betty Ford Clinic at this time. The thinking was,

"You're having a few too many? Just use your willpower and cut back." The idea that alcoholism was a disease wasn't in vogue yet, nor the idea that people drank for reasons other than a failure of character. Only later would Carver realize he had a genetic fault, a fatal orientation.

Maryann had virtually stopped drinking by this time, which further alienated Carver. "The sobers hate the drunks," he said, "and the drunks hate the sobers."[16] She had matched him drink for drink in the past, but she was not an alcoholic. She didn't drink in the mornings, for instance, nor did she miss work because of it. It wasn't a huge struggle for her to give it up. She did that after suffering her fourth blackout. She figured this was her brain telling her, "Enough, enough."[17] Afterward, AA helped her stay sober.

Carver, in contrast, didn't mind how many blackouts he had. He dressed shabbily and looked ten years older than his actual age. Carol Sklenicka wrote:

> His face and his body were bloated. When he wore the hip-hugger jeans and wide leather belts in style in the early seventies, his belly protruded above the belt. His hair was scruffy, his face sprouted sideburns. Continuous inebriation erased the timidity that used to make him look smaller than he really was. Now his big and lumbering presence could—and did—intimidate people.[18]

He was still being Bad Ray. He drank vodka straight from the bottle "as if it were cream soda" and was "ornery and inconsiderate" to people. "He lashed out," said Maryann, "ranted and raved. He seemed to be listening to voices in his head, conducting a dialogue that was a parody of what he used to write."[19] His life had turned into one of his stories. Mr. Whiskey was rising again.

Maryann tried to persuade him to go to AA meetings with her, but he always refused. One night he did accompany her—with a bottle in his hand. Not surprisingly, he was asked to leave.

Home life became crazier than ever. He still ordered his children around, but now they just looked at him, refusing to obey his (groggy) demands. His son Vance smoked pot and went to parties, unsupervised. He cut baseball practice and got away with it. Christine's school grades slipped. Their classmates were partly envious of their freedom and partly sympathetic—because they knew what was causing it.

The money situation became dire. Their credit cards were maxed out. Checks issued for household expenses bounced. Carver joked about their situation, commenting, "I felt so bad this morning, I could barely make it to the liquor store."[20]

Maryann kept preaching about the great things AA could achieve, but he wasn't ready to hear this yet. He had to *want* to dry out. That was the first step. If this wasn't the case, no amount of counseling would work.

By 1974, he was giving drunken readings of his work, sometimes being pulled offstage early. Maryann told him he was "pissing away" both his earnings and his talent. She wasn't far wrong. In 1973, he declared bankruptcy for the second time.

He tried to get sober that year, but the withdrawal led to seizures. His central nervous system was so accustomed to the presence of alcohol that it couldn't properly adjust to its absence. His body was depressed, but his brain was still hyperactive. He felt trapped. He hated the seizures, but also hated his addiction. If he drank he knew they'd stop but his doctor told him he could die from what he called "wet brain," i.e., permanent brain damage. He was afraid to drink and afraid *not* to drink. One seizure resulted in him splitting his forehead open after writhing on the floor. He was stitched up and sent home. He spent the rest of the evening drinking.[21]

One night he threw a bottle of wine at Maryann, hitting her on the side of the head. She was rushed to the hospital in an ambulance. Thankfully, the wound wasn't too deep and she made a full recovery. She didn't press charges against him, but soon afterward, he hit her again during another argument, this time dislocating her shoulder. His mood swings had become totally unpredictable. He flared up at her for no reason, and at others as well. He became jealous of any male attention she was given even though the marriage was effectively over.

He knew he was out of control. His life wasn't his own anymore. He had blackouts on a large scale: "You might drive a car, give a reading, teach a class, set a broken leg, go to bed with someone, and not have any memory of it later. You're on some kind of automatic pilot."[22]

In 1976, he entered the Garden Sullivan Hospital in San Francisco to be dried out. He came out feeling optimistic, but his resolve didn't last. At a party for Maryann's mother soon afterward he started knocking back some celebratory champagne. That year also saw the publication of his first short story collection, *Will You Please Be Quiet, Please?* It was shortlisted for the National Book Award. He was euphoric. He decided to give sobriety another shot.

Carver called Maryann from AA on New Year's Eve that year and her heart leapt with joy. He had gone there himself, without any urging from her. The signs looked good about him saying goodbye to Mr. Whiskey. He wanted to give it up. They were the words she had been longing to hear for years—the seminal first step of twelve.

Carver took his last drink on Thursday, June 2, 1977, at the Jambalaya bar in Arcata. "I'll always be an alcoholic," he said, "but I'm no longer a practicing alcoholic."[23] Or, to use the vernacular phrase, "A dry drunk."

"Good Ray" was reborn after that day. He promised Maryann not only to stay dry but also to reinvigorate the marriage. They tried to return to the simple life they had when they first got together. They bought fishing equipment to encourage them to live a healthy outdoor life again and had the phone cut off to protect them from unwanted callers (and debt collectors). Carver also continued attending AA meetings—sometimes two a day—and, upon returning home, shared his experiences with Maryann. Sometimes she went with him. Other nights they played bingo or went to horseraces. His creative juices were temporarily suspended, what little writing he did at this time being confined to letters.

But the second honeymoon with Maryann was not to last. Sobriety brought different problems, in particular one that Maryann hadn't expected: Carver's hunger for respectability. "Don't talk to people about my past," he warned her. "It doesn't look good." She found it hard to get her head around this directive. Was it really her husband speaking? It wasn't Good Ray or Bad Ray but some new phenomenon she called Squeaky Clean Ray. She didn't know how to deal with it. If she was to forget the past, would that not mean she was also to jettison the memory of the good things they had done together? As for him, how would he accommodate his new identity? After being the "town drunk" for ten years, how could he now envision himself as a "hot dog, a snob"?[24]

Once again, the writing was on the wall for the childhood sweethearts. They had gone from the brink of one disaster to a new, more worrisome one: How was Maryann going to deal with a sober spouse? Or, more to the point, how would a sober spouse deal with *her*?

Not very well, as it turned out. At a poetry reading in 1977 to promote his book *Furious Seasons* he met a woman who would become the nexus of his future: Tess Gallagher. They clicked immediately. By the end of the night, she had become a huge Carver fan. She bought his book and entered his heart. The feeling was obviously mutual.

After Carver broke up with Maryann he blamed her for his drinking, an outlandish accusation. If anything she made his literary career possible by rescuing him financially, time and again. He would have drunk if he never met her. Without her he might have been found in a gutter somewhere, another unknown writer who took to the bottle to drown his sorrows over a life punctuated by rejection slips and irate debtors.

The novelist Richard Ford met him at this time. He described him as being like a boxer on the ropes, making tentative baby steps back into another world. "He looked as if he'd stepped down of a Greyhound bus," Ford observed, "that was coming from someplace where he'd done mostly custodial duties."[25]

Gallagher promised to ease him through the rough patches. She said her life was like a "rehearsal" for meeting him. There was a sense, she proclaimed, in which all the failed alcoholics of her past were symbolically redeemed by his success. "He was drying out for all of them," she beamed.[26]

But drying out wasn't going to be easy. Nor was their relationship. One of their first arguments was about money. Carver asked her to lend him her credit card and she hesitated. He was, after all, an alcoholic, with two bankruptcies to his name. But, in the end, she gave it to him.

His life with Gallagher he likened to coming back from the grave. "I had to learn to teach sober," he said. "I had to learn to do nearly everything sober."[27]

They moved to Syracuse in 1980. He'd been appointed coordinator of a creative writing program at the university there. Two years later, he divorced Maryann. For her, it was the finality she never wanted.

Carver continued to fortify his reputation as the man who could revive the short story form almost single-handedly. Writing surged out of him like water from a well, as if serenading his recovery. His style was slightly different in his later work. The old minimalism was still there but it was less noticeable now, both because he was experimenting with different ways of saying things and because he wasn't a slave to the kind of cuts Gordon Lish made to his work when he was struggling with the bottle.

He published *Cathedral*, a short story anthology, in 1983. It was his crowning achievement. There were also a number of poetry collections in the offing—*Fires* later that year, *Where Water Comes Together with Other Water* in 1985, *Ultramarine* in 1986.

Gallagher kept him on the dry, but only just. One night, in 1988, he drove to an AA meeting in a town near Port Angeles but got lost *en route*. He dropped into a tavern and ordered a drink. Then he rang her. She asked him where he was, and he told her. He said he was about to break his pledge, that a drink was on the counter waiting for him.

"Have you started it yet?" she asked.

"No," he said.

"Then don't," she said. He took her advice and went home instead. At such times she was like his sponsor.

Carver was prouder of giving up drinking than anything else he had ever done in his life. But tragedy was to come. As was the case with his boozing buddy John Cheever, sobriety was shortly followed by cancer. He was only fifty when he contracted it. He was informed early on that it was aggressive and that his chances didn't look good, but he refused to take such a diagnosis seriously. He claimed he would beat the disease.[28] But it was too late: it was all over his system.

When he realized he wasn't going to make it he became more philosophical. What had he to complain about? He had a life many people envied, however brief it was. He'd got "the gravy."[29]

His name was a byword of American letters and he'd also secured the love of two women. Maryann Burk Carver, the first of these, put his life in a nutshell: "He was certain he would die young and never wavered in that intuitive belief. That made me want to give him everything he wanted as soon as was humanly possible."[30]

What more could a vodka-guzzling storywriter have asked for?

Chapter Notes

Introduction

1. Donald W. Goodwin, *Alcohol and the Writer* (London: Penguin, 1988), 176.
2. *London Magazine*, December 1974–January 1975.
3. Donald Newlove, *Those Drinking Days: Myself and Other Writers* (New York: Horizon Press, 1981), 125.
4. Barry Miles, *Jack Kerouac: King of the Beats: A Portrait* (New York: Henry Holt, 1998), 277.

Eugene O'Neill

1. Donald W. Goodwin, *Alcohol and the Writer* (London: Penguin, 1988), 32.
2. Stephen Black, *Eugene O'Neill: Beyond Mourning and Tragedy* (London: Yale University Press, 1999), 94.
3. Goodwin, *Alcohol and the Writer*, 129.
4. Black, *Beyond Mourning and Tragedy*, 98–99.
5. Arthur and Barbara Gelb, *Life with Monte Cristo* (New York: Applause Theater and Cinema Books, 2000), 293.
6. Arthur and Barbara Gelb, *O'Neill* (London: Jonathan Cape, 1962), 171.
7. William Davies King, ed., *Part of a Long Story: Eugene O'Neill as a Young Man in Love* (Jefferson, NC: McFarland, 2011), 96.
8. Arthur and Barbara Gelb, *Life with Monte Cristo*, 601.
9. *Ibid.*, 225.
10. Goodwin, *Alcohol and the Writer*, 134.
11. Arthur and Barbara Gelb, *Life with Monte Cristo*, 328.
12. *Ibid.*, 179.
13. Black, *Beyond Mourning and Tragedy*, 85.
14. Arthur and Barbara Gelb, *Life with Monte Cristo*, 348.
15. *Ibid.*, 622
16. *Ibid.*, 592.
17. Black, *Beyond Mourning and Tragedy*, 201.
18. Arthur and Barbara Gelb, *Life with Monte Cristo*, 525–26.
19. *Ibid.*, 525.
20. *Ibid.*, 526–27.
21. Arthur and Barbara Gelb, *O'Neill* (London: Jonathan Cape, 1962), 164.
22. Goodwin, *Alcohol and the Writer*, 133.
23. Tom Dardis, *The Thirsty Muse: Alcohol and the American Writer* (London: Sphere 1989), 221–22.
24. Goodwin, *Alcohol and the Writer*, 135.
25. Arthur and Barbara Gelb, *O'Neill*, 430.
26. Harry Kemp, "O'Neill of Provincetown," *Brentano's Book Chat* (May–June 1928), 45–7.
27. William Davies King, *Another Part of a Long Story: Literary Traces of Eugene O'Neill and Agnes Boulton* (Ann Arbor: University of Michigan Press, 2010), 142–43.
28. *Ibid.*, 140.
29. Robert M. Dowling, *Eugene O'Neill: A Life in Four Acts* (New Haven; London: Yale University Press, 2014), 313.
30. Louis Sheaffer, *Eugene O'Neill: Son and Playwright* (Boston: Little, Brown & Co., 1968), 388.
31. Newlove, *Those Drinking Days*, 135.
32. Dardis, *The Thirsty Muse*, 251.
33. Arthur and Barbara Gelb, *O'Neill*, 533.
34. *Ibid.*, 529.
35. Dowling, *Eugene O'Neill*, 311–12.
36. Arthur and Barbara Gelb, *O'Neill*, 573.
37. Travis Bogard and Jackson R. Bryer, eds., *Selected Letters of Eugene O'Neill* (New York: Limelight Editions, 1994), 399.
38. *Ibid.*, 224.
39. Dardis, *The Thirsty Muse*, 224.
40. King, *Agnes Boulton, Part of a Long Story*, 96.
41. Black, *Beyond Mourning and Tragedy*, 361.

42. Dardis, *The Thirsty Muse*, 240.
43. Bogard and Bryer, eds., *Selected Letters of Eugene O'Neill*, 210.
44. Ibid., 372.
45. Arthur and Barbara Gelb, *Life with Monte Cristo*, 311.
46. Ibid., 507.
47. Arthur and Barbara Gelb, *O'Neill*, 851–52.
48. Black, *Beyond Mourning and Tragedy*, 479.
49. Bogard and Bryer, eds., *Selected Letters of Eugene O'Neill*, 583.
50. Ibid., 573.
51. Black, *Beyond Mourning and Tragedy*, 499–500.
52. Bogard and Bryer, eds., *Selected Letters of Eugen O'Neill*, 574.
53. Arthur and Barbara Gelb, *O'Neill*, 934.
54. Ibid., 935.
55. Ibid., *O'Neill*, 938.
56. Ibid., 939.
57. Black, *Beyond Mourning and Tragedy*, 505.

Raymond Chandler

1. Tom Williams, *Raymond Chandler: A Life* (London: Aurum, 2012), 68.
2. Ibid., 203.
3. Tom Hiney, *Raymond Chandler: A Biography* (New York: Atlantic Monthly Press, 1997), 63.
4. Raymond Chandler, *Lady in the Lake* (London: Penguin, 1952), 38.
5. Williams, *Raymond Chandler: A Life*, 203.
6. Tom Hiney and Frank McShane, eds., *The Raymond Chandler Papers: Selected Letters and Non-Fiction, 1909–1959* (London: Hamish Hamilton, 2000), 196.
7. Chandler, *Lady in the Lake*, 54.
8. Hiney, *Raymond Chandler: A Biography*, 68.
9. Williams, *Raymond Chandler: A Life*, 99–100.
10. *New York Times*, April 1962.
11. Judith Freeman, *The Long Embrace: Raymond Chandler and the Woman He Loved* (New York: Pantheon Books, 2007), 106.
12. Hiney and McShane, eds., *The Raymond Chandler Papers*, 173–74.
13. Hiney, *Raymond Chandler: A Biography*, 272.
14. *Dime Detective Magazine*, March 1938.
15. Frank McShane, *The Life of Raymond Chandler* (Boston: G. K. Hall, 1978), 93–4.
16. Hiney and McShane, eds., *The Raymond Chandler Papers*, 147.
17. McShane, *The Life of Raymond Chandler*, 45.
18. Hiney and McShane, eds., *The Raymond Chandler Papers*, 194.
19. *The Times Quotations from Homer to Homer Simpson* (London: HarperCollins, 2006), 27.
20. John Robert Colombo, *Wit and Wisdom of the Movie-Makers* (London: Hamlyn, 1979), 149.
21. Hiney, *Raymond Chandler: A Biography*, 163.
22. Maurice Zolotow, *Billy Wilder in Hollywood* (New York: Limelight Editions, 1987), 115.
23. Hiney, *Raymond Chandler: A Biography*, 144.
24. Freeman, *The Long Embrace*, 213–18.
25. Hiney, *Raymond Chandler: A Biography*, 149.
26. McShane, *The Life of Raymond Chandler*, 115–16.
27. Hiney and McShane, eds., *The Raymond Chandler Papers*, 222.
28. Hiney, *Raymond Chandler: A Biography*, 121–22.
29. McShane, *The Life of Raymond Chandler*, 1.
30. Hiney, *Raymond Chandler: A Biography*, 206.
31. Freeman, *The Long Embrace*, 295.
32. Dorothy Gardiner and Katherine Sorley Walker, eds., *Raymond Chandler Speaking* (Berkeley: University of California Press, 1997), 216–17.
33. Hiney, *Raymond Chandler: A Biography*, 215.
34. Ibid., 216.
35. Raymond Chandler, *Playback* (London: Penguin, 2006), 193.
36. Freeman, *The Long Embrace*, 268.
37. McShane, *The Life of Raymond Chandler*, 214.
38. Freeman, *The Long Embrace*, 305.
39. Williams, *Raymond Chandler: A Life*, 316.
40. McShane, *The Life of Raymond Chandler*, 238–39.
41. *Daily Express*, January 14, 1956.
42. Gardiner and Walker, eds., *Raymond Chandler Speaking*, 32.
43. Hiney and McShane, eds., *The Raymond Chandler Papers*, 228.
44. Williams, *Raymond Chandler: A Life*, 317.
45. Hiney, *Raymond Chandler: A Biography*, 243.

46. Williams, *Raymond Chandler: A Life*, 343.
47. Hiney, *Raymond Chandler: A Biography*, 273.
48. *Ibid.*, 269.

Edna St. Vincent Millay

1. Daniel Mark Epstein, *What Lips My Lips Have Kissed: The Loves and Love Poems of Edna St. Vincent Millay* (New York: Henry Holt, 2001), 108.
2. Joan Dash, *A Life of One's Own: Three Gifted Women and the Men They Married* (New York: Paragon House, 1988), 120.
3. Nancy Milford, *Savage Beauty: The Life of Edna St. Vincent Millay* (New York: Random House, 2002), 64.
4. Dash, *A Life of One's Own*, 120.
5. Andrea Barnet, *All Night Party: The Women of Bohemian Greenwich and Harlem, 1913–1930* (Chapel Hill, NC: Algonquin Books, 2004), 95.
6. Epstein, *What Lips My Lips Have Kissed*, 81.
7. Miriam Gurko, *Restless Spirit: The Life of Edna St. Vincent Millay* (New York: Thomas Y. Crowell, 1962), 58.
8. Toby Shafter, *Edna St. Vincent Millay: America's Best-Loved Poet* (New York: Julian Messner Inc., 1957), 118.
9. Norman A. Brittin, *Edna St. Vincent Millay* (New York: George H. Doran, 1926), 39.
10. Barnet, *All Night Party*, 101.
11. Milford, *Savage Beauty*, 75.
12. Dash, *A Life of One's Own*, 142.
13. *Ibid.*, 144.
14. Milford, *Savage Beauty*, 279.
15. Elizabeth Atkins, *Edna St. Vincent Millay and Her Times* (New York: Russell & Russell, 1964), 70.
16. Barry Day, ed., *Dorothy Parker in Her Own Words* (Lanham, MD: Taylor Trade Publishing, 2004), 105.
17. Barnet, *All Night Party*, 125.
18. *Ibid.*, 125–26.
19. Dash, *A Life of One's Own*, 171.
20. Epstein, *What Lips My Lips Have Kissed*, 151.
21. *Ibid.*, 86.
22. Jean Gould, *The Poet and Her Book: A Biography of Edna St. Vincent Millay* (New York: Dodd, Mead, 1969), 162.
23. *Delineator*, October 1934.
24. *Ibid.*
25. Epstein, *What Lips My Lips Have Kissed*, 151.
26. *Ibid.*, 207.
27. Gurko, *Restless Spirit*, 167.
28. Epstein, *What Lips My Lips Have Kissed*, 223.
29. *Ibid.*, 196.
30. *Ibid.*, 227–28.
31. *Ibid.*, 241.
32. *Ibid.*, 217.
33. *Ibid.*, 245.
34. Milford, *Savage Beauty*, 373.
35. *Ibid.*
36. *Ibid.*
37. *Ibid.*
38. *Ibid.*, 375.
39. Gurko, *Restless Spirit*, 199.
40. Alan Ross McDougall, ed., *The Letters of Edna St. Vincent Millay* (New York: Harper & Row, 1952), 282.
41. Gurko, *Restless Spirit*, 228.
42. Barnet, *All Night Party*, 129.
43. *Ibid.*
44. Epstein, *What Lips My Lips Have Kissed*, 226.
45. *Ibid*, 259.
46. Upton Sinclair, *A Cup of Fury* (New York: Channel Press, 1956), 90.
47. Epstein, *What Lips My Lips Have Kissed*, 261.
48. *Ibid.*, 262–63.
49. *Ibid.*
50. Gurko, *Restless Spirit*, 229.
51. *New York Times*, September 23, 1962.
52. Gurko, *Restless Spirit*, 242.
53. Michele Brown and Ann O'Connor, eds., *Hammer and Tongues: A Dictionary of Women's Wit and Humor* (London: Grafton, 1988), 73.
54. Milford, *Savage Beauty*, 480.
55. Epstein, *What Lips My Lips Have Kissed*, 268.
56. Milford, *Savage Beauty*, 501.
57. Gurko, *Restless Spirit*, 254–55.

Dorothy Parker

1. Day, ed., *Dorothy Parker in Her Own Words*, 1.
2. Michelle Lovric, ed., *More Women's Wicked Wit* (London: Prion, 2004), 101.
3. Stuart Y. Silverstein, ed., *The Uncollected Dorothy Parker* (London: Duckbacks, 1999), 60.
4. Leslie Frewin, *The Late Mrs. Dorothy Parker* (New York: Macmillan, 1986), 64.
5. James M. Gaines, *Wits End: Days and Nights of the Algonquin Round Table* (United States: Book Surge Publishing, 2007).
6. Marion Meade, *What Fresh Hell Is This?* (New York: Penguin, 1989), 47.
7. Karen Weekes, ed., *Women Know*

Everything (Philadelphia: Quirk Books, 2007), 128.

8. George Eells, *Hedda and Louella: A Dual Biography of Hedda Hopper and Louella Parsons* (New York: G. P. Putnam & Sons, 1972), 50.

9. Silverstein, ed., *The Uncollected Dorothy Parker*, 67.

10. Colin Jarman, ed., *The Guinness Dictionary of Poisonous Quotations* (London: Guinness books, 1991), 130.

11. Sheilah Graham, *The Garden of Allah* (New York: Crown, 1970), 111.

12. *New York Times*, October 27, 1979.

13. Frewin, *The Late Mrs. Dorothy Parker*, 300–01.

14. *Associated Press*, January 15, 1951.

15. Day, ed., *Dorothy Parker in Her Own Words*, 74.

16. Frewin, *The Late Mrs. Dorothy Parker*, 321–22

17. *Ibid.*, 322.

18. Joan Mellen, *Hellman and Hammett* (London: HarperPerennial, 1997), 129.

19. Day, ed., *Dorothy Parker in Her Own Words*, 135.

20. Rosemarie Jarski, ed., *A Word from the Wise* (London: Ebury, 2006), 27.

21. Ned Sherrin, ed., *The Oxford Dictionary of Humorous Quotations* (London: Oxford University Press, 2001), 10.

22. Day, ed., *Dorothy Parker in Her Own Words*, 190.

23. Meade, *What Fresh Hell Is This?*, xviii.

24. Andrew Shaffer, *Literary Rogues A Scandalous History of Wayward Authors* (New York HarperPerennial, 2013), 119–20.

25. Allison Vale and Alison Rattle, eds., *Mother's Wit* (London: Prion, 2006), 204.

26. Robert Andrew, ed., *The New Penguin Dictionary of Modern Quotations* (London: Penguin, 2003), 437.

27. Day, ed., *Dorothy Parker in Her Own Words*, 138.

28. *Ibid.*, 132.

29. Jon Winokur, ed., *The Big Curmudgeon* (New York: Black Dog & Leventhal, 2007), 246.

30. Meade, *What Fresh Hell Is This?*, 159.

31. Ibid.

32. Ibid.

33. *New Yorker*, October 29, 1927.

34. Nicolas Gerogiannis, ed., *Ernest Hemingway: The Complete Poems* (Lincoln and London: University of Nebraska Press, 1992), 86.

35. Meade, *What Fresh Hell Is This?*, 235.

36. *New Yorker*, February 11, 1928.

37. *New York Telegram*, February 1, 1930.

38. *New York World*, February 1, 1930

39. John Keats, *You Might as Well Live: The Life and Times of Dorothy Parker* (London: Penguin, 1988), 156.

40. Jennifer Higgie, ed., *Far Too Noisy, My Dear Mozart: A Collection of Historical Insults* (London: Michael O'Mara, 1997), 61.

41. Meade, *What Fresh Hell Is This?*, 230–31.

42. Frewin, *The Late Mrs. Dorothy Parker*, 143.

43. Eells, *Hedda and Louella*, 118.

44. Ronald L. Davis, *The Glamour Factory: Inside Hollywood's Big Studio System* (Dallas, Texas: Southern Methodist University Press, 1993), 172.

45. Meade, *What Fresh Hell Is This?*, 268.

46. Keats, *You Might as Well Live*, 222–23.

47. *Ibid.*

48. Silverstein, ed., *The Uncollected Dorothy Parker*, 35–36.

49. Rosemarie Jarski, ed., *Hollywood Wit* (London: Prion, 2000), 234.

50. Winokur, ed., *The Big Curmudgeon*, 426.

51. Jessie Shiers, ed., *The Quotable Bitch* (Guildford, CT: Lyons Press, 2008), 237.

52. *New Yorker*, December 10, 1927.

53. Colin Jarman, ed., *I Said It My Way*, (Enfield: Middlesex Guinness Publishing, 1994), 153.

54. *New Masses*, March 14, 1939.

55. *New York Times*, January 8, 1939.

56. Day, ed., *Dorothy Parker in Her Own Words*, 169.

57. Frewin, *The Late Mrs. Dorothy Parker*, 154.

58. Meade, *What Fresh Hell Is This?*, 309.

59. Silverstein, ed., *The Uncollected Dorothy Parker*, 45.

60. *Ibid.*, 47.

61. Meade, *What Fresh Hell Is This?*, 339.

62. Silverstein, ed., *The Uncollected Dorothy Parker*, 47–8.

63. Day, ed., *Dorothy Parker In Her Own Words*, 158.

64. *Los Angeles Times*, June 18, 1962.

65. Keats, *You Might As Well Live*, 287.

66. *New York Herald Tribune*, October 13, 1963.

67. Shaffer, *Literary Rogues*, 127.

68. Meade, *What Fresh Hell Is This?*, 394–95.

69. Keats, *You Might as Well Live*, 297.

70. *Ibid.*

71. Meade, *What Fresh Hell is This?*, 405.

72. Silverstein, *The Uncollected Dorothy Parker*, 75.

73. Lillian Hellman, *An Unfinished Woman:*

A Memoir (London; Quartet Books, 1977), 180.
74. Keats, *You Might as Well Live*, 300.
75. Weekes, ed., *Women Know Everything*, 204.
76. Keats, *You Might as Well Live*, 306.
77. Meade, *What Fresh Hell is This?*, 406–07.
78. Jarman, ed., *The Guinness Dictionary of Poisonous Quotations*, 15.
79. Hellman, *An Unfinished Woman*, 173.
80. Weekes, ed., *Women Know Everything*, 104.
81. Frewin, *The Late Mrs. Dorothy Parker*, 93.

F. Scott Fitzgerald

1. Arthur Mizener, *The Far Side of Paradise* (New York: Avon Books, 1974), 34.
2. Nancy Milford, *Zelda: A Biography* (New York: Harper & Row, 1970), 27.
3. Scott Donaldson, *Fool for Love: A Biography of Scott Fitzgerald* (New York: Dell, 1983), 161–62.
4. *Ibid.*, 51.
5. Matthew J. Bruccoli and Judith S. Baugham, eds., *Conversations with F. Scott Fitzgerald* (University Press of Mississippi, 2003), 21.
6. Donaldson, *Fool for Love*, 161–62.
7. F. Scott Fitzgerald, *On Booze* (London: Picador, 2011), 20.
8. Marty Beckerman, *The Heming Way* (New York: St. Martin's Griffin, 2012), 55.
9. Donaldson, *Fool for Love*, 162.
10. Matthew J. Bruccoli, *The Notebooks of F. Scott Fitzgerald* (New York: Harcourt Brace, 1978), 148.
11. Donaldson, *Fool for Love*, 128.
12. Joshua Zeitz, *Flapper* (New York: Three Rivers Press, 2006), 271.
13. Malone, *On the Edge*, 136.
14. Goodwin, *Alcohol and the Writer*, 41.
15. Malone, *On the Edge*, 180.
16. Beckerman, *The Heming Way*, 165.
17. Donaldson, *Fool for Love*, 163.
18. Matthew J. Bruccoli, *Some sort of Epic Grandeur: The Life of F. Scott Fitzgerald* (London: Hodder & Stoughton, 1981), 185.
19. Anita Loos, *Cast of Thousands* (New York, Grosset & Dunlap, 1977), 128.
20. Matthew J. Bruccoli, *F. Scott Fitzgerald: A Descriptive Bibliography* (Pittsburgh: University of Pittsburgh Press, 1972), 265.
21. Ernest Hemingway, *A Moveable Feast* (London: Arrow Books, 2004), 86.
22. Malone, *On the Edge*, 175.
23. *Ibid*.
24. *Ibid.*, 103.
25. *Ibid.*, 107.
26. *Ibid*.
27. *Ibid.*,108.
28. Ibid.,109–10.
29. Andrew Turnbull, ed., *Dreams of Youth: The Letters of F. Scott Fitzgerald* (London: Max Press, 2011), 249.
30. Arthur Mizener, *F. Scott Fitzgerald and His World* (London: Thames & Hudson, 1972), 72.
31. Donaldson, *Fool for Love*, 172.
32. James R. Mellow, *Hemingway: A Life Without Consequences* (London: Hodder & Stoughton, 1994), 333.
33. Zeitz, *Flapper*, 272.
34. Gioia Diliberto, *Hadley: A Life of Hadley Richardson Hemingway* (London: Bloomsbury), 193.
35. Zeitz, *Flapper*, 275.
36. Matthew J. Bruccoli, *Fitzgerald and Hemingway: A Dangerous Friendship* (London: Andre Deutsch, 1994), 165.
37. Kenneth S. Lynn, *Hemingway* (London: Simon & Schuster, 1987), 287–88.
38. Ernest Hemingway, *The Snows of Kilimanjaro*, (London: Arrow Books, 1994), 20.
39. Mellow, *A Life Without Consequences*, 472.
40. Donaldson, *Fool for Love*, 170–71.
41. Ibid., 127.
42. Donaldson, *Fool for Love*, 127.
43. Matthew J. Bruccoli, *Some Sort of Epic Grandeur: The Life of F. Scott Fitzgerald* (London: Sphere, 1991), 311–13.
44. Donaldson, *Fool for Love*, 165.
45. *Ibid*.
46. Fitzgerald, *On Booze*, 74.
47. Lynn, *Hemingway*, 283.
48. Zeitz, *Flapper*, 274.
49. Mizener, *Scott Fitzgerald and his World*, 117.
50. Milford, *Zelda*, 222.
51. *Ibid.*, 171–2.
52. Donaldson, *Fool for Love*, 88–89.
53. *Ibid.*, 89–92.
54. *Ibid.*, 167.
55. *Ibid*.
56. *Ibid.*, 170.
57. Shaffer, *Literary Rogues*, 111–12.
58. Milford, *Zelda*, 201.
59. Aubrey Malone, *Hemingway: The Grace and the Pressure* (London: Robson Books, 1999), 185.
60. Mizener, *F. Scott Fitzgerald and His World*, 101.
61. Donaldson, *Fool for Love*, 171.
62. Shaffer, *Literary Rogues*, 111.
63. Tony Butitta, *After the Good Gay Times* (New York Viking, 1974), 4.

64. Donaldson, *Fool for Love*, 166.
65. Tom Dardis, *Some Time in the Sun* (New York: Limelight Editions, 1988), 24.
66. Aaron Latham, *Crazy Sundays: F. Scott Fitzgerald in Hollywood* (London: Secker & Warburg, 1972), 19–20.
67. Malone, *Hemingway*, 181–82.
68. Malone, *On the Edge*, 136.
69. *Ibid.*
70. Sheilah Graham, with Gerold Frank, *Beloved Infidel* (New York: Bantam Books, 1968), 212.
71. Sheilah Graham, *My Hollywood: A Celebration and a Lament* (London: Michael Joseph, 1984), 81.
72. Latham, *Crazy Sundays*, vii.
73. Sheilah Graham, *My Hollywood: A Celebration and a Lament* (London: Michael Joseph, 1984), 79.
74. Mizener, *Scott Fitzgerald and his World*, 104.
75. Bob Thomas, *Joan Crawford: A Biography* (London: Weidenfeld & Nicolson, 1978), 108.
76. Latham, *Crazy Sundays*, 171–72.
77. *Ibid.*, 173.
78. Thomas, *Joan Crawford*, 110.
79. Bruccoli, ed., *Dreams of Youth*, 295–96.
80. F. Scott Fitzgerald, *On Booze* (London: Picador, 2011), 20.
81. *Los Angeles Magazine*, January 1964.
82. Donaldson, *Fool for Love*, 214.
83. Mizener, *Scott Fitzgerald and his World*, 104.
84. Beckerman, *The Heming Way*, 168.
85. Arnold Samuelson, *With Hemingway: A Year in Key West and Cuba* (London: Severn House, 1985), 40.
86. Latham, *Crazy Sundays*, 244.
87. Malone, *On the Edge*, 186.
88. *Ibid.*, 230.
89. Goodwin, *Alcohol and the Writer*, 44.
90. Beckerman, *The Heming Way*, 169.
91. Fitzgerald, *On Booze*, 6.
92. Hiney and McShane, *The Raymond Chandler Papers*, 139–40.
93. Connie Robertson, ed., *Wordsworth Dictionary of Quotations* (Herefordshire, UK: Wordsworth Editions, 1998), 127.

William Faulkner

1. Goodwin, *Alcohol and the Writer*, 118.
2. *Esquire*, July 1963.
3. Goodwin, *Alcohol and the Writer*, 112.
4. Philip Gourevitch, ed., *The Paris Review Interviews*, Vol. II (New York: Picador, 2007), 50.
5. *Ibid.*, 38.
6. Jean-Francois Duval, *Bukowski and the Beats: A Commentary on the Beat Generation* (Northville, MI: Sun Dog Press, 2002), 184.
7. Dardis, *The Thirsty Muse*, 25.
8. *Ibid.*, 62.
9. Howard Mumford Jones and Walter B. Rideout, eds., *The Letters of Sherwood Anderson* (New York: Little, Brown & Co., 1953), 252.
10. Dardis, *Some Time in the Sun*, 104.
11. Newlove, *Those Drinking Days*, 147–48.
12. Joseph Blotner, *Faulkner: A Biography* (New York: Vintage, 1991), 225.
13. Goodwin, *Alcohol and the Writer*, 111.
14. Blotner, *Faulkner*, 387.
15. Philip Greene, *To Have and Have Another: A Hemingway Cocktail Companion* (New York: Perigree, 2012), 127.
16. Newlove, *Those Drinking Days*, 146–47.
17. Shaffer, *Literary Rogues*, 139.
18. Robert Coughlan, *The Private World of William Faulkner* (New York: Harper & Brothers, 1954), 134.
19. Dardis, *The Thirsty Muse*, 78.
20. George Plimpton, *Truman Capote* (New York, Picador, 1998), 243.
21. Newlove, *Those Drinking Days*, 35–36.
22. Dardis, *The Thirsty Muse*, 93.
23. *Ibid.*

Ernest Hemingway

1. Scott Donaldson, *By Force of Will: The Life and Art of Ernest Hemingway* (New York: Penguin, 1978), 267.
2. Henry S. Villard and James Nagel, *Hemingway in Love and War: The Lost Diary of Agnes von Kurowsky* (Boston: Northeastern University Press, 189), 21–22.
3. Lynn, *Hemingway*, 98.
4. Hemingway, *A Moveable Feast*, 18.
5. Carlos Baker, ed., *Selected Letters of Ernest Hemingway*, 1917–1961 (London: Panther, 1985), 169.
6. Diliberto, *Hadley*, 193.
7. Brenda Maddox, *Nora* (London: Hamish Hamilton, 1988), 297.
8. Beckerman, *The Heming Way*, 75.
9. Lynn, *Hemingway*, 370.
10. Donaldson, *By Force of Will*, 267.
11. Greene, *To Have and Have Another*, xx.
12. Beckerman, *The Heming Way*, 52.
13. Denis Brian, *The Faces of Hemingway:*

Intimate Portraits of Ernest Hemingway By Those Who Knew Him (London: Grafton Books, 1988), 245.
14. *Ibid.*, 266.
15. Goodwin, *Alcohol and the Writer*, 55.
16. Lynn, *Hemingway*, 359.
17. Kurt Singer, *Hemingway: Life and Death of a Giant* (London: Consul, 1962), 207.
18. Baker, ed., *Selected Letters of Ernest Hemingway*, 420.
19. Malone, *Hemingway*, 163.
20. Baker, ed., *Selected Letters of Ernest Hemingway*, 500.
21. Lynn, *Hemingway*, 500–01.
22. Malone, *Hemingway*, 220.
23. Peter Buckley, *Ernest* (New York: Dial Press, 1978), 148.
24. Carl Rollyson, *Nothing Ever Happens to the Brave: The Story of Martha Gellhorn* (New York: St. Martin's Press, 1990), 324.
25. A. E. Hotchner, *Papa Hemingway* (London: Simon & Schuster, 1999), 87.
26. Malone, *Hemingway*, 207.
27. Baker, ed., *Selected Letters of Ernest Hemingway*, 593.
28. *Argosy*, September 1958.
29. Hotchner, *Papa Hemingway*, 194.
30. Lynn, *Hemingway*, 528.
31. Lynn, *Hemingway*, 529.
32. Goodwin, *Alcohol and the Writer*, 62
33. Donaldson, *By Force of Will*, 267.
34. Baker, ed., *Selected Letters of Ernest Hemingway*, 772.
35. Christopher Ondaatje, *Hemingway in Africa: The Last Safari* (Toronto: HarperCollins, 2003), 98.
36. Ernest Hemingway, *The Snows of Kilimanjaro* (Middlesex, UK: Penguin, 1972), 57.
37. John Raeburn, *Fame Became of Him: Hemingway as Public Writer* (Bloomington: Indiana University Press, 1984), 134.
38. Anthony Burgess, *Ernest Hemingway and His World* (London: Thames & Hudson, 1978), 58.
39. Dardis, *The Thirsty Muse*, 192.
40. Greene, *To Have and Have Another*, 203–04.
41. Burgess, *Ernest Hemingway and his World*, 101.
42. Brian, *The Faces of Hemingway*, 238.
43. Lynn, *Hemingway*, 529.
44. *New York Times*, January 26, 1954.
45. Mellow, *A Life Without Consequences*, 587.
46. Michael Reynolds, *Hemingway: The Final Years* (New York: W. W. Norton, 1999), 274.
47. Beckerman, *The Heming Way*, 77.

48. Peter Viertel, *Dangerous Friends: Hemingway, Huston and Others* (London: Viking, 1992), 9.
49. Malone, *Hemingway*, 260.
50. Stephen King, *On Writing: A Memoir of the Craft* (New York: Simon & Schuster, 2002), 87.
51. Hotchner, *Papa Hemingway*, 173.
52. *Ibid.*
53. Dardis, *The Thirsty Muse*, 201.
54. Hotchner, *Papa Hemingway*, 173.
55. *Ibid.*, 184.
56. Donaldson, *By Force of Will*, 268.
57. Hotchner, *Papa Hemingway*, 188.
58. Malone, *Hemingway*, 271.
59. Mellow, *A Life Without Consequences*, 600.
60. Malone, *Hemingway*, 270.
61. Reynolds, *The Final Years*, 355.
62. Lynn, *Hemingway*, 591.
63. Mellow, *A Life Without Consequences*, 604.
64. Ernest Hemingway, *The Snows of Kilimanjaro* (Middlesex, UK: Penguin, 1972), 193.

John Cheever

1. Susan Cheever, *Note Found in a Bottle: My Life as a Drinker* (New York: Simon & Schuster, 1999), 17.
2. *Ibid.*, 33.
3. Cheever, *Note Found in a Bottle*, 187–88.
4. Susan Cheever, *Home Before Dark* (London: Weidenfeld & Nicholson, 1984), 161-63.
5. Blake Bailey, *Cheever: A Life* (London: Picador, 2009), 78.
6. *Ibid.*, 144.
7. John Cheever, *The Journals* (London: Vintage, 1991), 101.
8. *Ibid.*, 212.
9. Bailey, *Cheever: A Life*, 332.
10. Cheever, *The Journals*, 286.
11. Bailey, *Cheever: A Life*, 463.
12. Cheever, *The Journals*, 277.
13. Cheever, *Home Before Dark*, 42–43.
14. Benjamin Cheever, ed., *The Letters of John Cheever* (London: Vintage, 2009), 126.
15. Cheever, *The Journals*, 94.
16. Bailey, *Cheever*, 302–03.
17. Olivia Laing, *The Trip to Echo Spring: Why Writers Drink* (Edinburgh: Canongate, 2013), 267–68.
18. *Ibid.*
19. Bailey, *Cheever*, 40.
20. Cheever, *The Journals*, 270.
21. Jared Brown, *Alan J. Pakula: His Film

and His Life (New York: Backstage Books, 2005) 63.
22. Bailey, *Cheever*, 422.
23. Scott Donaldson, *John Cheever: A Biography* (New York: Random House, 1988), 238.
24. Cheever, *The Journals*, 287.
25. *Ibid.*, 275.
26. John Cheever, *The Collected Stories* (London: Vintage, 2010), 875.
27. Cheever, *The Journals*, 159.
28. *Ibid.*, 230.
29. *Ibid.*, 233.
30. *Ibid.*
31. Cheever, *Note Found in a Bottle*, 178.
32. Cheever, *The Journals*, 233–34.
33. *Ibid.*, 234.
34. Cheever, ed., *The Letters of John Cheever*, 266.
35. Bailey, *Cheever*, 382.
36. *Ibid.*, 410.
37. *Ibid.*, 410–11.
38. Cheever, *Home Before Dark*, 176.
39. *Ibid.*, 163.
40. Donaldson, *John Cheever: A Biography*, 253.
41. *Ibid.*, 254.
42. Cheever, *The Journals*, 287.
43. Donaldson, *John Cheever: A Biography*, 225.
44. *Ibid.*
45. Bailey, *Cheever*, 462.
46. *Ibid.*, 457.
47. Donaldson, *John Cheever: A Biography*, 268.
48. Cheever, *Home Before Dark*, 181.
49. Cheever, ed., *The Letters of John Cheever*, 195.
50. Bailey, *Cheever*, 470.
51. *Ibid.*, 472.
52. Goodman, *Alcohol and the Writer*, 187.
53. Cheever, *Home Before Dark*, 225.
54. Cheever, *The Journals*, 105.
55. Cheever, *Home Before Dark*, 189.
56. Donaldson, *John Cheever: A Life*, 279.
57. Ibid., 287.
58. Carol Sklenicka, *Raymond Carver: A Writer's Life* (New York: Scribner, 2009), 258.
59. Donaldson, *John Cheever: A Biography*, 288–89.
60. *Ibid.*
61. *Ibid.*, 290.
62. Cheever, *Note Found in a Bottle*, 124.
63. Donaldson, *John Cheever: A Biography*, 292.
64. *Ibid.*
65. Cheever, *Note Found in a Bottle*, 150.
66. Cheever, *The Journals*, 365.
67. *Ibid.*
68. Cheever, *Note Found in a Bottle*, 147.
69. Bailey, *Cheever*, 658.

John Berryman

1. Eileen Simpson, *Poets in Their Youth: A Memoir* (New York: Farrar, Straus & Giroux, 1990), 14.
2. Laing, *A Trip to Echo Spring*, 166.
3. Paul Mariani, *Dream Song: The Life of John Berryman* (New York: William Morrow, 1990), 12–13.
4. Richard J. Kelly, ed., *We Dream of Honor: John Berryman's Letters to His Mother* (New York: W. W. Norton, 1988), 378.
5. Simpson, *Poets in Their Youth*, 63.
6. John Haffenden, *The Life of John Berryman* (London: Ark, 1983), 274.
7. *Ibid.*, 31.
8. *Ibid.*, 192.
9. Simpson, *Poets in Their Youth*, 140.
10. E. M. Halliday, *John Berryman and the Thirties: A Memoir* (Amherst: University of Massachusetts Press, 1987), 207.
11. Eileen Simpson, *The Maze* (New York: Simon & Schuster, 1975), 197.
12. Simpson, *Poets in Their Youth*, 154.
13. Mariani, *Dream Song*, 161.
14. *Poetry Review* 73 (1983).
15. Simpson, *Poets in Their Youth*, 180.
16. *Ibid.*, 234.
17. Simpson, *Poets in Their Youth*, 211.
18. *Ibid.*, 188.
19. Simpson, *The Maze*, 199.
20. Mariani, *Dream Song*, 272.
21. *Paris Review* (Winter 1972).
22. Paul Ferris, *Dylan Thomas* (London: Penguin, 1985), 334.
23. Mariani, *Dream Song*, 273.
24. Shaffer, *Literary Rogues*, 172.
25. Mariani, *Dream Song*, 285–86.
26. Kelly, ed., *We Dream of Honor*, 303.
27. *Ibid.*, 322.
28. *Ibid.*, 44.
29. *Ibid.*, 301.
30. Haffenden, *The Life of John Berryman*, 298.
31. Mariani, *Dream Song*, 368.
32. Laing, *The Trip to Echo Spring*, 230.
33. Simpson, *The Maze*, 142.
34. Haffenden, *The Life of John Berryman*, 285.
35. *Ibid.*, 118.
36. *Hibernia*, May 24, 1974.
37. *Ibid.*
38. Mariani, *Dream Song*, 428–29.
39. Allan Luks, *Four Authors Discuss Drinking and Writing* (New York: New York

Affiliate of the National Council on Alcoholism, 1980), 20.
40. Haffenden, *The Life of John Berryman*, 362–63.
41. *Ibid.*, 375–6.
42. *Ibid.*, 378.
43. *Ibid.*, 379.
44. Mariani, *Dream Song*, 476–77.
45. Simpson, *Poets in Their Youth*, 249.
46. Mariani, *Dream Song*, 494.
47. *Ibid.*, 500.
48. Shaffer, *Literary Rogues*, 178.
49. Haffenden, *The Life of John Berryman*, 78.

Carson McCullers

1. Virginia Spencer Carr, *The Lonely Hunter: A Biography of Carson McCullers* (Athens: University of Georgia Press, 175), 112.
2. Carson McCullers, *Illumination and Night Glare: The Unfinished Autobiography* (Madison: University of Wisconsin Press, 1999), 7.
3. Carr, *The Lonely Hunter*, 159.
4. *Ibid.*, 190.
5. Virginia Spencer Carr, *Understanding Carson McCullers* (Columbia: University of South Carolina Press, 1990), 39.
6. *Ibid.*, 5.
7. Oliver Evans, *The Ballad of Carson McCullers* (New York: Coward McCall, 1966), 23.
8. McCullers, *Illumination and Night Glare*, 14.
9. *Ibid.*, 16.
10. *Ibid.*, 121.
11. Josyane Savigneau, *Carson McCullers: A Life* (New York: Houghton Mifflin, 1995), 43.
12. Lawrence Graver, *Carson McCullers* (Minneapolis: University of Minnesota Press, 1969), 6–7.
13. *New Republic*, August 5, 1940.
14. McCullers, *Illumination and Night Glare*, 35.
15. *Ibid.*, 31.
16. Maurice Leonard, *Montgomery Clift* (London: Hodder & Stoughton, 1997), 286.
17. Peschal, *Writers Gone Wild*, 201.
18. Sherill Tippins, *February House* (London: Simon & Schuster, 2005), 222.
19. Weekes, ed., *Women Know Everything*, 118.
20. Carr, *The Lonely Hunter*, 105.
21. Tippins, *February House*, 25.
22. *Ibid.*
23. Carr, *The Lonely Hunter*, 245.
24. McCullers, *Illumination and Night Glare*, 86–145.
25. Savigneau, *Carson McCullers*, 144.
26. McCullers, *Illumination and Night Glare*, 153.
27. *Ibid.*, 92.
28. *Ibid.*, 145.
29. *Ibid.*, 146.
30. Tennessee Williams, *Memoirs* (London: W. H. Allen, 1977), 107.
31. Donald Spoto, *The Kindness of Strangers: The Life of Tennessee Williams* (New York: Ballantine Books, 1965).
32. George Plimpton, *Truman Capote* (London: Picador, 1999), 55–56.
33. *Ibid.*, 124–25.
34. Savigneau, *Carson McCullers*, 170.
35. *Ibid.*, 189–90.
36. Carr, *The Lonely Hunter*, 290.
37. *Ibid.*, 295.
38. Carr, *Understanding Carson McCullers*, 157.
39. McCullers, *Illumination and Night Glare*, 30.
40. Graver, *Carson McCullers*, 9.
41. McCullers, *Illumination and Night Glare*, 39
42. *Ibid.*, 43.
43. *Ibid.*, 17.
44. Carr, *The Lonely Hunter*, 400.
45. *Ibid.*
46. *Ibid.*
47. *Ibid.*, 401–02.
48. Williams, *Memoirs*, 249.
49. Savigneau, *Carson McCullers*, 239.
50. Carr, *The Lonely Hunter*, 451.
51. Spoto, *The Kindness of Strangers*, 216.
52. Carr, *The Lonely Hunter*, 454.
53. McCullers, *Illumination and Night Glare*, 51.
54. Evans, *The Ballad of Carson McCullers*, 170.
55. *New York Times*, April 16, 1967.
56. Carr, *The Lonely Hunter*, 489.
57. McCullers, *The Mortgaged Heart* (Boston: Houghton Mifflin, 1971), xv.
58. Leonard, *Montgomery Clift*, 286.
59. David Downing, *Marlon Brando* (New York: Stein & Day, 1984), 122.
60. Tony Thomas, *The Films of Marlon Brando* (New York: Citadel, 1992), 188.
61. David Shipman, *Marlon Brando* (London: Sphere, 1974), 168.
62. Carr, *The Lonely Hunter*, 533.

Charles Bukowski

1. Charles Bukowski, *Ham on Rye* (Edinburgh: Canongate, 2001), 34–35.

2. Jim Christy, *The Buk Book: Musings on Charles Bukowski* (Toronto, Ontario: ECW Press, 1997), 15–16.
3. Bukowski, *Ham on Rye*, 101.
4. *Ibid.*, 101–2.
5. Barry Miles, *Charles Bukowski* (London: Virgin, 2005), 43.
6. Howard Sounes, *Charles Bukowski: Locked in the Arms of a Crazy Life* (Edinburgh: Canongate, 1999), 15–16.
7. *Ibid.*, 20.
8. Sounes, *Locked in the Arms of a Crazy Life*, 21.
9. Miles, *Charles Bukowski*, 71–72.
10. *Ibid.*, 73.
11. *The Charles Bukowski Tapes.* Barbet Schroeder, M&N Media, Barrel Entertainment.
12. Howard Sounes, *Bukowski in Pictures* (Edinburgh: Rebel Inc.), 37.
13. Neeli Cherkovski, *Bukowski: A Life* (Vermont: Steerforth Press, 1999), 81.
14. *Ibid.*, 82.
15. *Ibid.*
16. Ben Pleasants, *Visceral Bukowski: Inside the Sniper Landscape of L. A. Writers* (Northville, MI: Sun Dog Press, 2004), 93.
17. Cherkovski, *Bukowski*, 84–85.
18. Aubrey Malone, *The Hunchback of East Hollywood*, (Manchester: Critical Vision, 2003), 35.
19. David Stephen Calonne, ed., *Bukowski: Portions from a Wine-Stained Notebook: Uncollected Stories and Essays, 1944–1990* (San Francisco: City Lights, 2008), 96.
20. Duval, *Bukowski and the Beats*, 176.
21. A.D. Winans, *The Charles Bukowski/Second Coming Years* (Coventry: Beat Scene Press, 1996), 120.
22. Charles Bukowski, *The Bell Tolls For No One* (San Francisco: City Lights, 2015), 122.
23. *Paris Metro*, October 11, 1978.
24. Pleasants, *Visceral Bukowski*, 156.
25. Sounes, *Locked in the Arms of a Crazy Life*, 36–41.
26. Charles Bukowski, *Hollywood* (Santa Rosa, CA: Black Sparrow Press, 1989), 88.
27. Seamus Cooney, ed., *Screams From the Balcony: Selected Letters of Charles Bukowski, 1960–1970*, (Santa Rosa, CA: Black Sparrow Press, 1998), 72.
28. Cherkovski, *Bukowski*, 142.
29. *Chicago Literary Times*, March 1963.
30. *Los Angeles Times*, January 4, 1981.
31. Malone, *On the Edge*, 484.
32. Cooney, ed., *Screams from the Balcony*, 353.
33. *The Charles Bukowski/Second Coming Years*, 112.
34. Abel Debritto, ed., *Essential Bukowski* (Edinburgh: Fourth Estate, 2016), back cover citation.
35. Cherkovski, *Bukowski*, 294.
36. *Weekend Guardian*, December 14–15, 1991.
37. Sounes, *Locked in the Arms of a Crazy Life*, 1.
38. Miles, *Charles Bukowski*, 39–40.
39. Fernanda Pivano, *Charles Bukowski: Laughing with the Gods* (Northville, MI: Sun Dog Press, 2000), 94.
40. Cherkovski, *Bukowski*, 294.
41. Miles, *Charles Bukowski*, 117.
42. Duval, *Bukowski and the Beats*, 142.
43. *Ibid.*, 137.
44. Howard Sounes, *Bukowski in Pictures* (Edinburgh, Canongate, 2000), 17.
45. Sounes, *Locked in the Arms of a Crazy Life*, 171.
46. Winans, *The Charles Bukowski/Second Coming Years*, 110.
47. Pivano, *Laughing with the Gods*, 129.
48. Sounes, *Locked in the Arms of a Crazy Life*, 183.
49. Sounes, *Locked in the Arms of a Crazy Life*, 182–84.
50. Malone, *The Hunchback of East Hollywood*, 183.
51. *Ibid.*, 196.
52. *Ibid.*, 207.
53. Miles, *Charles Bukowski*, 250.
54. Daniel Weizmann, ed., *Drinking with Bukowski: Recollections of the Poet Laureate of Skid Row* (New York: Thunders Mouth Press, 2000), 187–88.
55. Charles Bukowski, *Women* (London: Virgin, 1993), 171–72.
56. Pivano, *Laughing With the Gods*, 49.
57. Malone, *The Hunchback of East Hollywood*, 107.
58. Sounes, *Locked in the Arms of a Crazy Life*, 219.
59. Harold Norse thought of Bukowski – and himself – like this. He called his autobiography *Memoirs of a Bastard Angel* (New York: William Morrow, 1989).

Anne Sexton

1. Anne Sexton, *The Last Summer* (New York: St. Martin's Press, 2000), 2.
2. Diane Wood Middlebrook, *Anne Sexton: A Biography* (London: Virago, 1991), 37.
3. John Lloyd and John Mitchinson, eds., *Advanced Banter* (London: Faber & Faber, 2008), 117.
4. Middlebrook, *Anne Sexton: A Biography*, 13.

5. *Ibid.*, 14.
6. Anne Sexton, *A Self Portrait in Letters* (Boston: Houghton Mifflin, 1977), 5.
7. Middlebrook, *Anne Sexton: A Biography*, 14.
8. Sexton, *A Self Portrait in Letters*, 21.
9. Middlebrook, *Anne Sexton: A Biography*, 39.
10. Sexton, *A Self Portrait in Letters*, 417.
11. Linda Gray Sexton, *Half in Love: Surviving the Legacy of Suicide* (Berkeley, CA: Counterpoint, 2011), 63.
12. Bill Peschel, *Writers Gone Wild* (New York: Perigree, 2010), 160.
13. Sexton, *A Self Portrait in Letters*, 270.
14. Middlebrook, *Anne Sexton: A Biography*, 35.
15. *Hudson Review* (Winter 1965/66).
16. Sexton, *The Last Summer*, 6.
17. *The Paris Review Interviews*, Fourth Series.
18. Middlebrook, *Anne Sexton: A Biography*, 333–34.
19. Sexton, *Half in Love*, 55–59.
20. Middlebrook, *Anne Sexton: A Biography*, 36.
21. *Ibid.*, 389.
22. Sexton, *A Self Portrait in Letters*, 125.
23. Middlebrook, *Anne Sexton: A Biography*, 152.
24. *Ibid.*, 246.
25. *Ibid.*
26. *Ibid.*, 147.
27. *Ibid.*, 147–48.
28. Sexton, *A Self Portrait in Letters*, 75.
29. Middlebrook, *Anne Sexton: A Biography*, 309.
30. *Ibid.*, 143.
31. Sexton, *A Self Portrait in Letters*, 261.
32. *Ibid.*, 237.
33. *Ibid.*, 249.
34. Middlebrook, *Anne Sexton: A Biography*, 226.
35. *Ibid.*, 36.
36. Anne Sexton, *No Evil Star: Selected Essays, Interviews and Prose* (Ann Arbor: University of Michigan Press, 1985), 197.
37. *Ibid.*
38. Linda Gray Sexton, *Searching for Mercy Street: My Journey Back to My Mother, Anne Sexton* (Berkeley, CA: Counterpoint, 2011), 81.
39. Sexton, *A Self Portrait in Letters*, 163.
40. Sexton, *The Last Summer*, 54.
41. Sexton, *Searching for Mercy Street*, 184.
42. Sexton, *The Last Summer*, 79.
43. *Ibid.*, 78–9.
44. Sexton, *Searching for Mercy Street*, 31.
45. Middlebrook, *Anne Sexton: A Biography*, 355.
46. Sexton, *A Self Portrait in Letters*, 349.
47. Middlebrook, *Anne Sexton: A Biography*, 381.
48. *Ibid.*, 380.
49. *Ibid.*
50. Sexton, *Searching for Mercy Street*, 165.
51. Sexton, *A Self Portrait in Letters*, 132.
52. *Ibid.*, 15–16.
53. *Boston Magazine*, August 1968.
54. Sexton, *Searching for Mercy Street*, 91.
55. *Ibid.*, 92.
56. *Ibid.*, 91–92.
57. *Ibid.*, 176.
58. *Ibid.*, 178.
59. *Ibid.*, 176.
60. Sexton, *A Self Portrait in Letters*, 137.
61. Middlebrook, *Anne Sexton: A Biography*, 381.
62. Sexton, *The Last Summer*, 32.
63. *Ibid.*, xii
64. *Ibid.*
65. Sexton, *Searching for Mercy Street*, 162–63.
66. Middlebrook, *A Biography*, 395.
67. Donaldson, *John Cheever*, 282.
68. Bailey, *Cheever*, 505.
69. *Ibid.*, 505.
70. Sexton, *A Self Portrait in Letters*, 408.
71. Middlebrook, *Anne Sexton: A Biography*, 396.
72. *Ibid.*
73. *Ibid.*
74. *Ibid.*, 240.
75. Bailey, *Cheever*, 505.
76. Sexton, *Half in Love*, 192.
77. *Ibid.*, 300.
78. *Ibid.*, 306.
79. Middlebrook, *Anne Sexton: A Biography*, 282.

Raymond Carver

1. Sklenicka, *Raymond Carver: A Writer's Life*, 18.
2. Raymond Carver, *Where I'm Calling From: The Selected Stories* (London: Harvill Press, 1988), 417.
3. Maryann Burk Carver, *What It Used to Be Like: A Portrait of My Marriage to Raymond Carver* (New York: St. Martin's Griffin, 2006), 104.
4. Shaffer, *Literary Rogues*, 207.
5. *Ibid.*, 246.
6. *Ibid.*, 242–43.
7. Marshall Gentry and William Stull, eds., *Conversations with Raymond Carver* (Jackson: University of Mississippi Press, 1990), 192.

8. Carver, *What It Used to Be Like*, 270–71.
9. *Ibid.*, 272.
10. *Ibid.*, 272–73.
11. Sklenicka, *Raymond Carver*, 264.
12. *Ibid.*, 264–5.
13. Carver, *What It Used to Be Like*, 247.
14. *Ibid.*, 247–48.
15. *Ibid.*, 248.
16. Sklenicka, *Raymond Carver: A Writer's Life*, 258.
17. Carver, *What It Used To Be Like*, 301.
18. Sklenicka, *Raymond Carver: A Writer's Life*, 262.
19. Carver, *What It Used to Be Like*, 305.
20. Sklenicka, *Raymond Carver: A Writer's life*, 254.
21. *Ibid.*
22. Gentry and Stull, eds., *Conversations with Raymond Carver*, 38.
23. *Ibid.*, 38–39.
24. Carver, *What It Used to Be Like*, 319.
25. *New Yorker*, October 5, 1998.
26. Sklenicka, *Raymond Carver: A Writer's Life*, 341.
27. *Ibid.*, 341.
28. *New York Times*, May 15, 1988.
29. "Gravy" is the title of one of his poems on this theme. See Sklenicka, *Raymond Carver: A Writer's Life*, 460.
30. Carver, *What It Used To Be Like*, 146.

Bibliography

Abadie, Ann J., ed. *William Faulkner: A Life on Paper*. Jackson: University Press of Mississippi, 1980.

Arpin, Gary Q. *The Poetry of John Berryman*. New York: Kennikat Press, 1978.

Atkins, Elizabeth. *Edna St. Vincent Millay and Her Times*. New York: Russell & Russell, 1964.

Bailey, Blake. *Cheever: A Life*. London: Picador, 2009.

Baker, Carlos. *Ernest Hemingway: A Life Story*. London: Literary Guild, 1969.

———, ed. *Selected Letters of Ernest Hemingway, 1917–1961*. London: Panther, 1985.

Barnet, Andrea. *All Night Party: The Women of Bohemian Greenwich Village and Harlem, 1913–1930*. Chapel Hill, NC: Algonquin Books, 2004.

Beckerman, Marty. *The Heming Way*. New York: St. Martin's Griffin, 2012.

Black, Stephen A. *Eugene O'Neill: Beyond Mourning and Tragedy*. London: Yale University Press, 1999.

Bogarde, Travis, and Jackson R. Bryer, eds. *Selected Letters of Eugene O'Neill*. New York: Limelight Editions, 1964.

Bold, Alan, ed. *Drink to Me Only*. London: Robin Clark, Ltd., 1982.

Blotner, Joseph. *Faulkner: A Biography*. New York: Vintage, 1991.

Boon, Marcus. *The Road to Excess: A History of Writers on Drugs*. Boston: Harvard University Press, 2002.

Breit, Harvey, with Margerie Bonner Lowry, eds. *Selected Letters of Malcolm Lowry*. New York: Capricorn Books, 1965.

Brian, Denis. *The Faces of Hemingway*. London: Grafton Books, 1988.

Brittin, Norman. *Edna St. Vincent Millay*. New York: George H. Doran, 1926.

Bruccoli, Matthew J. *Conversations with Ernest Hemingway*. Jackson; London: University Press of Mississippi. 1986.

———. *Fitzgerald and Hemingway: A Dangerous Friendship*. London: Andre Deutsch, 1995.

Buckley, Peter. *Ernest*. New York: Dial Press, 1978.

Bukowski, Charles. *Factotum*. Santa Rosa: Black Sparrow Press, 1998.

———. *Ham on Rye*. Santa Rosa: Black Sparrow Press, 1999.

Calonne, David Stephen, ed. *Charles Bukowski: Interviews & Encounters, 1963–1993*. Northville, MI: Sun Dog Press, 2003.

———. *Charles Bukowski: Portions from a Wine-Stained Notebook*. San Francisco: City Lights, 2008.

Carr, Virginia Spencer. *Understanding Carson McCullers*. Columbia: University of South Carolina Press, 1990.

———. *The Lonely Hunter: A Biography of Carson McCullers*. Athens: University of Georgia Press, 2003.

Carver, Raymond. *Where I'm Calling From: The Selected Stories*. London: Harvill Press, 1995.

Carver, Maryann Burk. *What It Used to Be Like: A Portrait of My Marriage to Raymond Carver*. New York: St. Martin's Press, 2006.

Charters, Ann. *Kerouac: A Biography*. New York: St. Martin's Press, 1994.

Cheever, Benjamin, ed. *The Letters of John Cheever*. London: Vintage, 2009.

Cheever, John. *The Journals*. London: Vintage, 1991.

———. *Collected Stories*. London: Vintage, 2010.

Cheever, Susan. *Home Before Dark*. London: Weidenfeld & Nicolson, 1984.

_____. *Note Found in a Bottle: My Life as a Drinker.* New York: Washington Square Press, 1999.

Cheney, Anne. *Millay in Greenwich Village.* Tuscaloosa: University of Alabama Press, 1975.

Cherkovski, Neeli. *Bukowski: A Life.* Vermont: Steerforth Press, 1999.

Clark, Tom. *Jack Kerouac: A Biography.* London: Plexus, 1984.

Coale, Samuel. *John Cheever.* New York: Frederick Ungar, 1977.

Coughlan, Robert. *The Private World of William Faulkner.* New York: Harper Brothers, 1954.

Cowley, Malcolm. *The Dream of the Golden Mountains: Remembering the 1930s.* New York: Viking, 1980.

Cronin, Harry C. *Eugene O'Neill: Irish and American.* New York: Ayer Company, 1976.

Dardis, Tom. *Some Time in the Sun.* New York: Limelight Editions, 1988.

_____. *The Thirsty Muse: Alcohol and the American Writer.* London: Sphere, 1990.

Dash, Joan. *A Life of One's Own: Three Gifted Women and the Men They Married.* New York: Paragon House, 1988.

Day, Barry, ed. *Dorothy Parker in Her Own Words.* Lanham, MD: Taylor Trade Publishing, 2004.

Diliberto, Gioia. *Hadley: A Life of Hadley Richardson Hemingway.* London: Bloomsbury, 1992.

Donaldson, Scott. *Fool for Love: A Biography of F. Scott Fitzgerald.* New York: Delta, 1983.

_____. *John Cheever: A Biography.* New York: Random House, 1988.

Duval, Jean-Francois. *Bukowski and the Beats.* Northville, MI: Sun Dog Press, 2002.

Eastman, Max. *Great Companions: Critical Memories of Some Famous Friends.* New York: Farrar, Straus & Cudahy, 1959.

Eells, George. *Hedda and Louella: A Dual Biography of Hedda Hopper and Louella Parsons.* New York: G. P. Putnam's Sons, 1972.

Epstein, Daniel Mark. *What Lips My Lips Have Kissed: The Loves and Love Poems of Edna St. Vincent Millay.* New York: Henry Holt & Co., 2001.

Evans, Oliver. *The Ballad of Carson McCullers.* New York: Coward McCann, 1966.

Exley, Frederick. *A Fan's Notes.* New York: Vintage, 1988.

Faulkner, John. *My Brother Bill: An Affectionate Reminiscence.* New York: Trident Press, 1963.

Fenton, Charles A. *The Apprenticeship of Ernest Hemingway.* New York: Farrar, Straus & Young, 1954.

Fitzgerald, F. Scott. *The Crack-Up, with Other Pieces and Stories.* London: Penguin, 1965.

_____. *The Last Tycoon.* London: Penguin, 1965.

_____. *On Booze.* London: Picador, 2011.

Floyd, Virginia. *The Plays of Eugene O'Neill: A New Assessment.* New York: Frederick Ungar, 1985.

Freeman, Judith. *The Long Embrace: Raymond Chandler and the Woman He Loved.* New York: Pantheon, 2007.

Frewin, Leslie. *The Late Mrs. Dorothy Parker.* New York: Macmillan, 1986.

Gaines, James R. *Wit's End: Days and Nights of the Algonquin Round Table.* North Charleston, SC: BookSurge Publishing, 2007.

Gardiner, Dorothy, and Kathrine Sorley Walker, eds. *Raymond Chandler Speaking.* Berkeley: University of California Press, 1997.

Gelb, Arthur, and Barbara Gelb. *O'Neill.* London: Jonathan Cape, 1962.

_____. *O'Neill: Life with Monte Cristo.* New York: Applause Theater and Cinema Books, 2000.

Gilmore, Christopher Cook. *Hemingway: A Novel.* New York: St. Martin's Press, 1988.

Gilmore, Thomas B. *Equivocal Spirits: Alcoholism and Drinking in Twentieth-Century Literature.* Chapel Hill: University of North Carolina Press, 1987.

Goodwin, Donald W. *Alcohol and the Writer.* New York: Penguin, 1988.

Gould, Jean. *The Poet and Her Book: A Biography of Edna St. Vincent Millay.* New York: Dodd, Mead, 1969.

Gourevitch, Philip, ed. *The Paris Review Interviews,* Vol. II. New York: Picador, 2007.

Graham, Sheilah. *My Hollywood: A Celebration and a Lament.* London: Michael Joseph, 1984.

Greene, Philip. *To Have and Have Another: A Hemingway Cocktail Companion.* New York: Perigree, 2012.

Gurko, Miriam. *The Life of Edna St. Vincent Millay*. New York: Thomas Y. Crowell, 1962.

Halliday, E. M. *John Berryman and the Thirties*. Amherst: University of Massachusetts Press, 1987.

Hamill, Peter. *A Drinking Life: A Memoir*. London: Little Brown, 1994.

Heffenden, John. *The Life of John Berryman*. London: Ark, 1983.

Hellman, Lillian. *An Unfinished Woman: A Memoir*. London: Quartet, 1977.

Hemingway, Ernest. *A Moveable Feast*. London: Arrow Books, 2004.

Hemingway, Gregory H. *Papa: A Personal Memoir*. Boston: Houghton Mifflin, 1976.

Hemingway, Jack. *Misadventures of a Fly Fisherman*. Dallas: Taylor, 1986.

Hemingway, Leicester. *My Brother, Ernest Hemingway*. London: Weidenfeld & Nicholson, 1962.

Hemingway, Mary Welsh. *How It Was*. London: Futura, 1978.

Hemingway, Valerie. *Running with the Bulls: My Years with the Hemingways*. Waterville, ME: Thorndike Press, 2004.

Hiney, Tom. *Raymond Chandler: A Biography*. New York: Atlantic Monthly Press, 1997.

Hiney, Tom, with Frank McShane, eds. *Selected Letters and Non-Fiction of Raymond Chandler, 1909–59*. London: Hamish Hamilton, 2000.

Hotchner, A. E. *Hemingway and His World*. London: Viking, 1989.

_____. *Papa Hemingway*. London: Simon & Schuster, 1999.

Howe, Irving. *William Faulkner: A Critical Study*. Chicago: University of Chicago Press, 1975.

Johnson, Joyce. *The Voice is All: The Lonely Victory of Jack Kerouac*. London: Penguin, 2012.

Keats, John. *You Might as Well Live: The Life and Times of Dorothy Parker*. London: Penguin, 1988.

Kelly, Richard J., ed. *We Dream of Honor: John Berryman's Letters to His Mother*. New York: W. W. Norton, 1988.

King, William Davis, ed. *Part of a Long Story: Eugene O'Neill as a Young Man in Love*. Garden City, NY: Doubleday, 1958.

Kukil, Karen V., ed. *The Journals of Sylvia Plath, 1950–62*. London: Faber & Faber, 2000.

Laing, Olivia. *The Trip to Echo Spring: Why Writers Drink*. Edinburgh: Canongate, 2013.

Latham, Aaron. *Crazy Sundays: F. Scott Fitzgerald in Hollywood*. London: Secker & Warburg, 1972.

Laurence, Frank M. *Hemingway and the Movies*. New York: Da Capo, 1981.

Linebarger, J. M. *John Berryman*. Boston: Twayne, 1974.

London, Jack. *John Barleycorn*. New York: Macmillan, 1913.

Lynn, Kenneth S. *Hemingway*. London: Simon & Schuster, 1987.

Maddox, Brenda. *Nora: A Biography of Nora Joyce*. London: Hamish Hamilton, 1988.

Mariani, Paul. *Dream Song: The Life of John Berryman*. New York: William Morrow, 1990.

McCaffrey, John K. M., ed. *Ernest Hemingway: The Man and His Work*. Cleveland: World Publishing, 1950.

McCullers, Carson. *The Mortgaged Heart*. Boston: Houghton Mifflin, 1971.

_____. *Illumination and Night Glare: The Unfinished Autobiography*. Madison: University of Wisconsin Press, 1999.

Macdougall, Alan Ross, ed. *The Letters of Edna St. Vincent Millay*. New York: Harper & Row, 1952.

Meade, Marion. *Dorothy Parker: What Fresh Hell Is This?* London: Penguin, 1987.

Mellow, James R. *Hemingway: A Life Without Consequences*. London: Hodder & Stoughton, 1994.

Middlebrook, Diane Wood. *Anne Sexton: A Biography*. London: Virago, 1992.

Miles, Barry. *Jack Kerouac: King of the Beats*. New York: Henry Holt & Co., 1998.

Milford, Nancy. *Zelda: A Biography*. New York: Harper & Row, 1970.

_____. *Savage Beauty: The Life of Edna St. Vincent Millay*. New York: Random House, 2002.

Miller, Madelaine Hemingway. *Ernie: Hemingway's Sister "Sunny" Remembers*. New York: Crown, 1975.

Mizener, Arthur. *Scott Fitzgerald and His World*. London: Thames & Hudson, 1972.

Nagel, James, ed. *Ernest Hemingway: The Oak Park Legacy*. Tuscaloosa: University of Alabama Press, 1996.

Newlove, Donald. *Those Drinking Days.* New York: Horizon, 1981.

Olsen, Eric, and Glenn Schaeffer. *We Wanted to be Writers: Life, Love and Literature at the Iowa Writers' Workshop.* New York: Skyhorse, 2011.

Ondaatje, Christopher. *Hemingway in Africa: The Last Safari.* Toronto: HarperCollins, 2003.

Peschel, Bill. *Writers Gone Wild.* New York: Perigree, 2010.

Pivano, Fernanda. *Charles Bukowski: Laughing with the Gods.* Northville, MI: Sun Dog Press, 2000.

Pleasants, Ben. *Visceral Bukowski: Inside the Sniper Landscape of L.A. Writers.* Northville, MI: Sun Dog Press, 2004.

Plimpton, George. *Truman Capote.* London: Picador, 1999.

Raeburn, John. *Fame Became of Him: Hemingway as Public Writer.* Bloomington: Indiana University Press, 1984.

Reynolds, Michael. *Hemingway: The Final Years.* New York: W. W. Norton, 1999.

Richmond, Steve. *Spinning off Bukowski.* Northville, MI: Sun Dog Press, 1996.

Rollyson, Carl. *Nothing Ever Happens to the Brave: The Story of Martha Gellhorn.* New York: St. Martin's Press, 1990.

Rorabaugh, W. J. *The Alcoholic Republic.* New York: Oxford University Press, 1979.

Russo, William, and Jan Merlin. *Troubles in a Golden Eye.* CreateSpace Independent Publishing Platform, 2012.

Samuelson, Arnold. *With Hemingway: A Year in Key West and Cuba.* London: Severn House, 1985.

Sanford, Marcelline Hemingway. *At the Hemingways.* London: Putnam, 1963.

Saroyan, William. *Darkness Visible.* London: Vintage, 2004.

Savigneau, Josyane. *Carson McCullers: A Life.* New York: Houghton Mifflin, 2001.

Sexton, Anne. *A Self-Portrait in Letters.* Boston: Houghton Mifflin, 1977.

_____. *The Complete Poems.* Boston: Houghton Mifflin, 1981.

_____. *No Evil Star: Selected Essays, Interviews, and Prose.* Ann Arbor: University of Michigan Press, 1985.

Sexton, Linda Gray. *Mirror Images.* London: Futura, 1985.

_____. *Searching for Mercy Street: My Journey Back to My Mother.* Berkeley, CA: Counterpoint, 2011.

_____. *Half in Love: Surviving the Legacy of Suicide.* Berkeley, CA: Counterpoint, 2011.

Shaffer, Andrew. *Literary Rogues: A Scandalous History of Wayward Authors.* New York: Harper Perennial, 2013.

Shafter, Toby. *Edna St. Vincent Millay: America's Best Loved Poet.* New York: Julian Messner, 1957.

Sheaffer, Lewis. *O'Neill: Son and Playwright.* Boston: Little, Brown & Co., 1968.

Silverstein, Stuart Y., ed. *The Uncollected Dorothy Parker.* London: Duckworth, 1999.

Simpson, Eileen. *Poets in Their Youth: A Memoir.* New York: Farrar, Straus and Giroux, 1990.

Sinclair, Upton. *A Cup of Fury.* New York: Channel Press, 1956.

Sklenicka, Carol. *Raymond Carver: A Writer's Life.* New York: Simon & Schuster, 2009.

Smith, Jules. *Art, Survival and So Forth: The Poetry of Charles Bukowski.* East Yorkshire: Wrecking Ball Press, 2000.

Sokoloff, Alice Hunt. *Hadley: The First Mrs. Hemingway.* New York: Dodd, Mead, 1973.

Sounes, Howard. *Charles Bukowski: Locked in the Arms of a Crazy Life.* Edinburgh: Canongate, 1998.

Spoto, Donald. *The Kindness of Strangers: The Life of Tennessee Williams.* New York: Ballantine, 1998.

Tippins, Sherill. *February House.* London: Simon & Schuster, 2005.

Turnbull, Andrew, ed. *The Letters of F. Scott Fitzgerald.* London: Max Press, 2011.

Viertel, Peter. *Dangerous Friends: Hemingway, Huston, and Others.* London: Viking, 1992.

Villard, Henry S., and James Nagel. *Hemingway in Love and War: The Lost Diary of Agnes von Kurowsky.* Boston: Northeastern University Press, 1989.

Wagner, Linda W. *Ernest Hemingway: Six Decades of Criticism.* Ann Arbor: Michigan State University Press, 1987.

Wasson, Ben. *Count No'count: Flashbacks to Faulkner.* Jackson: University Press of Mississippi, 1983.

Weizmann, Daniel, ed. *Drinking with Bukowski: Recollections of the Poet Laureate of Skid Row.* New York: Thunders Mouth Press, 2000.

Williams, Tennessee. *Memoirs*. London: W. H. Allen, 1977.
Winans, W. D. *The Charles Bukowski/Second Coming Years*. North Coventry: Beat Scene Press, 1996.
Wood, Naomi. *Mrs. Hemingway*. London: Picador, 2014.
Zeitz, Joshua. *Flapper*. New York: Three Rivers Press, 2006.
Zolotow, Maurice. *Billy Wilder in Hollywood*. New York: Limelight Editions, 1996.

Index

Numbers in ***bold italics*** indicate pages with illustrations

Across the River and Into the Trees 92, 99, 100
Adams, Franklin Pierce 45
The Aeneid 44
After Such Pleasures 50
After the Fall 183, 190
Agee, James 2, 53
Albee, Edward 53
Alcoholics Anonymous 1, 51, 60, 73, 117, 119, 122, 123–24, 137, 149, 200–201, 202, 203
Algonquin Circle 45–47, 56
All My Pretty Ones 182
Altman, Robert 197
Anderson, Sherwood 3, 84
The Angel Intrudes 37
Angus, John 126–127
Apostrophes 170–171
Auden, W.H. 143

Bacall, Lauren ***87***
Baker, Fred ***172***
Baker, Jane Cooney 159–161, 163, 164–165, 172
The Ballad of the Harp Weaver 38
Ballad of the Sad Café 142
Bankhead, Tallulah 46, 49
Barach, Alvin 49
Barfly 172, ***173***
Bauman, Ann 165
Beach, Sylvia 67
The Beautiful and the Damned 60
Behan, Brendan 20
Beighle, Linda Lee *see* Bukowski, Linda
Bellow, Saul 128, 192
Beloved Infidel 76, ***77***
Benchley, Robert 45, 46, 49, 51, 55, 74
Berlin, Irving 49
Bernstein, Leonard 55
Berryman, Ethel 126
Berryman, Jill (Martha) 126–128, 132–133, 137
Berryman, John 120, 126–138, ***127***, 169, 177; accidents while drinking 131, 133–134, 135–36; affairs 129, 130; Ann Levine 132, 133: eccentric behavior 131, 132; Eileen Simpson 128–130, 134, 137; fainting spells 134, 137; Ireland 134–35, 136; Kate Donahue 133, 134–135, 136, 138; mother complex 132–133; nervous temperament 129, 132, 133, 136; phobias 129, 135, 136; suicidal impulses 128, 129–130, 138
Berryman, Robert 126
Beyond the Horizon 11
Bierce, Ambrose 3
The Big Sleep 26, 28
Bisch, Louis 11–12
Bishop, John 39
Black, Stephen 6
Black Mask 25
Black Sparrow Press 166, 168
The Blue Dahlia 28
Bogart, Humphrey 53, 85–86, ***87***, 171
Boissevain, Eugene 38–43
Bono 175
Boulton, Agnes 10, 11, 14–15, 16, 17
Bowen, Elizabeth 154
Brando, Marlon 51, 153
Breen, Joseph 76
Breit, Harvey 98
Brennan, Walter 87
Brinnin, John Malcolm 131
Brittin, Benjamin 143
Broun, Heywood 45, 46
Brown, Simone 150
Brunner-Orne, Martha 178
Brunner-Orne, Martin 178–179, 183, 187, 191
Brush, Katharine 69
Bryan, Joseph 51
Bukowski, Charles 2, 155–175, ***157***, ***170***, ***172***, 196; acne 155, 156; alcohol as "happy drug" 155, 156, 161, 162, 168; alcohol as writing stimulant 160–161, 165, 169, 173–174; arrest for alleged draft-dodging 157; Barbara Frye 163–64; The Beats 168–9; cruelty of father 155, 156; daughter 165;

223

Frances Dean 165; German origins 155; Jane Cooney Baker 159–161, 163, 164–165, 172; John Martin 166, 168, 171–172; Linda King 167; Linda Lee Beighle 169, 170, 171–72, 175; murder threat 158–159; Nazi leanings 156; readings 166, 167, 168–169, 171; suicidal impulses 161, 165; track attendances 163, 172–173; tuberculosis 174
Bukowski, Linda 169, 170, 171–172, 175
Bukowski, Marina 165
Bullet Park 116
Burgess, Anthony 99
Bynner, Witter 41

Caddie 55
Callaghan, Morley 92
Campbell, Alan 51–56
Capote, Truman 3, 88, 124, 146
Carlin, Terry 9
Carpenter, Meta 83
Carr, Virginia Spencer 150
Carruth, Hayden 123
Carson, Johnny 124
Carver, Christine 193, 194, 198, 200
Carver, Maryanne 83, 193–202, 204
Carver, Raymond 1, 16, 83, 119, 120, 124, 167, 193–204, *195*; bankruptcy 195, 201; drinking with wife 194, 195–96; dual identity 194, 196, 197, 200, 202; fatherhood 193; money problems 193–195, 200, 203; sobriety 202–204; violence 198, 201
Carver, Vance 193, 200
Cathedral 203
Cecily, Diane 196, 198, 199
Cervantes, Miguel de 134
Chamson, Andre 67
Chandler, Cissy *see* Pascal, Cissy
Chandler, Raymond 21–34, *30*, 80, 100; *The Big Sleep* 26, 28; Cissy (wife) 21–31; *Double Indemnity* 25–6, *27*, 28; infidelity 21–2, 26–27; *Lady in the Lake* 22, *23*; loses job 23; Natasha Spender 31–33; Philip Marlowe 24–25, 33–34; *Playback* 33; RAF 21; *Strangers on a Train* 29; suicidal behavior 21, 22, 30–31
Chaplin, Charlie 17, 19
Cheever, Ben 107, 120
Cheever, Federico 107, 110–111, 113, 119, 121
Cheever, Fred 109, 122
Cheever, John 83, 86, 107–125, *108*, 177, 189, 191, 199, 204; bisexuality 111, 112, 113, 116, 118, 124; *Bullet Park* 116; Falconer 118; hallucinations 120; Hope Lange *112*, 113, 114, 117, 124; infidelity 111, 112; lecturing 119–122; motivation to drink 109, 110, 120; Smithers Alcoholism Center 122–123; sobriety 121–124; *The Swimmer* 111, 116, 117; *Wapshot Scandal* 111, 112
Cheever, Mary 107, 110, 111, 113–119, 122, 124

Cheever, Susan 83, 107–108, 109, 110, 114, 115, 118, 120, 121, 122, 123, 124
Chekhov, Anton 142
Chicago Daily News 136–137
Clarac-Schwarzenbach Annemarie 141–142
Clarke, Anne 183
Clift, Montgomery 153
Clock Without Hands 152
Cohen, Leonard 166
Cohn, Harry 24
Collins, Elizabeth 109
Conant, Louise 190
Condon, James 6–7
Connelly, Marc 45
Coolidge, Calvin 51
Cooper, Gary 93
The Count of Monte Cristo 6
Coward, Noel 46
Cowley, Malcolm 109, 118
Crane, Hart 138
Crane, Stephen 132
Crawford, Joan 75–76
"Crazy Sunday" 74–75
Crosby, Bing 27
Crucifix in a Deathhand 165–166

Daily Express 32
Daly, Blyth 46
Dardis, Tom 174
Davies, Marion 46
Davis, Bill 104–105
Davis, George 143
The Dead 154
Dean, Frances 165
Death and Taxes 50
Dell, Floyd 37, 38
Delong, Katherine 90
De Niro, Robert **79**
Desire Under the Elms **14**
De Wilde, Brandon 147, **148**
Diamond, David 142–143, 148–149
Dietz, Howard 53
Dillman, Bradford **84**
Dillon, George 39–40
The Dime 25
Dirks, Mary 122
Domench, Dan 198–199
A Domestic Dilemma 147
Dominguin, Luis Miguel 92–93, 104
Don Quixote 134
Donahue, Kate 133, 134–135, 136, 138
Donaldson, Scott 67
Dos Passos, John 60, 91
Double Indemnity 25–26, *27*, 28
The Dream Songs 135
Dreiser, Theodore 3
Dubliners 154
Dunaway, Faye 172
Duncan, Isadora 68

Index

Edwards, Eric 181
Einstein, Albert 147
Engle, Paul 42–43
Enough Rope 49
Epstein, Daniel Mark 35
Esquire 55, 66, 71, 72, 195
Exley, Frederick 115

A Fable 88
Falconer 118
A Farewell to Arms 68, 90, 92, 93, 94, 100
The Farmer's Daughter 53
Farrell, Sharon **89**
Fatal Interview 40
Faulkner, Alabama 84
Faulkner, Jill 86, 88
Faulkner, Jimmy 87–88
Faulkner, William 1, 2, 46, 75, 81–89, **82**, 94, 98, 174, 177, 194; accidents while drinking 83, 85, 86; alcoholic heritage 81; hallucinations 86; Hollywood 85; marriage 83; medical properties of alcohol 81; motivation for drinking 81–82, 85–86; nightmares 83; Nobel Prize 88; screenwriting 85, 86; sexism 83; withdrawal symptoms 83; work attitudes 82
February House 143
Ferber, Edna 46
Ferreri, Marco 171
A Few Figs from Thistles 37–38
Ficke, Arthur 37
Fields, W.C. 167
Fires 203
Fitzgerald, Barry 27
Fitzgerald, F. Scott 1, 2, 16, 46, 50, 52–53, 58–80, **59**, **62**, **65**, 86, 94, 98, 100, 102, 110, 169, 174; childhood 58; "crack-up" 59, 72; depression 59, 70, 71, 78, 79; Ernest Hemingway 63–66, 68, 71, 72–73, 78; gin 60, 66, 67, 70, 71, 74, 76, 78, 80; illogicality 69–70; insecurity 60; misbehavior with drink 62, 64–68, 71–72, 74, 75, 76, 79; Princeton 58; screenwriting 67, 71, 72, 75–76; suicidal tendencies 59, 66–67, 74; tolerance for alcohol 60, 63–64
Fitzgerald, Scottie **59**, 67, 71
Fitzgerald, Zelda 52–53, 58, **59**, 60–61, **62**, 63–71, 73, 76, 78, 95
Fleming, Ian 33
For Whom the Bell Tolls 92, 93, 94
Ford, Richard 202–203
Foster, Sally 55
Fracasse, Jean 33
Franco, Francisco 52, 72, 95
Franklin, Benjamin 110
Fraser, Katharine 138
Fred Baker Films 171
Freud 153
Frye, Barbara 163–164

Fuentes, Norberto 97
Furious Seasons (book) 202
"Furious Seasons" (story) 194

Gallagher, Tess 202–203
Gandhi, Mahatma 42
Gardner, Ava **96**, 97
Gazzara, Ben 171
Gellhorn, Martha 94–96
Genet, Jean 159
Gillmore, Margalo 46
Gingrich, Arnold 71, 74
Going My Way 27
Goodwin, Donald 60, 81
Graham, Sheilah 73–74, 76–80
Grant, Jane 46
The Great Gatsby 58, 63
Green Hills of Africa 98
Greene, Helga 31, 33
Greene, Philip 92, 102
Gurganos, Allan 119

The Hairy Ape 15
Hale, Ruth 45
Halliday, Milt 128
Hamilton, Clayton 11
Hamlet 128, 174
Hammett, Dashiell 25, 47, 55, 56, 74
Harper's Bazaar 143
Harris, Julie 147, **148**, **153**
Hayes, Helen 76
Hayward, Susan 53, **54**
The Heart Is a Lonely Hunter 141, 142
Hecht, Anthony 182
Hellman, Lillian 56, 72–73
Hemingway, Ernest 1, 2, 46, 47, 50, 52, 61, 63–8, 70, 71, 72–73, 78, 86, 90–106, **98**, **99**, 111, 128, 133, 168, 169, 174, 182, 183, 190; accidents with drink 92, 94, 97, 101–102; Adriana Ivancich 99, 101; Agnes von Kurowsky 90–91; electric shock treatment 104; extremism 92, 93; F. Scott Fitzgerald 63–66, 68, 71–73, 78, 91–92; Hadley Richardson 65, 66, 68, 91–92; insomnia 95, 102; macho image 93–94, 95, 99; Martha Gellhorn 94–96; Mary Welsh 95–96, 101, 103–106; paranoia 104–105; Pauline Pfeiffer 92, 94; war 90, 95; Zelda Fitzgerald 64, 68
Hemingway, Gregory 95
Hemingway, Patrick 95
Henry, O. 3, 110
Hepburn, Katharine 18
"Her Kind" 184
Hergesheimer, Joseph 80
Hitchcock, Alfred 29
Hollywood 172
Homage to Mistress Bradstreet 132
Hopkins, Miriam 84
Hopper, Dennis 173

Hotchner, A.E. 97, 103, 105
House Beautiful 46
Houseman, John 28
HUAC 52, 53–54
Hudson, Rock 93
Huston, John 152–154

Ibsen, Henrik 179
The Iceman Cometh 17
Infidelity 75–76
Instant of the Hour After 147
Isherwood, Christopher 143
It Catches My Heart in Its Hands 165
Ivancich, Adriana 99, 101

James, Henry 63, 108
Jenkins, Katherine 7
Johnson, Lyndon B. 134
Johnson, Nunnally 76
Jones, Jennifer 93
Jordan, Neil 2
Joyce, James 67, 91–92, 154
Joyce, Nora 91

Kaloyme, Louis 15–16
Kashkeen, Ivan 94
Kaufman, Beatrice 46
Kaufman, George S. 45, 47
Keats, John 56, 186
Kelly, Richard J 133
Kemp, Harry 111
Kerouac, Jack 3
Kerr, Deborah 76, *77*
The Killers 96
King, Ginevra 58
King, Linda 167
King, Martin Luther 57
King, Stephen 3, 102
Knopf Alfred A. 117
Knopf, Edwin H. 72
Kramer, Stanley 148
Kroll, Francis 78
Kumin, Maxine 187, 190
Kurowsky, Agnes von 90–91, 101

Ladd, Parker 56
Ladies of the Corridor 54
Lady in the Lake 22, *23*
Lake, Veronica 28
Laments for the Living 50
Lancaster, Burt *96*, 97, 116, *117*
Landgard, Janet *117*
Lange, Hope *112*, 113, 114, 117, 124
Lanham, Buck 92
Lardner, Ring 3, 46
The Last Tycoon 78, *79*
Lawson, John Howard 53
Lee, Gypsy Rose 143
Leech, Margaret 46
Le Gallienne, Eva 46

Leigh, Vivien *75*
Lemmon, Elizabeth 60
Lenya, Lotte 143
Levine, Ann 132, 133
Lewis, Sinclair 2
Life 116
A Light in August 83
Lish, Gordon 195, 203
Live or Die 184
London, Jack 2
Long Day's Journey into Night 5, 6, 12, 13, 17, *18*
The Long Goodbye 29, 31
Loos, Anita 62
Loren, Sophia *14*
The Lost Weekend 28, 115
Lowell, Robert 131
Lowry, Malcolm 2

MacArthur, Charles 48, 76
MacBride, Maud Gonne 129
MacCracken, Henry 36
MacLeish, Archibald 92, 102
MacMurray, Fred 26, *27*, 28
Manhattan, Jane 170
Mann, Golo 143
March, Frederic *18*
Marlowe, Philip 24, 29, 31, 33–4
Marre, Albert 151
Martin, John 166, 168, 171–172
Marx, Groucho 48
Marx, Harpo 46, 49
Masse, Jordan 152
Mayer, William 147
McAdoo, Richard 190
McCarey, Leo 27
McCarthy, Joseph 52
McCullers, Carson 139–154, *140*; androgynous feelings 139, 140; complexity 150–151; divorce 143; eccentricity 139; husband's rivalry 141, 142, 147; husband's suicide 149–150; husband's wartime exploits 144; ill health 140, 141, 142, 146–147, 148, 151, 152; lesbian rumors 141, 143; outcast status 139, 142; re-marriage 144
McCullers, Reeves 140–144, 145–147, 148–50
McGinley, Art 8, 11, 12
McMein, Neysa 46
McQueen, Steve *89*
The Member of the Wedding 139, 144–145, 146, 147, *148*
Mercy Street 186
Middlebrook, Diane Wood 191
Milford, Nancy 71
Milland, Ray 28, 115
Millay, Cara 35–36, 40
Millay, Edna St. Vincent 35–44, *36*; academic brilliance 36; acting prowess 37; car accident 41; depression 42, 43; disor-

derliness 39; drug addiction 41–43; Eugene Boissevain 38–43; gender confusion 36; ill health 40; lesbian encounters 37; liberal attitudes 35, 37, 39; open marriage 39–40; personality 35, 40; political views 37; Pulitzer Prize 38; recklessness 36, 37, 40; resilience 43; sexual dalliances 37, 39; war time involvements 42; war propaganda 42–43
Millay, Henry 35
Millay, Kathleen 35, 40
Millay, Norma 35, 37
Miller, Alice Duar 46
Miller, Arthur 183, 190
Miller, Henry 174
Modine, Matthew *197*
Mok, Michael 66
Le Monde 171
Monroe, Marilyn 183, 190
Montague, John 134–135
Monterey, Carlotta 15–20
Montgomery, Robert *23*
A Moon for the Misbegotten 17
Moore, Julianne *197*
Moran, Lois 67
Mourning Becomes Electra 16
Mulholland, Inez 38
Mulligan, Robert 112
Mullinax, William 160
Murphy, Gerald 65, 68
Murphy, Sara 65
Murray, Natalia 146

NAACP 57
Near Klamath 194
New Republic 107
New York Post 66
New York Times 57, 120
The New Yorker 52, 55, 57, 107, 109
Newlove, Donald 2, 12, 86–87
No Evil Star 179
Norse, Harold 175

O'Connor, Flannery 148
O'Hara, John 74
The Old Man and the Sea 100, *101*
Oldham, Estelle 83
O'Neill, Ella 5, 13, 14
O'Neill, Eugene 2, 5–20, *15*, 22, 37, 86, 107, 174; acting experiences 8; bravado 7, 8; DTs 7, 9; depression 8, 9, 17–20; divorce 15; drunken behavior 5–10; jobs 7; mother complex 12; motivation to drink 11–12, 15; suicidal tendencies 6, 8, 18; tremors 12, 16–17, 20
O'Neill, Eugene (Junior) 7, 12, 19
O'Neill, James 5, 6, 8, 11, 13
O'Neill, Jamie 6, 10, 11, 13, 17
O'Neill, Oona 10, 17, 19
O'Neill, Shane 10, 19

Oppenheimer, George 50
Ordonez, Antonio 104

Pakula, Alan J. 112, 117
Parker, Dorothy 38, 45–57, *49*, 68, 72–73; abortion 48; Alan Campbell 51–56; bingeing 49, 51–52, 56; divorce 53; eccentricity 48, 56, 57; entertaining 51–2; epitaphs 57; Ernest Hemingway 50, 52; F. Scott Fitzgerald 50, 52–53; hangovers 47; Hollywood 51–52, 53; hysterectomy 53; miscarriage 53; money 52, 56, 57; motivation to drink 47–48; reclusiveness 54; screenwriting 51–52, 53–54; socialist tendencies 52, 53–54; suicide attempts 48–49
Pascal, Cissy 21–31
Pascal, Lavinia 24
Peck, Gregory 76, *77*, 93
Penn, Sean 172–173
Perkins, Anthony *14*
Perkins, Maxwell 66, 70, 77, 94, 96
Pfeiffer, Pauline 68, 92, 94
Pinter, Harold 115
Pivano, Fernanda 170, 174
Pivot, Bernard 170–171
Plath, Sylvia 180, 182–183, 191
Playback 33
Plimpton, George 101
Poe, Edgar Allan 23
Pollack, Channing 46
Pond, Edwin Parker 45, 46, 48
Poodle Springs 34
Porter, Katharine Anne 142, 148
Portfolio 159
Post Office 166
Production Code Administration 28

Red Headed Woman 69
Reflections in a Golden Eye 141, *153*, 154
The Reivers *89*
Remick, Lee *84*
Reynolds, Michael 102
Richardson, Hadley 65, 66, 68, 91–92
Robards, Jason *18*
Robinson, Edward G 26, *27*
Roethke, Theodore 3
Rose, Alexander 134
Ross, Harold 45, 52
Ross, Lillian 99
Rourke, Mickey 172, *173*
Russell, Theresa *79*

Saint Judas 180
San Diego Tribune 33
Sanctuary *84*
Sartre, Jean-Paul 159
Saviers, George 105
Sayre, Zelda *see* Fitzgerald, Zelda
Schroeder, Barbet 172
Schulberg, Budd 75

Schwartz, Barbara 185, 190
Schwartz, Delmore 131
Searching for Mercy Street 191
Selznick, David O 146
77 Dream Songs 134
Sexton, Alfred (Kayo) 177, 178–80, 181, 185, 186–9
Sexton, Anne 42, 121–122, 175–92, *177*; affairs 181, 183, 188; breakdowns 178, 180; depression 178, 186; diva-like behavior 188; elation 183, 188, 190; hippie attitudes 181; infidelity 182; marital strife 180, 187–8; masochism 187, 192; poems as living things 179; promiscuity 178–179; rebirth through writing 179, 190; self loathing 176, 187; sexuality 178–179, 182; suicidal impulses 182–183, 184, 186, 188, 190–191; temper tantrums 178; therapy 178–179, 184, 187, 190; upbringing 176–177; violence 180, 187, 188
Sexton, Billie 178, 179, 181, 187
Sexton, George 178, 179
Sexton, Joy 177, 179, 180, 181, 183, 184, 185, 191
Sexton, Linda 177, 178, 180, 181, 183–184, 185, 186, 188, 189, 191–192
Shakespeare, William 1, 86, 88, 128
Shaw, George Bernard 16
Shay, Frank 11, 16
Sheen, Vincent 47
Sheen, Wilfred 116
Sherwood, Robert E. 45
Short Cuts **197**
"The Short, Happy Life of Francis Macomber" 98
Shroyer, Fred 57
Silverberg, Dr 118–119
Simpson, Eileen 128–130, 134, 137
Sinatra, Frank 113
Singer, Kurt 93–94
Sklenicka, Carol 200
Smash-Up 53, *54*
Smith, Bill 90
Smith, John Allyn 126–127
The Snows of Kilimanjaro 66, 93, 97
The Spanish Earth 72
Spender, Natasha 31–32, 33
Spoto, Donald 151
The Square Root of Wonderful 151
Stanwyck, Barbara 26–8
Stein, Gertrude 91
Steinbeck, John 2
Stevens, Ken 136
Stewart, Donald Ogden 46
The Story of Temple Drake 84
Strangers on a Train 29
Sullivan, Frank 46
The Sun Also Rises 91, 92, 94, 97, 99
The Swimmer 111, 116, *117*

Tales of a Jazz Age 60
Tales of Ordinary Madness 171, *172*
Tate, Allen 136
Taylor, Deems 46
Taylor, Elizabeth *153*
Taylor, Robert *75*
Teasdale, Sara 38
Tender Is the Night 69, 70, 98
Thalberg, Irving 79
The Thirsty Muse 174
This Side of Paradise 58–59
Thomas, Caitlin 131
Thomas, Dylan 130–131, 135, 169, 196
Thompson, Hunter S. 2–3
Three Comrades 72
"The Three Day Blow" 98–99
Thurber, James 2
Time 66, 111
To Have and Have Not 87
Tookey, John Peter 45
Totter, Audrey *23*
A Touch of the Poet 17
Tracy, Spencer 100, *101*
True at First Light 98
Twain, Mark 102
Tyndale, Jessica 32

Ultramarine 203
Untermeyer, Louis 139

Vanity Fair 45, 57
Viertel, Peter 102
Vogue 45
Vorse, Mary 8

"Waiting to Die" 183
Walsh, Ernest 91
Wanger, Walter 75
The Wapshot Scandal 111, 112
Waters, Ethel 147, *148*
Weissner, Carl 166
Welles, Orson 23
Welsh, Mary 95–96, 101, 103–106
Welty, Eudora 142, 148
West, Kay 33
When Water Comes Together with Other Water 203
Who's Afraid of Virginia Woolf? 53
Widdemer, Margaret 38
Wilder, Billy 25–26, 28
Will You Please Be Quiet, Please? (book) 201
"Will You Please Be Quiet, Please?" (story) 195
Williams, Rose 145
Williams, Tennessee 3, *145*, 150, 151
Wilson, Edmund 38, 46
Wilson, Mary Ann 134
Wilson, Woodrow 6
Winter Carnival 75

Winternitz, Mary see Cheever, Mary
Winwood, Estelle 46
Women 173–174
Wood, Peggy 46
Woolcott, Alexander 45
The World of Apples 120
Wright, James 180–181
Wunderkind 140

A Yank at Oxford 75
Yeats, W.B. 129, 130
Yevtushenko, Yevgeny 119
Young Loretta 53

Zanuck, Darryl F. 85
Zaphiro, Denis 97
Zinnemann, Fred 148

www.ingramcontent.com/pod-product-compliance
Lightning Source LLC
Chambersburg PA
CBHW032050300426
44116CB00007B/683